NOW who do we blame?

Political Cartoons by Tom Toles

Andrews McMeel
Publishing

Kansas City

Tom Toles is syndicated internationally by Universal Press Syndicate.

Now Who Do We Blame? copyright © 2005 by Tom Toles. All rights reserved. Printed in the United States of America. No part of this book may be used or reproduced in any manner whatsoever without written permission except in the case of reprints in the context of reviews. For information, write Andrews McMeel Publishing, an Andrews McMeel Universal company, 4520 Main Street, Kansas City, Missouri 64111.

05 06 07 08 09 BBG 10 9 8 7 6 5 4 3 2 1

ISBN-13: 978-0-7407-5558-3
ISBN-10: 0-7407-5558-7

Library of Congress Control Number: 2005929088

www.andrewsmcmeel.com

For Seth

"Dear Mr. Toles,
   I am enclosing 2 of your cartoons, one of which I don't understand and the other one offends me a great deal.
   I happen to think Mr. Bush is a fine looking man and your portrait of him makes him look like some kind of little animal. I think it is highly disrespectful of you to do this. His ears are on his head in the same place as everyone else's are."

The writer also enclosed a photograph of the president, in case I hadn't seen one. It looked just like my caricature, to me.

—Tom Toles

Contents

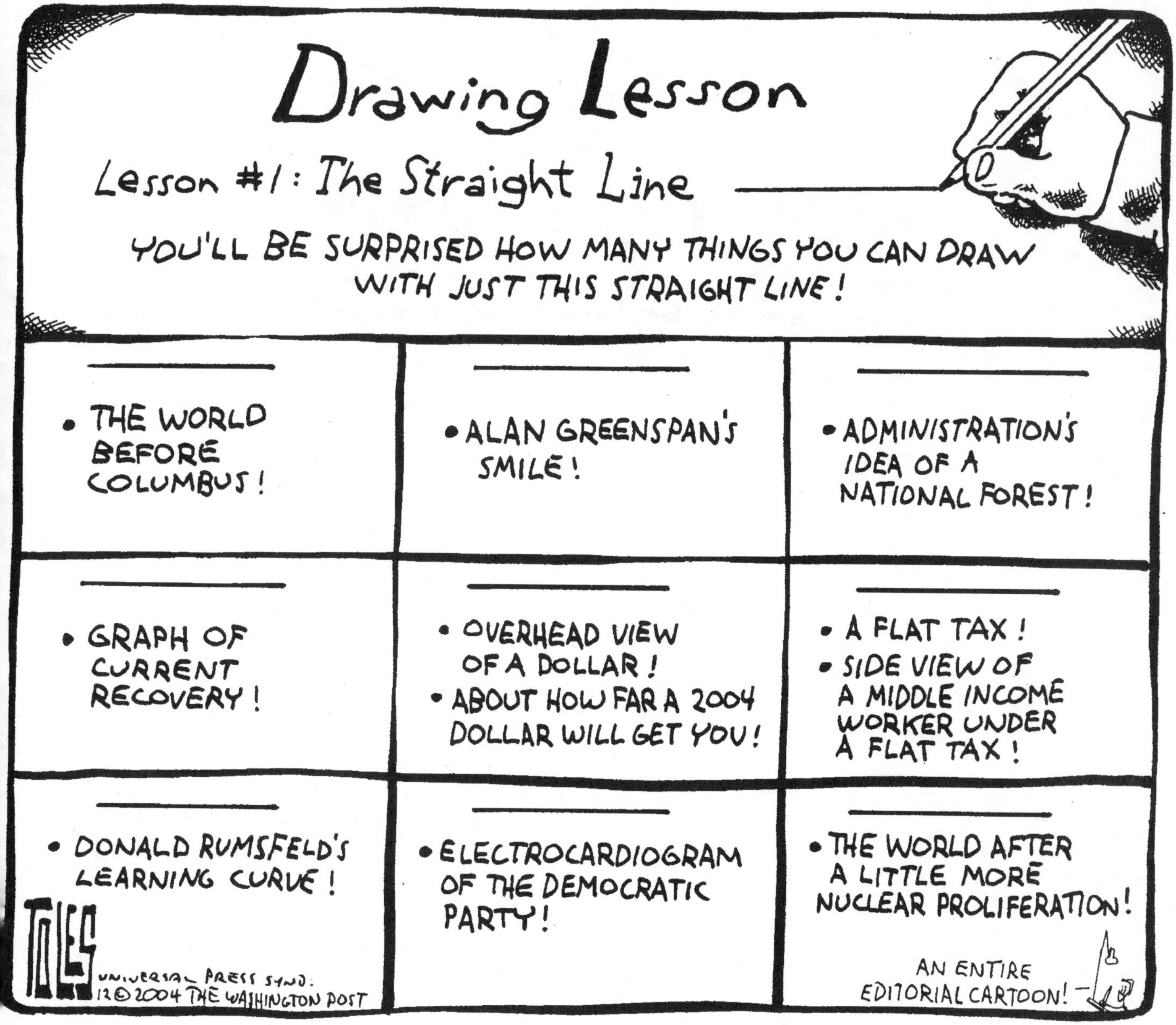
Drawing Lesson
Lesson #1: The Straight Line
YOU'LL BE SURPRISED HOW MANY THINGS YOU CAN DRAW WITH JUST THIS STRAIGHT LINE!
• THE WORLD BEFORE COLUMBUS!
• ALAN GREENSPAN'S SMILE!
• ADMINISTRATION'S IDEA OF A NATIONAL FOREST!
• GRAPH OF CURRENT RECOVERY!
• OVERHEAD VIEW OF A DOLLAR!
• ABOUT HOW FAR A 2004 DOLLAR WILL GET YOU!
• A FLAT TAX!
• SIDE VIEW OF A MIDDLE INCOME WORKER UNDER A FLAT TAX!
• DONALD RUMSFELD'S LEARNING CURVE!
• ELECTROCARDIOGRAM OF THE DEMOCRATIC PARTY!
• THE WORLD AFTER A LITTLE MORE NUCLEAR PROLIFERATION!
AN ENTIRE EDITORIAL CARTOON!
TOLES
UNIVERSAL PRESS SYND.
12 © 2004 THE WASHINGTON POST

12-8-04

POLITICS AND THE ELECTION

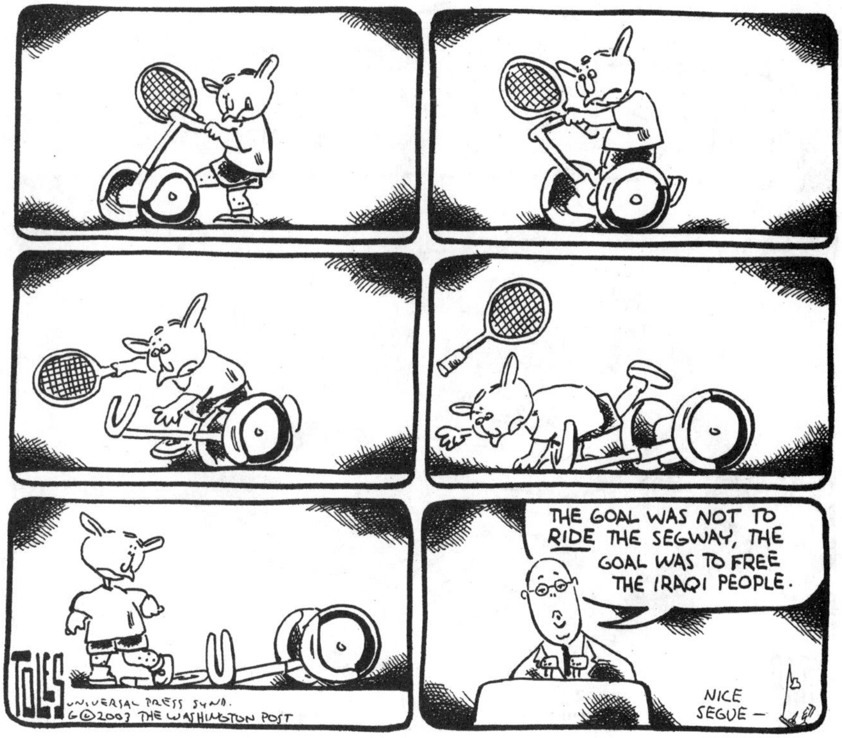
THE GOAL WAS NOT TO RIDE THE SEGWAY, THE GOAL WAS TO FREE THE IRAQI PEOPLE.
NICE SEGUE —
TOLES
UNIVERSAL PRESS SYND.
6©2003 THE WASHINGTON POST

6-18-03

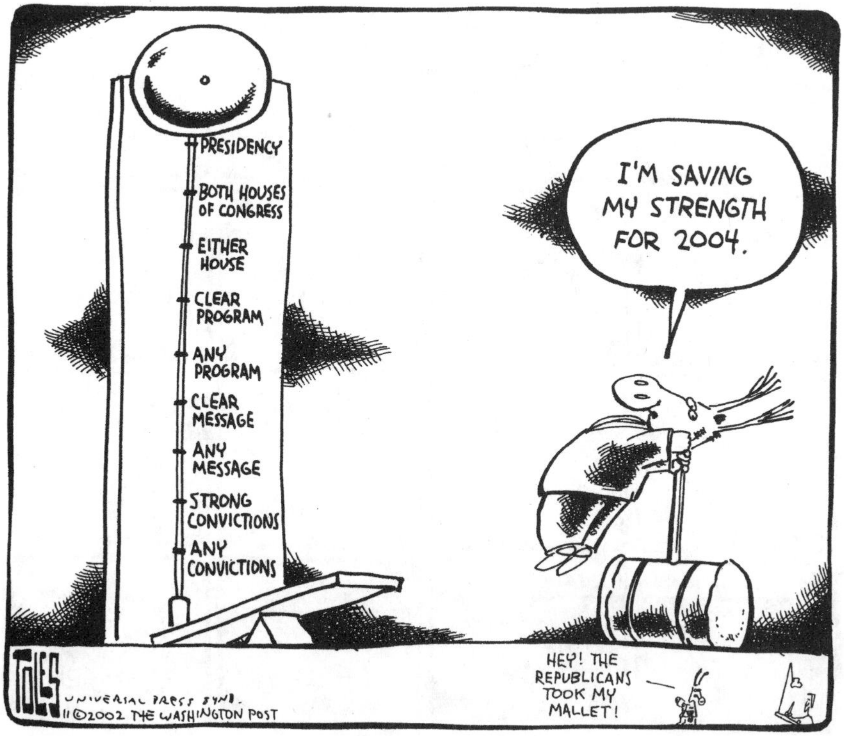
PRESIDENCY
BOTH HOUSES OF CONGRESS
EITHER HOUSE
CLEAR PROGRAM
ANY PROGRAM
CLEAR MESSAGE
ANY MESSAGE
STRONG CONVICTIONS
ANY CONVICTIONS
I'M SAVING MY STRENGTH FOR 2004.
HEY! THE REPUBLICANS TOOK MY MALLET!
TOLES
UNIVERSAL PRESS SYND.
11©2002 THE WASHINGTON POST

11-11-02

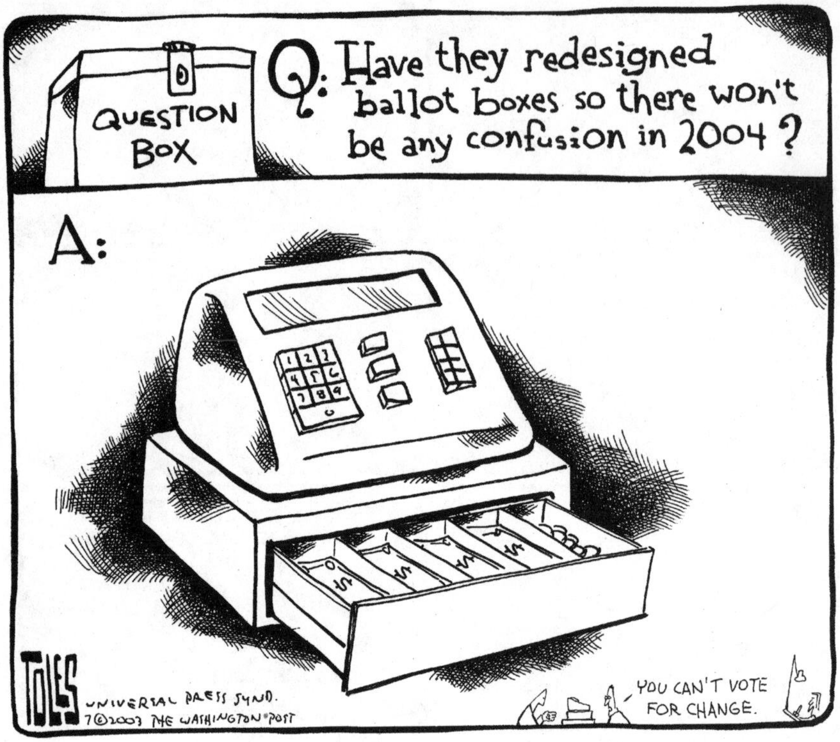
QUESTION BOX
Q: Have they redesigned ballot boxes so there won't be any confusion in 2004?
A:
TOLES
UNIVERSAL PRESS SYND.
7©2003 THE WASHINGTON POST
YOU CAN'T VOTE FOR CHANGE.

7-7-03

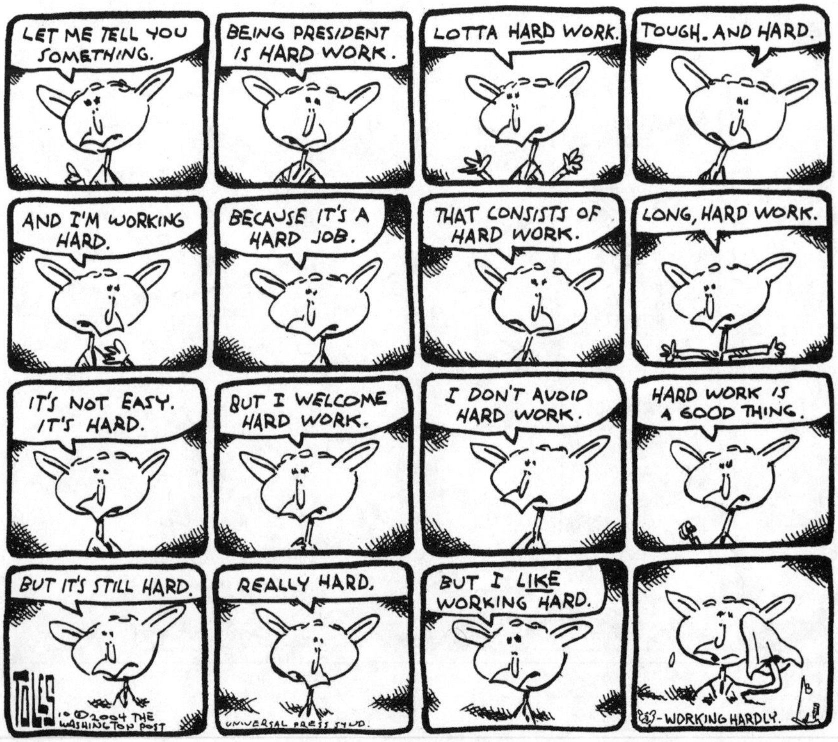
LET ME TELL YOU SOMETHING.
BEING PRESIDENT IS HARD WORK.
LOTTA HARD WORK.
TOUGH. AND HARD.
AND I'M WORKING HARD.
BECAUSE IT'S A HARD JOB.
THAT CONSISTS OF HARD WORK.
LONG, HARD WORK.
IT'S NOT EASY. IT'S HARD.
BUT I WELCOME HARD WORK.
I DON'T AVOID HARD WORK.
HARD WORK IS A GOOD THING.
BUT IT'S STILL HARD.
REALLY HARD.
BUT I LIKE WORKING HARD.
TOLES
10©2004 THE WASHINGTON POST
UNIVERSAL PRESS SYND.
-WORKING HARDLY.

10-8-04

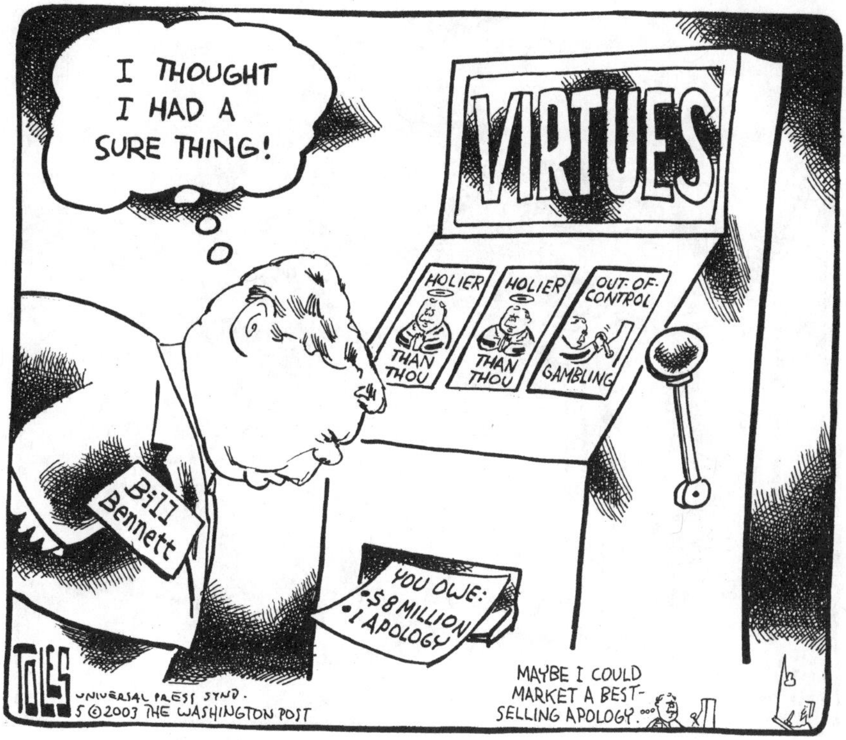
I THOUGHT I HAD A SURE THING!
VIRTUES
HOLIER THAN THOU
HOLIER THAN THOU
OUT-OF-CONTROL GAMBLING
Bill Bennett
YOU OWE: •$8 MILLION •1 APOLOGY
MAYBE I COULD MARKET A BEST-SELLING APOLOGY...
TOLES
UNIVERSAL PRESS SYND.
5 ©2003 THE WASHINGTON POST

5-6-03

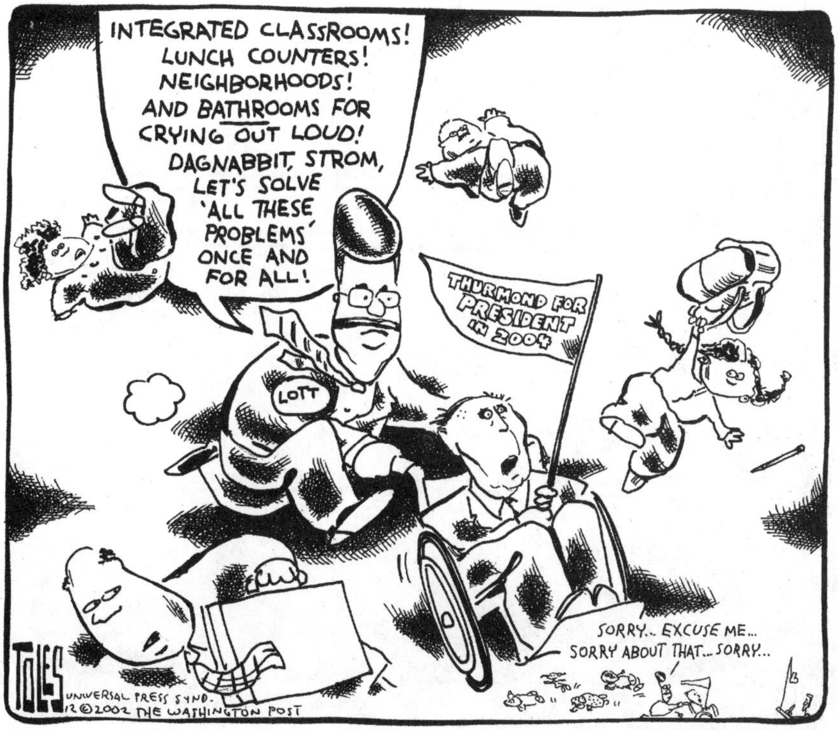
INTEGRATED CLASSROOMS! LUNCH COUNTERS! NEIGHBORHOODS! AND BATHROOMS FOR CRYING OUT LOUD! DAGNABBIT, STROM, LET'S SOLVE 'ALL THESE PROBLEMS' ONCE AND FOR ALL!
THURMOND FOR PRESIDENT IN 2004
LOTT
SORRY.. EXCUSE ME... SORRY ABOUT THAT... SORRY...
TOLES
UNIVERSAL PRESS SYND.
12 ©2002 THE WASHINGTON POST

12-12-02

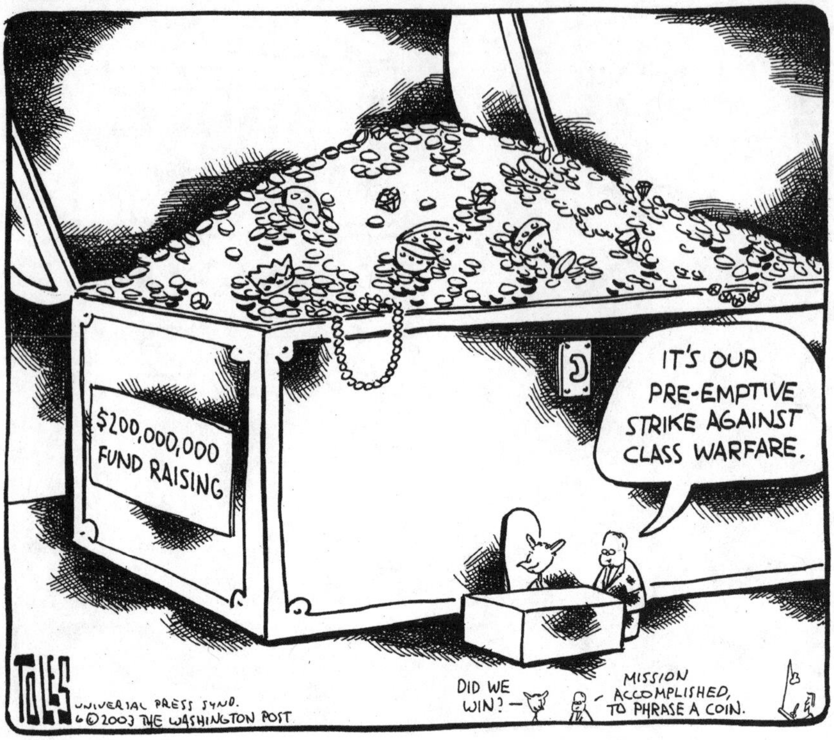
$200,000,000 FUND RAISING
IT'S OUR PRE-EMPTIVE STRIKE AGAINST CLASS WARFARE.
TOLES
UNIVERSAL PRESS SYND.
6 © 2003 THE WASHINGTON POST
DID WE WIN?
MISSION ACCOMPLISHED, TO PHRASE A COIN.

6-19-03

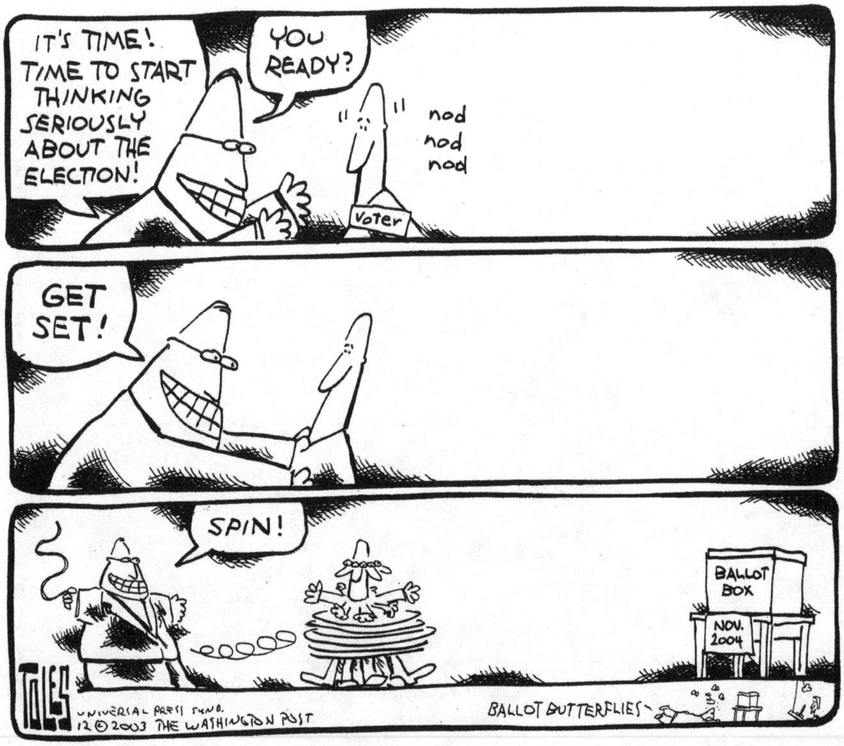
IT'S TIME! TIME TO START THINKING SERIOUSLY ABOUT THE ELECTION!
YOU READY?
nod nod nod
Voter
GET SET!
SPIN!
BALLOT BOX
NOV. 2004
TOLES
UNIVERSAL PRESS SYND.
12 © 2003 THE WASHINGTON POST
BALLOT BUTTERFLIES

12-28-03

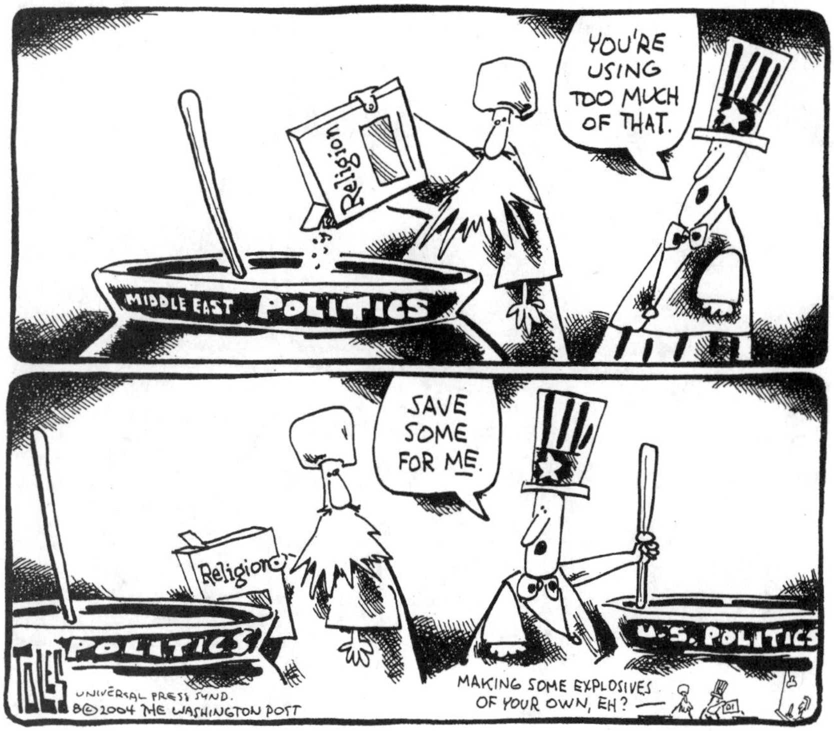
YOU'RE USING TOO MUCH OF THAT.
Religion
MIDDLE EAST POLITICS
SAVE SOME FOR ME.
Religion
POLITICS
U.S. POLITICS
TOLES
UNIVERSAL PRESS SYND.
8 © 2004 THE WASHINGTON POST
MAKING SOME EXPLOSIVES OF YOUR OWN, EH?

8-5-04

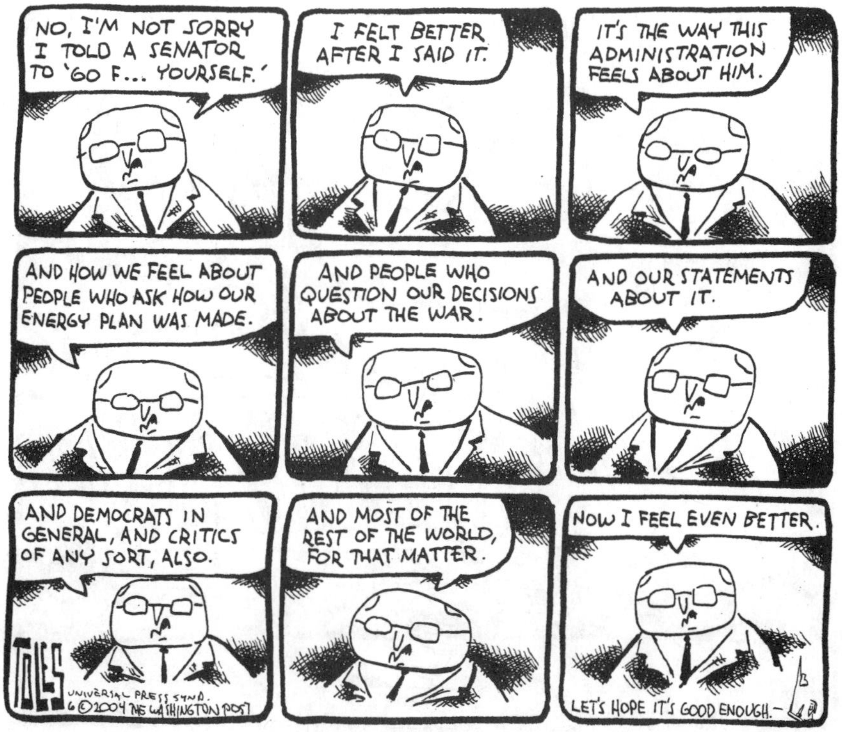
NO, I'M NOT SORRY I TOLD A SENATOR TO 'GO F... YOURSELF.'
I FELT BETTER AFTER I SAID IT.
IT'S THE WAY THIS ADMINISTRATION FEELS ABOUT HIM.
AND HOW WE FEEL ABOUT PEOPLE WHO ASK HOW OUR ENERGY PLAN WAS MADE.
AND PEOPLE WHO QUESTION OUR DECISIONS ABOUT THE WAR.
AND OUR STATEMENTS ABOUT IT.
AND DEMOCRATS IN GENERAL, AND CRITICS OF ANY SORT, ALSO.
AND MOST OF THE REST OF THE WORLD, FOR THAT MATTER.
NOW I FEEL EVEN BETTER.
TOLES
UNIVERSAL PRESS SYND.
6 © 2004 THE WASHINGTON POST
LET'S HOPE IT'S GOOD ENOUGH.

6-29-04

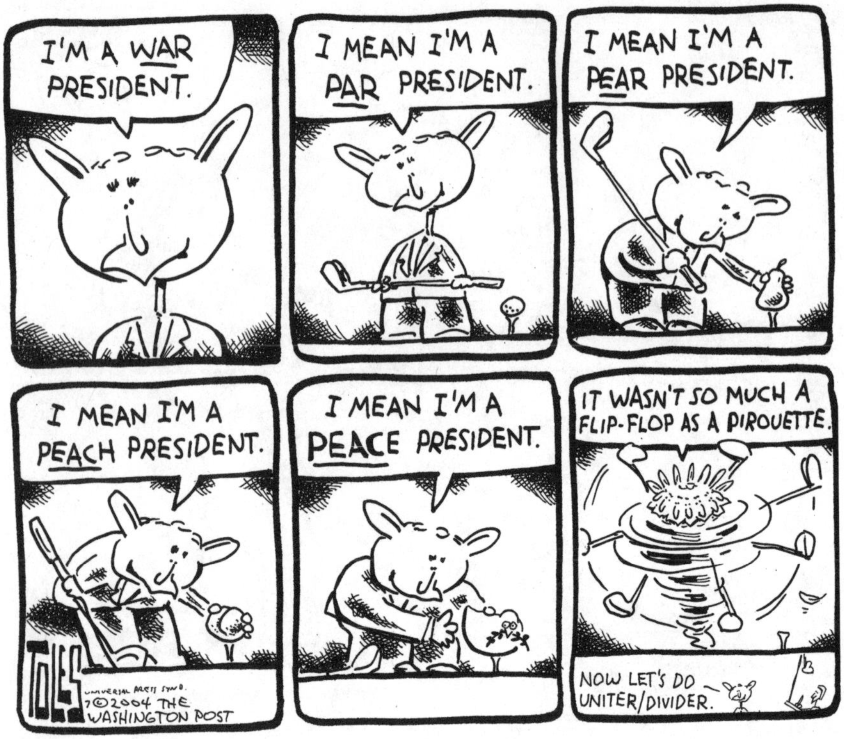
I'M A WAR PRESIDENT.
I MEAN I'M A PAR PRESIDENT.
I MEAN I'M A PEAR PRESIDENT.
I MEAN I'M A PEACH PRESIDENT.
I MEAN I'M A PEACE PRESIDENT.
IT WASN'T SO MUCH A FLIP-FLOP AS A PIROUETTE.
NOW LET'S DO UNITER/DIVIDER.
TOLES
UNIVERSAL PRESS SYND.
7 © 2004 THE WASHINGTON POST

7-25-04

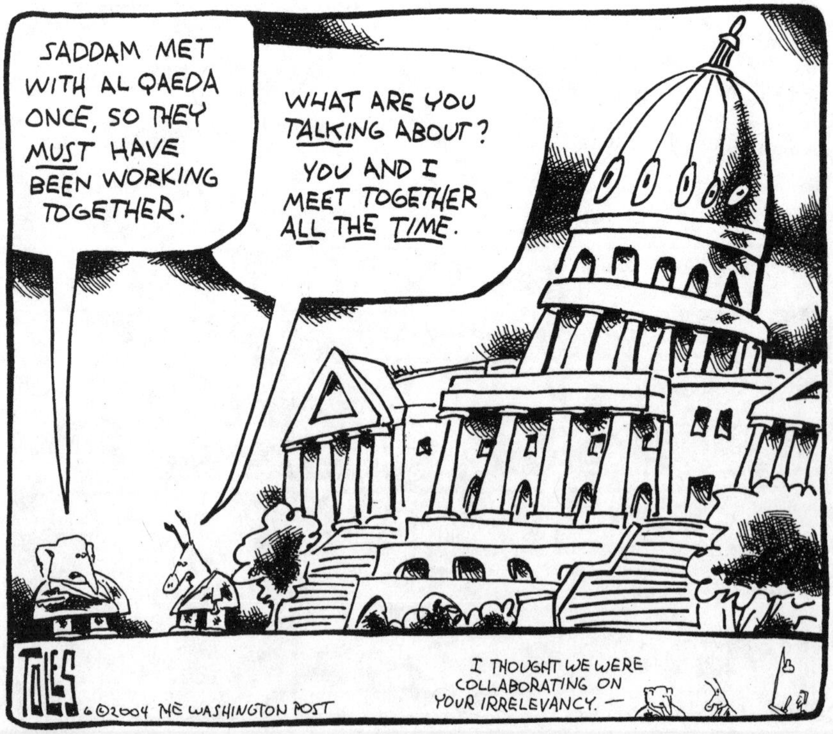
SADDAM MET WITH AL QAEDA ONCE, SO THEY MUST HAVE BEEN WORKING TOGETHER.
WHAT ARE YOU TALKING ABOUT? YOU AND I MEET TOGETHER ALL THE TIME.
I THOUGHT WE WERE COLLABORATING ON YOUR IRRELEVANCY.
TOLES
6 © 2004 THE WASHINGTON POST

6-20-04

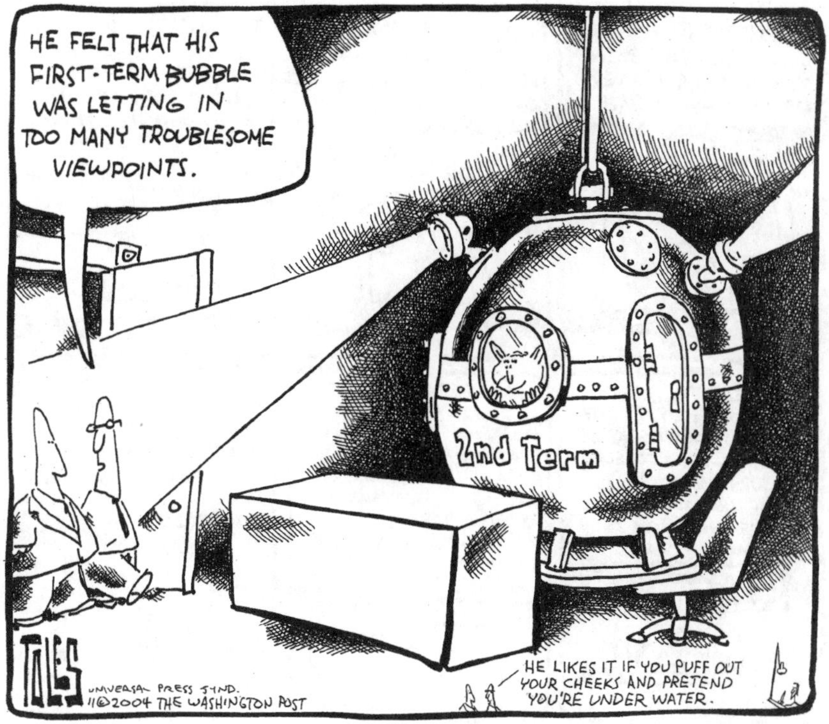
HE FELT THAT HIS FIRST-TERM BUBBLE WAS LETTING IN TOO MANY TROUBLESOME VIEWPOINTS.
2nd Term
TOLES
UNIVERSAL PRESS SYND.
11© 2004 THE WASHINGTON POST
HE LIKES IT IF YOU PUFF OUT YOUR CHEEKS AND PRETEND YOU'RE UNDER WATER.

11-23-04

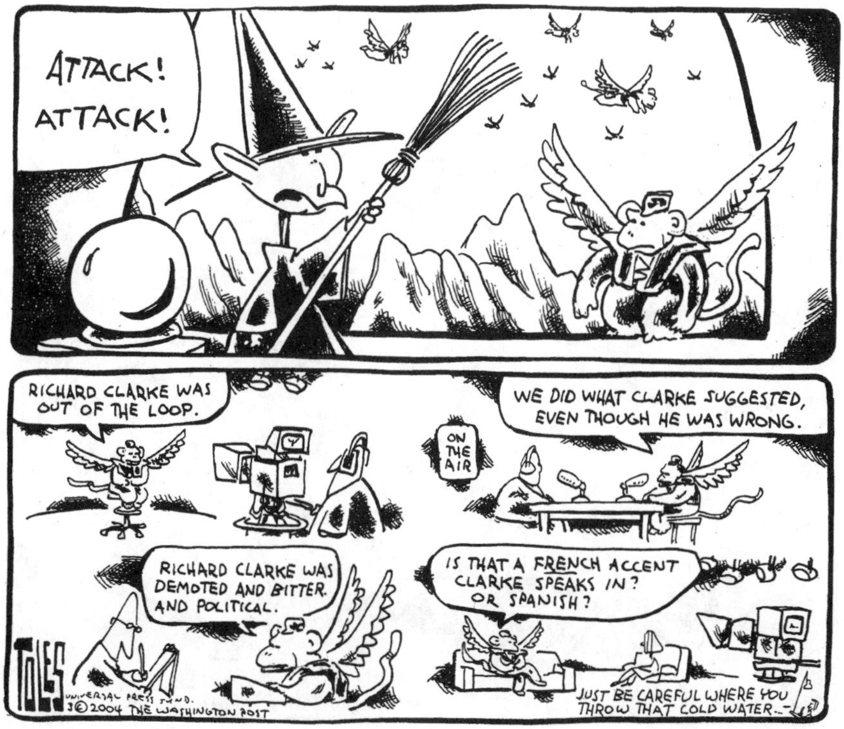
ATTACK! ATTACK!
RICHARD CLARKE WAS OUT OF THE LOOP.
WE DID WHAT CLARKE SUGGESTED, EVEN THOUGH HE WAS WRONG.
ON THE AIR
RICHARD CLARKE WAS DEMOTED AND BITTER. AND POLITICAL.
IS THAT A FRENCH ACCENT CLARKE SPEAKS IN? OR SPANISH?
TOLES
UNIVERSAL PRESS SYND.
3© 2004 THE WASHINGTON POST
JUST BE CAREFUL WHERE YOU THROW THAT COLD WATER...

3-24-04

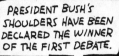

PRESIDENT BUSH'S SHOULDERS HAVE BEEN DECLARED THE WINNER OF THE FIRST DEBATE.
THURSDAY NIGHT'S TOPIC OF FOREIGN AFFAIRS PROVIDED REPORTERS AN EXCELLENT OPPORTUNITY TO ASSESS THE ALL-IMPORTANT BODY LANGUAGE DIMENSION OF THE RACE.
TO A QUESTION ABOUT CAR BOMBINGS IN IRAQ, THE PRESIDENT RESPONDED WITH A DECISIVE OUTWARD-TURNING OF THE ARMS, WHILE KERRY'S HANDS RESTED ON HIS PODIUM, HELPLESSLY?
IN HIS REBUTTAL, KERRY SCORED POINTS BY HAVING BOTH EYES LOOKING AT THE SAME THING SIMULTANEOUSLY, BUT TURNING HIS HEAD SIDE-TO-SIDE BROUGHT TO MIND OUR PRECONCEPTION OF YOU-KNOW-WHAT.
AND WHEN THE PRESIDENT SAID THAT THE WORLD WAS BETTER OFF NOW THAT OSAMA BIN LADEN WAS NO LONGER DICTATOR OF IRAQ, KERRY AVOIDED THE FATAL SIGHING AND EYE-ROLLING, BUT LET HIS JAW DROP, THOUGH SOME ANALYSTS INSIST IT'S ALWAYS THAT LONG.
WE NOW TURN OUR ATTENTION TO THE DOMESTIC ISSUES DEBATE, WHERE REPORTERS WILL HAVE AN OPPORTUNITY TO DISCUSS THE CANDIDATES' ONE-LINERS, ANECDOTES AND ZINGERS.
THE MEDIA WINS THE 'LOWERED EXPECTATIONS' CONTEST—
TOLES
UNIVERSAL PRESS SYND.
© 2004 THE WASHINGTON POST

9-29-04

2 HOUR WAIT FROM THIS POINT
WHERE DO I GO TO VOTE AGAINST THIS?
U.S. ELECTION SYSTEM
PATENT 1804
POPULAR VOTE
RED
BLUE
ELECTORS
NON-SWING STATES
J-H
—THAT WOULD BE A DIFFERENT COUNTRY.
TOLES
UNIVERSAL PRESS SYND
© 2004 THE WASHINGTON POST

11-7-04

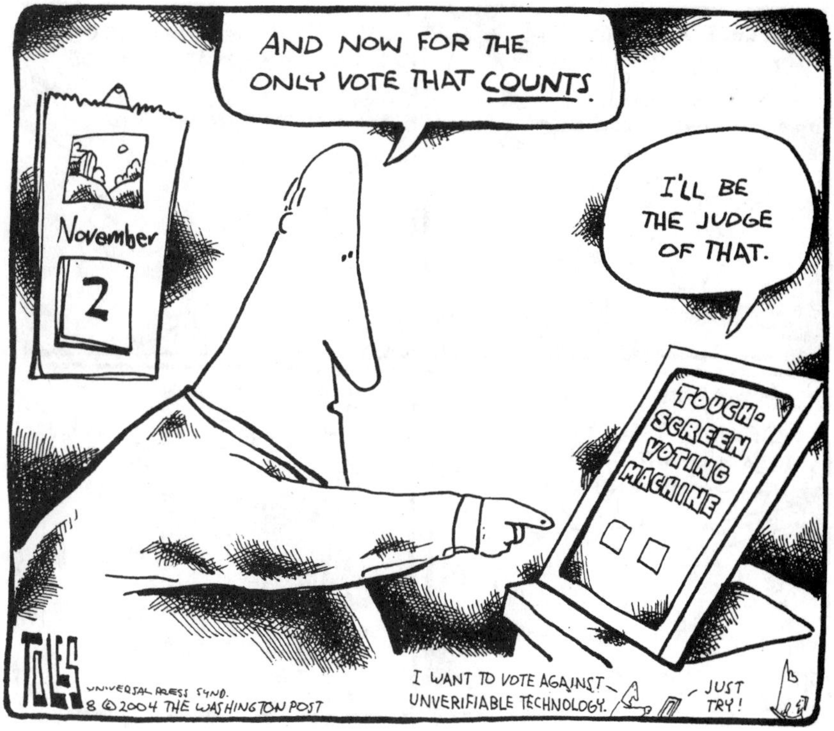
AND NOW FOR THE ONLY VOTE THAT COUNTS.
November
2
I'LL BE THE JUDGE OF THAT.
TOUCH-SCREEN VOTING MACHINE
TOLES
UNIVERSAL PRESS SYND.
8 © 2004 THE WASHINGTON POST
I WANT TO VOTE AGAINST UNVERIFIABLE TECHNOLOGY.
JUST TRY!

8-16-04

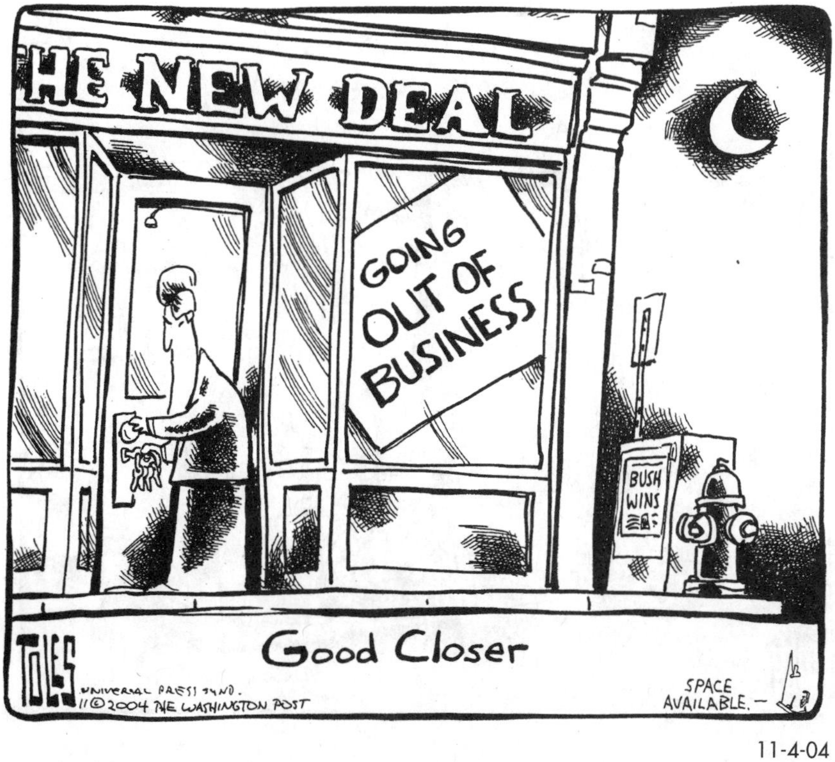
THE NEW DEAL
GOING OUT OF BUSINESS
BUSH WINS
Good Closer
TOLES
UNIVERSAL PRESS SYND.
11 © 2004 THE WASHINGTON POST
SPACE AVAILABLE.

11-4-04

REELECTION MEANS THE VOTERS AGREE I MADE NO MISTAKES.
THAT THEY AGREE THAT NO ONE IN MY ADMINISTRATION MADE ANY MISTAKES.
THAT THE VOTERS DON'T EXPECT ANY REASSESSMENT, ACCOUNTABILITY OR LEARNING TO TAKE PLACE.
A CAMPAIGN SPEECH I DECIDED WOULD BE MORE EFFECTIVE AFTER THE ELECTION.
THAT'S THE KIND OF FREEDOM I'M TALKING ABOUT! —
TOLES
UNIVERSAL PRESS SYND.
1©2005 THE WASHINGTON POST

1-23-05

WE JUST MADE OFFICIAL THE JOB KARL HAS BEEN DOING ALL ALONG ANYWAY...
HEY!
ROVE
DICK
PRESIDENT OF THE UNITED STATES
SO NOW WHAT WILL YOU DO? —
I'LL ASK!
TOLES
UNIVERSAL PRESS SYND.
2©2005 THE WASHINGTON POST

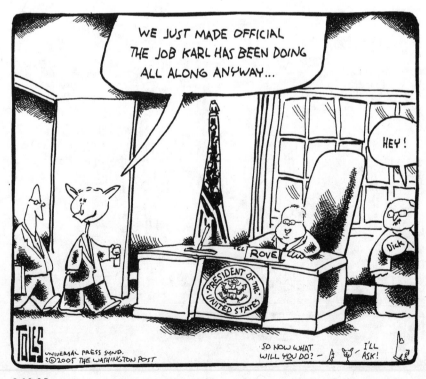

2-10-05

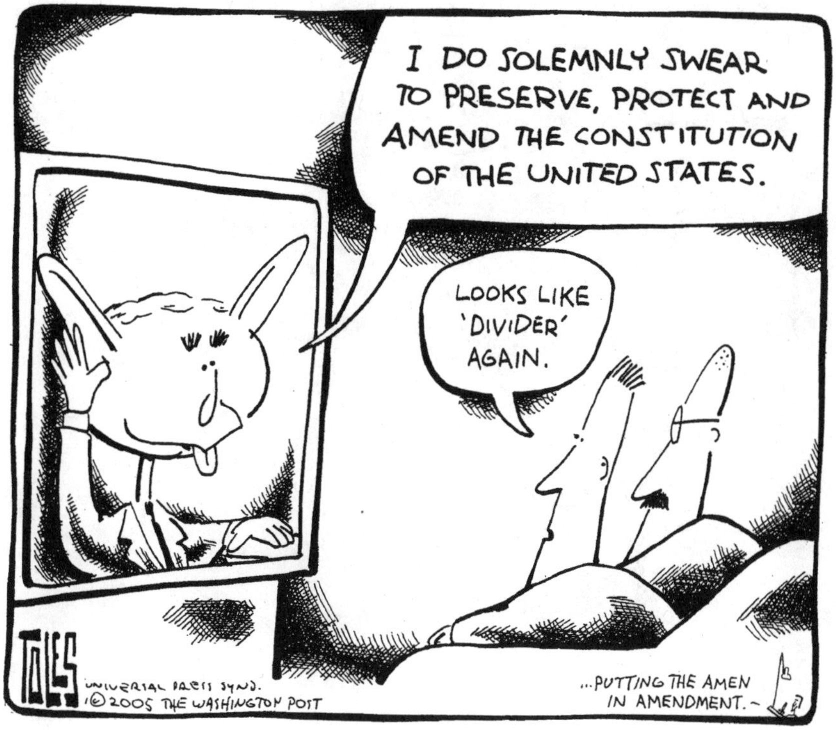
I DO SOLEMNLY SWEAR TO PRESERVE, PROTECT AND AMEND THE CONSTITUTION OF THE UNITED STATES.
LOOKS LIKE 'DIVIDER' AGAIN.
TOLES
UNIVERSAL PRESS SYND.
1 © 2005 THE WASHINGTON POST
...PUTTING THE AMEN IN AMENDMENT.

1-18-05

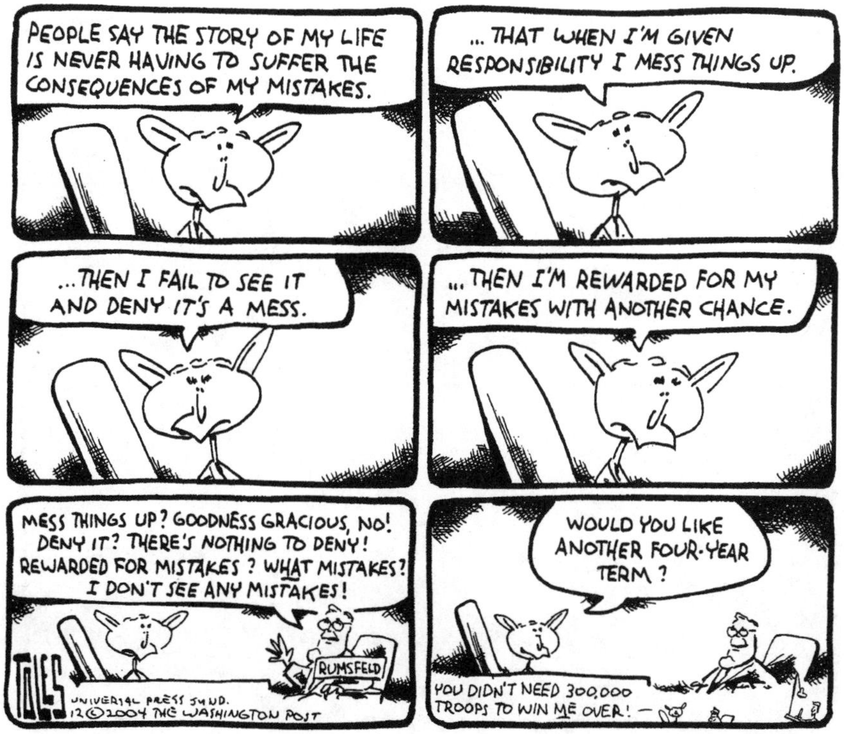
PEOPLE SAY THE STORY OF MY LIFE IS NEVER HAVING TO SUFFER THE CONSEQUENCES OF MY MISTAKES.
... THAT WHEN I'M GIVEN RESPONSIBILITY I MESS THINGS UP.
...THEN I FAIL TO SEE IT AND DENY IT'S A MESS.
...THEN I'M REWARDED FOR MY MISTAKES WITH ANOTHER CHANCE.
MESS THINGS UP? GOODNESS GRACIOUS, NO! DENY IT? THERE'S NOTHING TO DENY! REWARDED FOR MISTAKES? WHAT MISTAKES? I DON'T SEE ANY MISTAKES!
RUMSFELD
TOLES
UNIVERSAL PRESS SYND.
12 © 2004 THE WASHINGTON POST
WOULD YOU LIKE ANOTHER FOUR-YEAR TERM?
YOU DIDN'T NEED 300,000 TROOPS TO WIN ME OVER!

12-7-04

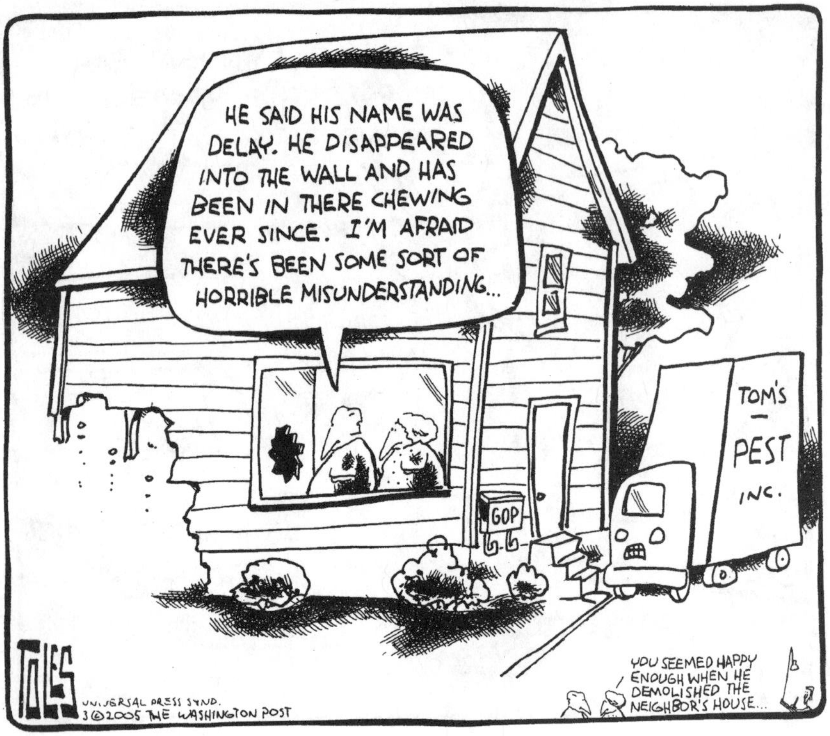
HE SAID HIS NAME WAS DELAY. HE DISAPPEARED INTO THE WALL AND HAS BEEN IN THERE CHEWING EVER SINCE. I'M AFRAID THERE'S BEEN SOME SORT OF HORRIBLE MISUNDERSTANDING...
GOP
TOM'S — PEST INC.
YOU SEEMED HAPPY ENOUGH WHEN HE DEMOLISHED THE NEIGHBOR'S HOUSE...
TOLES
UNIVERSAL PRESS SYND.
3 © 2005 THE WASHINGTON POST

3-27-05

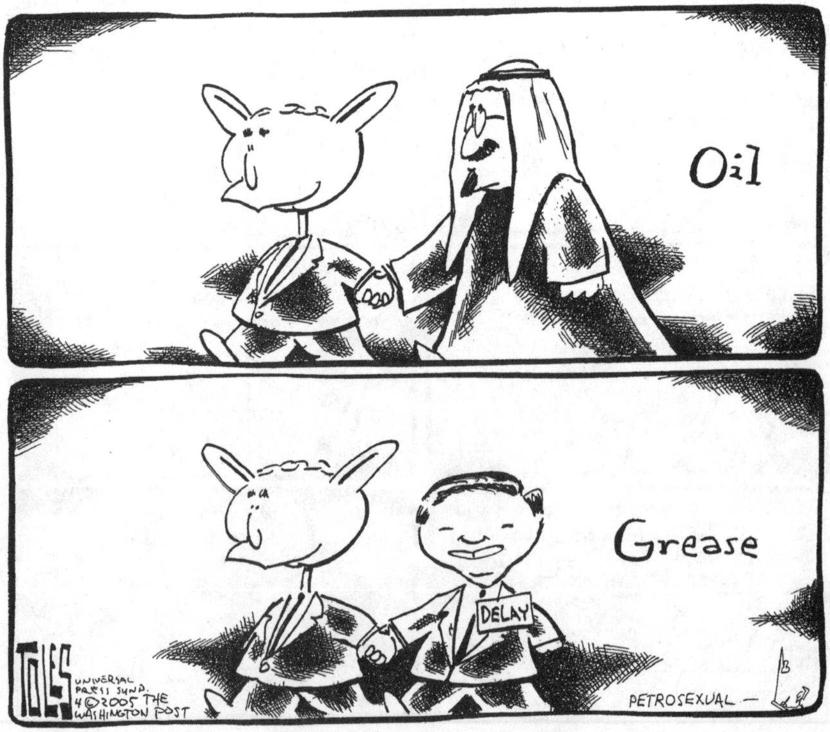
Oil
Grease
DELAY
PETROSEXUAL —
TOLES
UNIVERSAL PRESS SYND.
4 © 2005 THE WASHINGTON POST

4-28-05

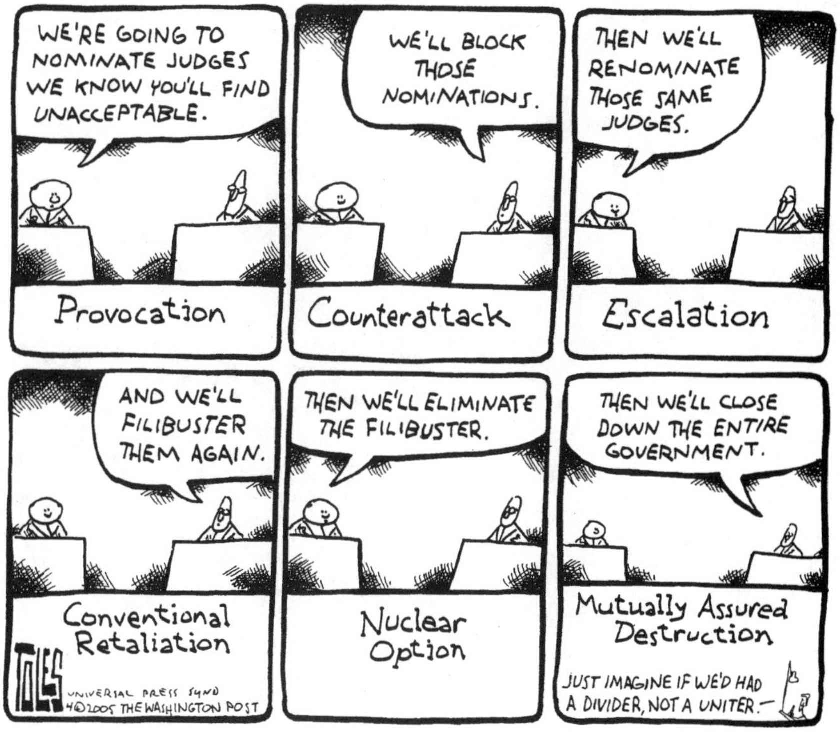
WE'RE GOING TO NOMINATE JUDGES WE KNOW YOU'LL FIND UNACCEPTABLE.
Provocation
WE'LL BLOCK THOSE NOMINATIONS.
Counterattack
THEN WE'LL RENOMINATE THOSE SAME JUDGES.
Escalation
AND WE'LL FILIBUSTER THEM AGAIN.
Conventional Retaliation
THEN WE'LL ELIMINATE THE FILIBUSTER.
Nuclear Option
THEN WE'LL CLOSE DOWN THE ENTIRE GOVERNMENT.
Mutually Assured Destruction
TOLES
UNIVERSAL PRESS SYND
4©2005 THE WASHINGTON POST
JUST IMAGINE IF WE'D HAD A DIVIDER, NOT A UNITER.

4-17-05

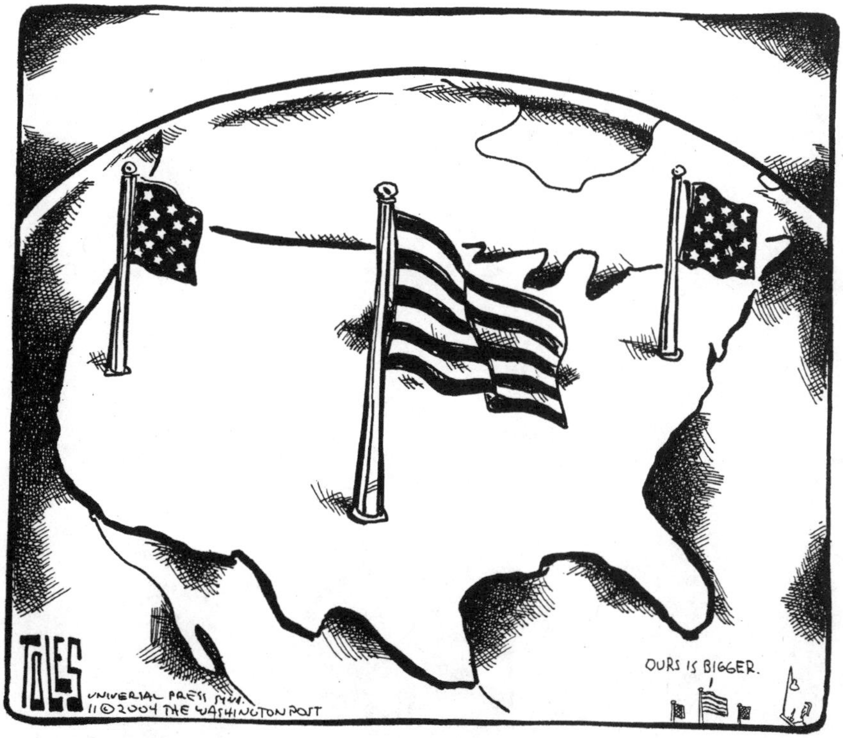
TOLES
UNIVERSAL PRESS SYND.
11©2004 THE WASHINGTON POST
OURS IS BIGGER.

11-14-04

GAYS AND RELIGION

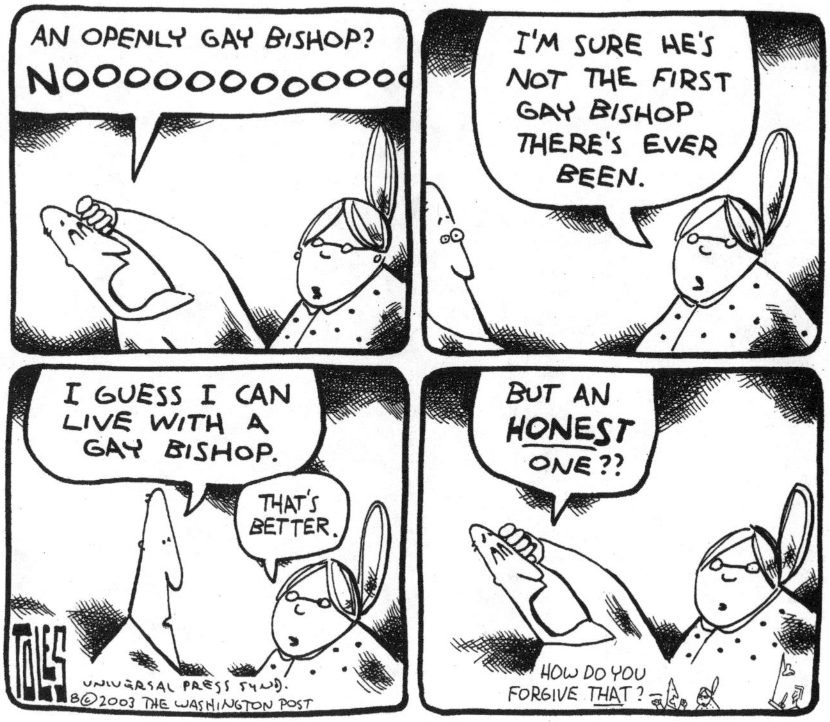
AN OPENLY GAY BISHOP?
NOOOOOOOOOOOO
I'M SURE HE'S NOT THE FIRST GAY BISHOP THERE'S EVER BEEN.
I GUESS I CAN LIVE WITH A GAY BISHOP.
THAT'S BETTER.
BUT AN HONEST ONE??
TOLES
UNIVERSAL PRESS SYND.
8©2003 THE WASHINGTON POST
HOW DO YOU FORGIVE THAT?

8-7-03

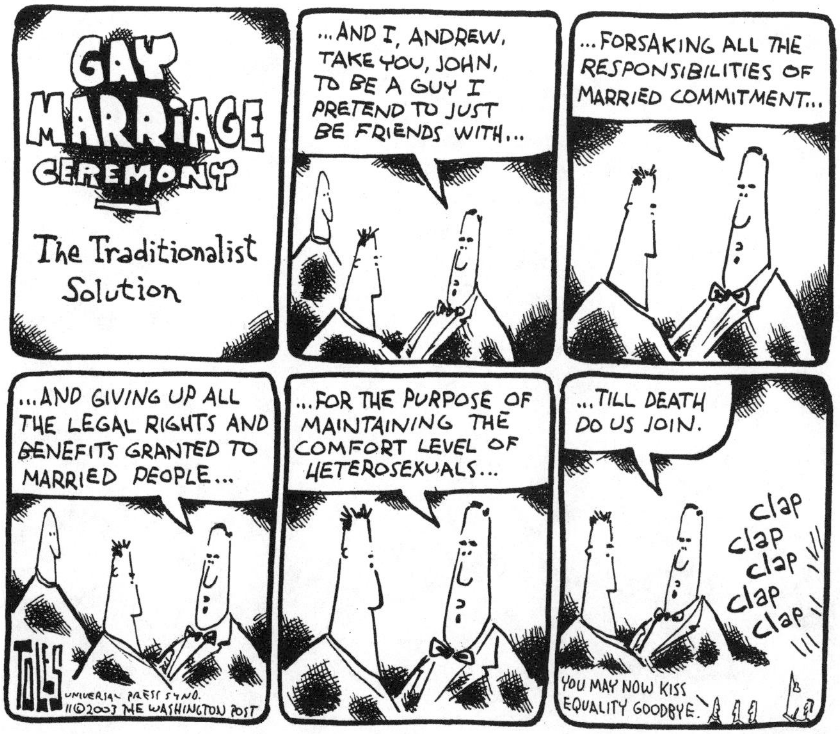
GAY MARRIAGE CEREMONY
The Traditionalist Solution
...AND I, ANDREW, TAKE YOU, JOHN, TO BE A GUY I PRETEND TO JUST BE FRIENDS WITH...
...FORSAKING ALL THE RESPONSIBILITIES OF MARRIED COMMITMENT...
...AND GIVING UP ALL THE LEGAL RIGHTS AND BENEFITS GRANTED TO MARRIED PEOPLE...
...FOR THE PURPOSE OF MAINTAINING THE COMFORT LEVEL OF HETEROSEXUALS...
...TILL DEATH DO US JOIN.
clap
clap
clap
clap
clap
TOLES
UNIVERSAL PRESS SYND.
11©2003 THE WASHINGTON POST
YOU MAY NOW KISS EQUALITY GOODBYE.

11-20-03

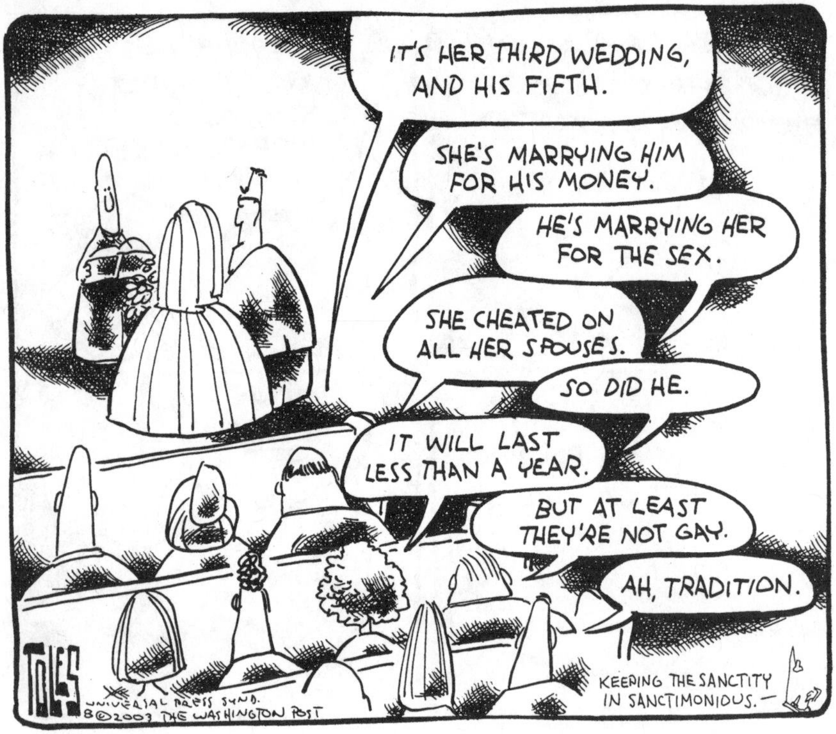
IT'S HER THIRD WEDDING, AND HIS FIFTH.
SHE'S MARRYING HIM FOR HIS MONEY.
HE'S MARRYING HER FOR THE SEX.
SHE CHEATED ON ALL HER SPOUSES.
SO DID HE.
IT WILL LAST LESS THAN A YEAR.
BUT AT LEAST THEY'RE NOT GAY.
AH, TRADITION.
TOLES
UNIVERSAL PRESS SYND.
8©2003 THE WASHINGTON POST
KEEPING THE SANCTITY IN SANCTIMONIOUS.—

8-3-03

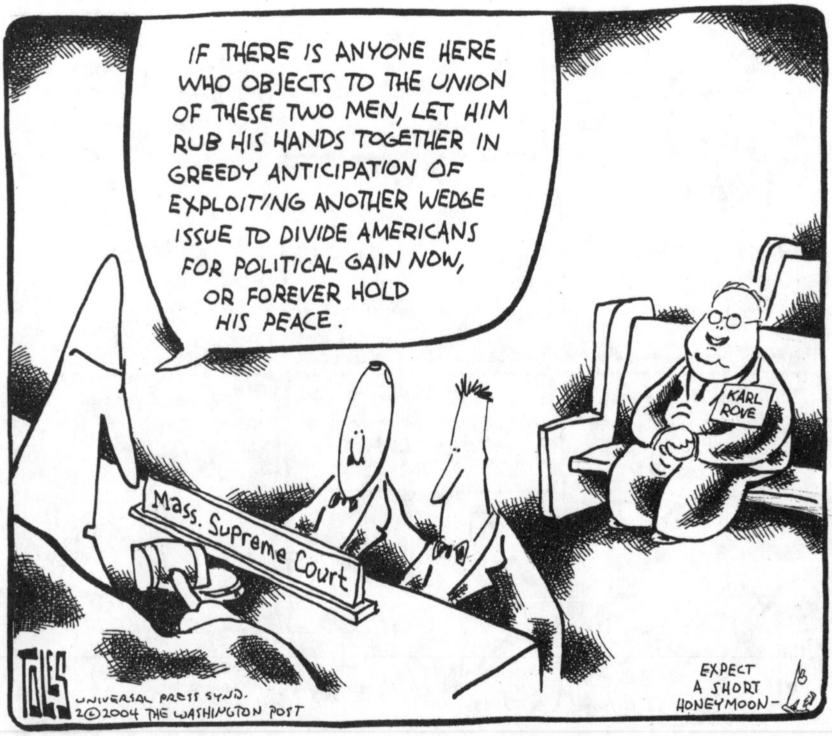
IF THERE IS ANYONE HERE WHO OBJECTS TO THE UNION OF THESE TWO MEN, LET HIM RUB HIS HANDS TOGETHER IN GREEDY ANTICIPATION OF EXPLOITING ANOTHER WEDGE ISSUE TO DIVIDE AMERICANS FOR POLITICAL GAIN NOW, OR FOREVER HOLD HIS PEACE.
KARL ROVE
Mass. Supreme Court
TOLES
UNIVERSAL PRESS SYND.
2©2004 THE WASHINGTON POST
EXPECT A SHORT HONEYMOON—

2-8-04

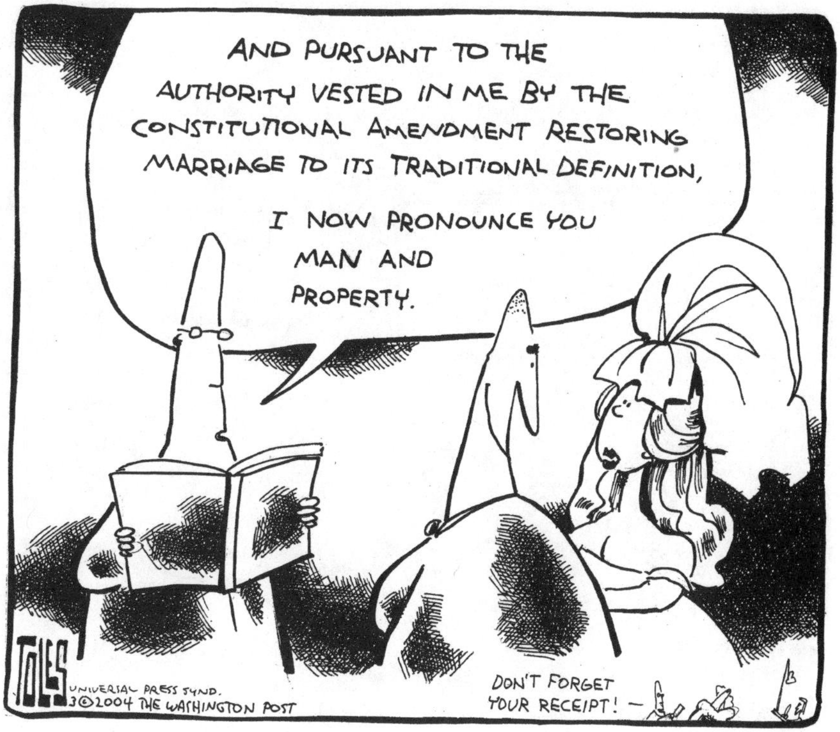
AND PURSUANT TO THE AUTHORITY VESTED IN ME BY THE CONSTITUTIONAL AMENDMENT RESTORING MARRIAGE TO ITS TRADITIONAL DEFINITION,
I NOW PRONOUNCE YOU MAN AND PROPERTY.
TOLES
UNIVERSAL PRESS SYND.
3©2004 THE WASHINGTON POST
DON'T FORGET YOUR RECEIPT! —

3-31-04

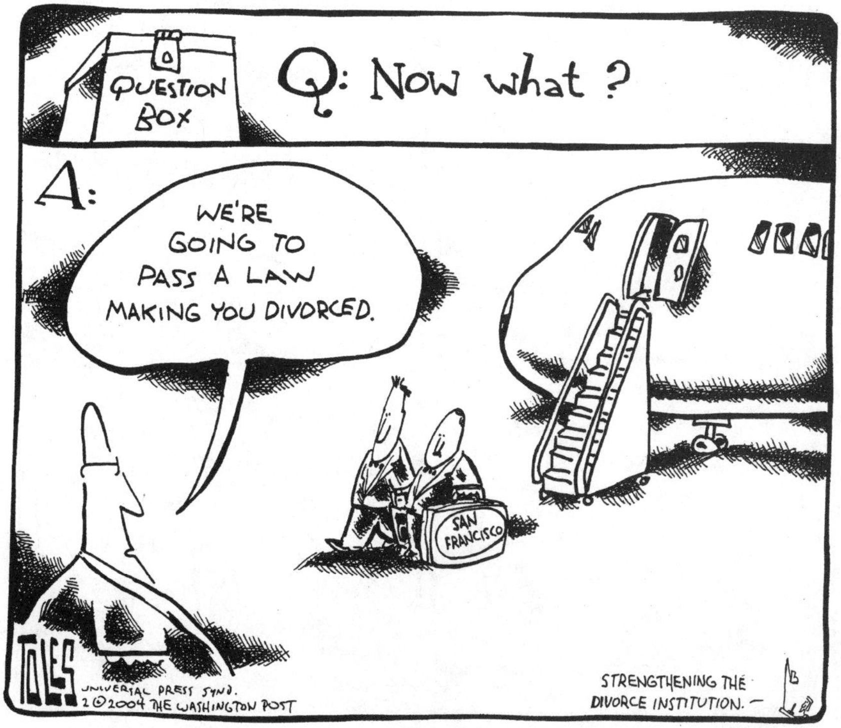
QUESTION BOX
Q: Now what?
A:
WE'RE GOING TO PASS A LAW MAKING YOU DIVORCED.
SAN FRANCISCO
TOLES
UNIVERSAL PRESS SYND.
2©2004 THE WASHINGTON POST
STRENGTHENING THE DIVORCE INSTITUTION. —

2-18-04

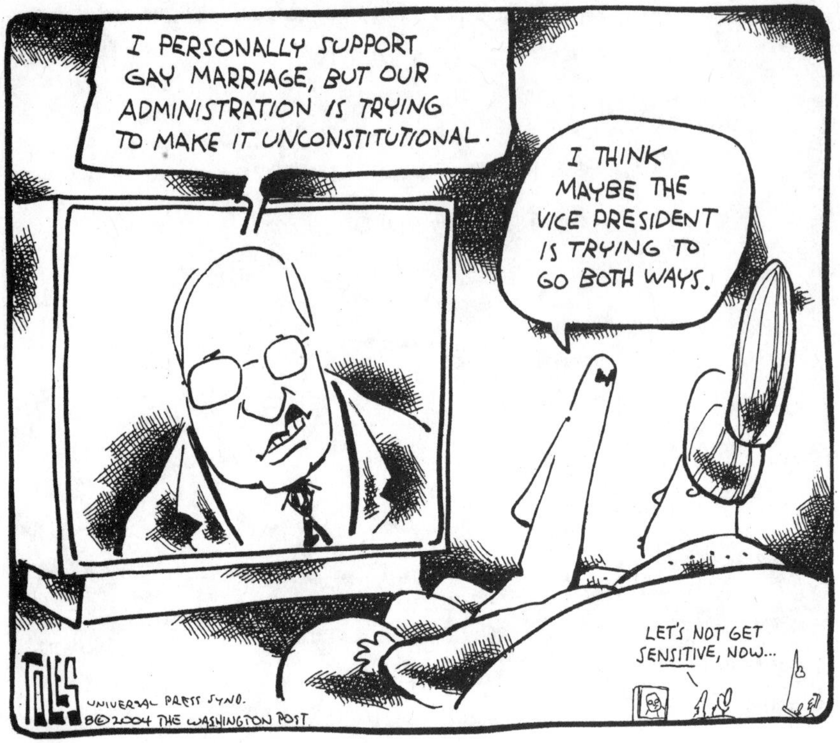
I PERSONALLY SUPPORT GAY MARRIAGE, BUT OUR ADMINISTRATION IS TRYING TO MAKE IT UNCONSTITUTIONAL.
I THINK MAYBE THE VICE PRESIDENT IS TRYING TO GO BOTH WAYS.
LET'S NOT GET SENSITIVE, NOW...
TOLES
UNIVERSAL PRESS SYND.
8©2004 THE WASHINGTON POST

8-26-04

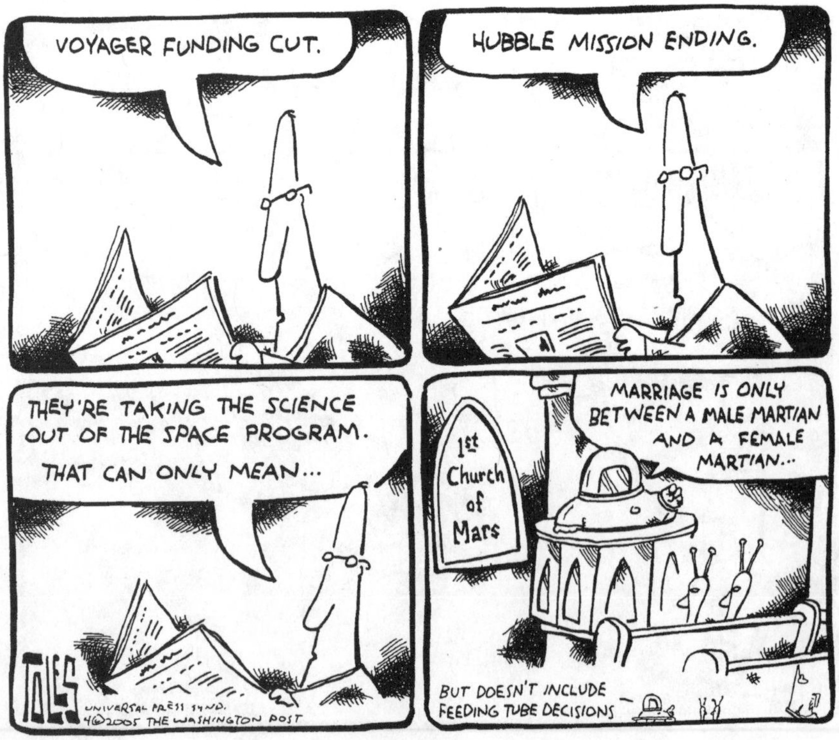
VOYAGER FUNDING CUT.
HUBBLE MISSION ENDING.
THEY'RE TAKING THE SCIENCE OUT OF THE SPACE PROGRAM.
THAT CAN ONLY MEAN...
1st Church of Mars
MARRIAGE IS ONLY BETWEEN A MALE MARTIAN AND A FEMALE MARTIAN...
BUT DOESN'T INCLUDE FEEDING TUBE DECISIONS
TOLES
UNIVERSAL PRESS SYND.
4©2005 THE WASHINGTON POST

4-13-05

WE'LL GET RID OF SOMETHING TO MAKE ROOM FOR IT.
RELIGION
Ethics
TOLES
UNIVERSAL PRESS SYND.
3©2005 THE WASHINGTON POST
SERMON ON THE HILL —

3-23-05

Terri Schiavo
POLITICS
Feeding Tube
TOLES
UNIVERSAL PRESS SYND.
3©2005 THE WASHINGTON POST
A PERSISTENT EXPLOITATIVE STATE —

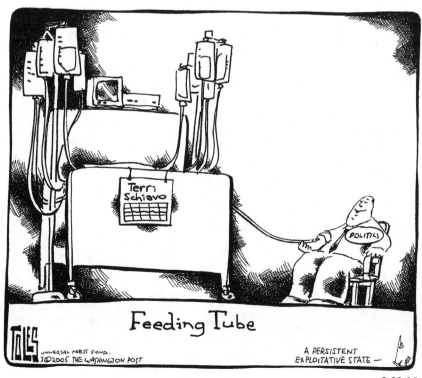

3-22-05

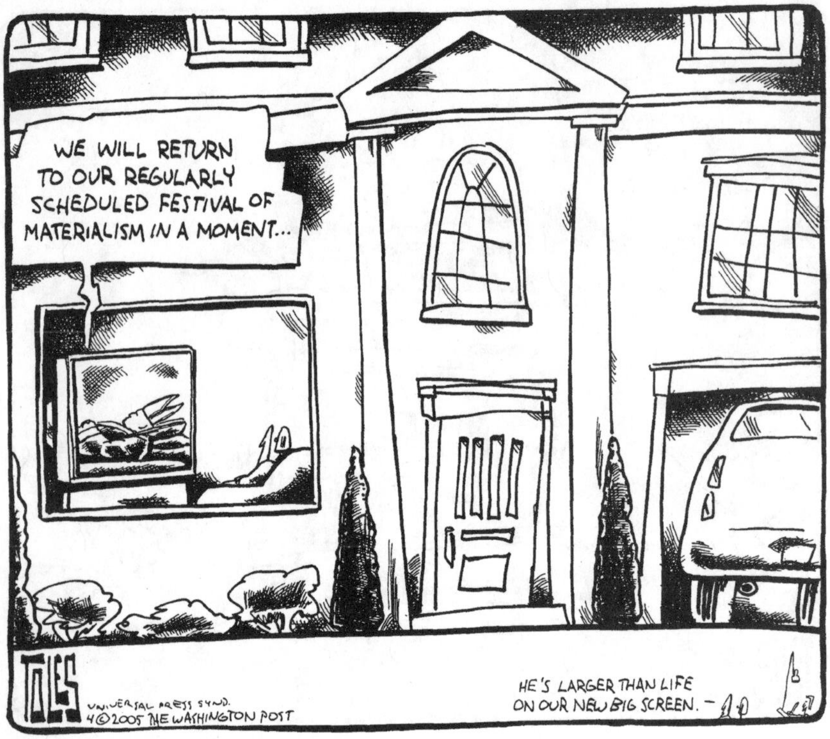
WE WILL RETURN TO OUR REGULARLY SCHEDULED FESTIVAL OF MATERIALISM IN A MOMENT...
TOLES
UNIVERSAL PRESS SYND.
4 © 2005 THE WASHINGTON POST
HE'S LARGER THAN LIFE ON OUR NEW BIG SCREEN.

4-5-05

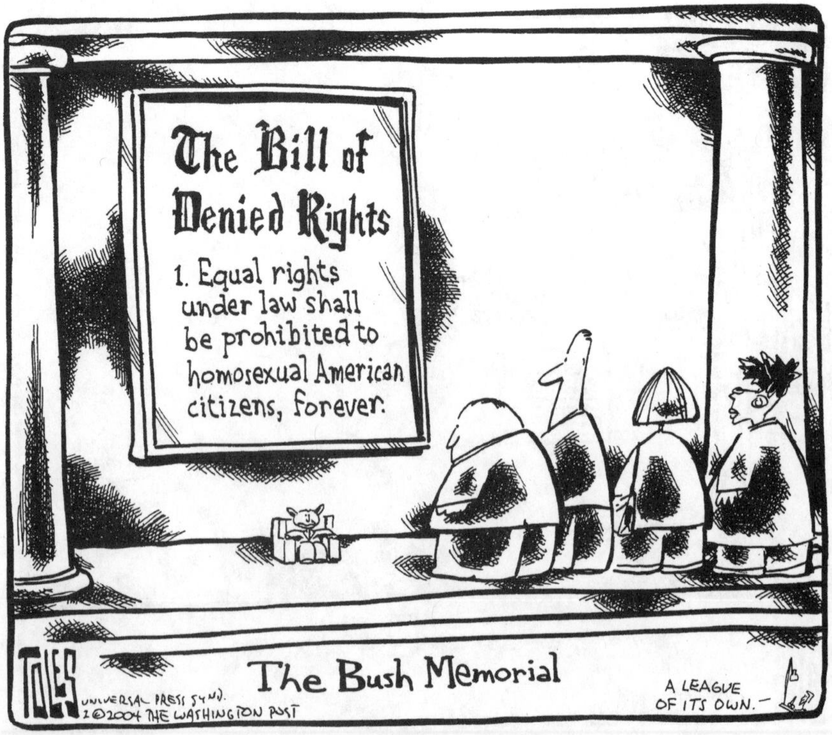
The Bill of Denied Rights
1. Equal rights under law shall be prohibited to homosexual American citizens, forever.
The Bush Memorial
TOLES
UNIVERSAL PRESS SYND.
2 © 2004 THE WASHINGTON POST
A LEAGUE OF ITS OWN.

2-26-04

LAW AND REGULATIONS

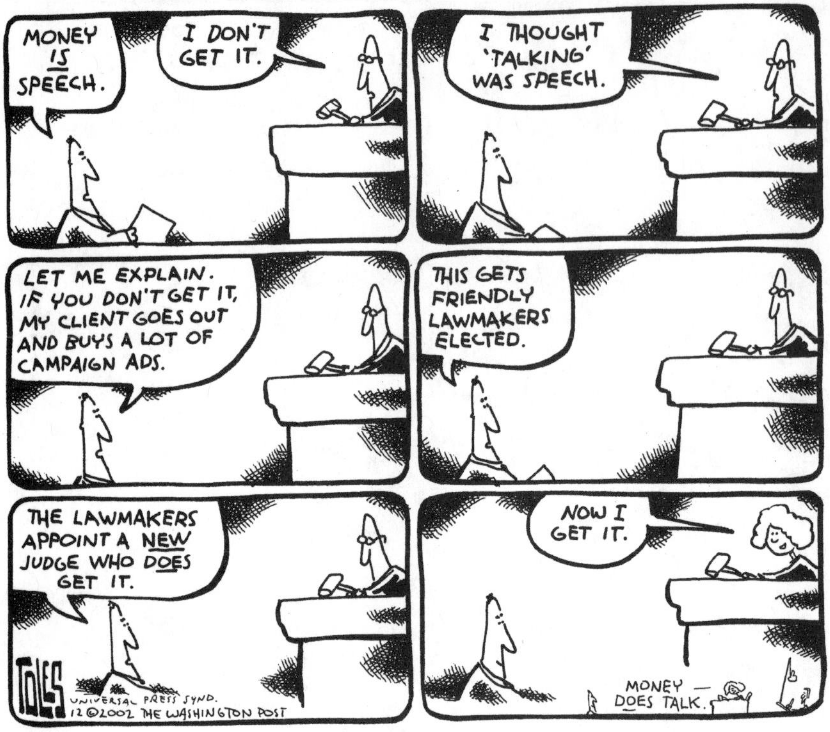
MONEY IS SPEECH.
I DON'T GET IT.
I THOUGHT 'TALKING' WAS SPEECH.
LET ME EXPLAIN. IF YOU DON'T GET IT, MY CLIENT GOES OUT AND BUYS A LOT OF CAMPAIGN ADS.
THIS GETS FRIENDLY LAWMAKERS ELECTED.
THE LAWMAKERS APPOINT A NEW JUDGE WHO DOES GET IT.
NOW I GET IT.
MONEY — DOES TALK.
TOLES
UNIVERSAL PRESS SYND.
12 ©2002 THE WASHINGTON POST

12-8-02

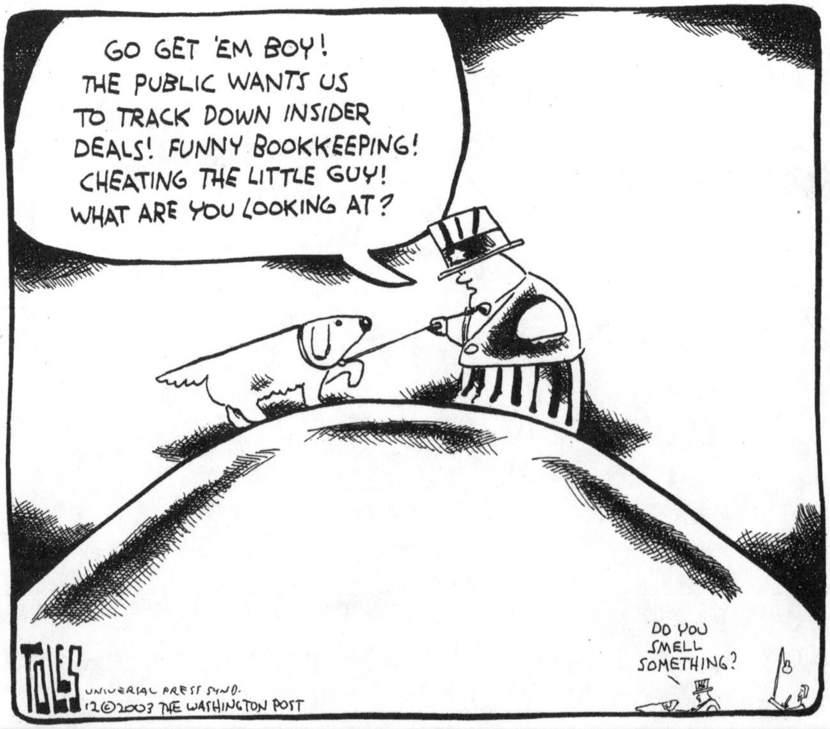
GO GET 'EM BOY! THE PUBLIC WANTS US TO TRACK DOWN INSIDER DEALS! FUNNY BOOKKEEPING! CHEATING THE LITTLE GUY! WHAT ARE YOU LOOKING AT?
DO YOU SMELL SOMETHING?
TOLES
UNIVERSAL PRESS SYND.
12 ©2003 THE WASHINGTON POST

12-29-03

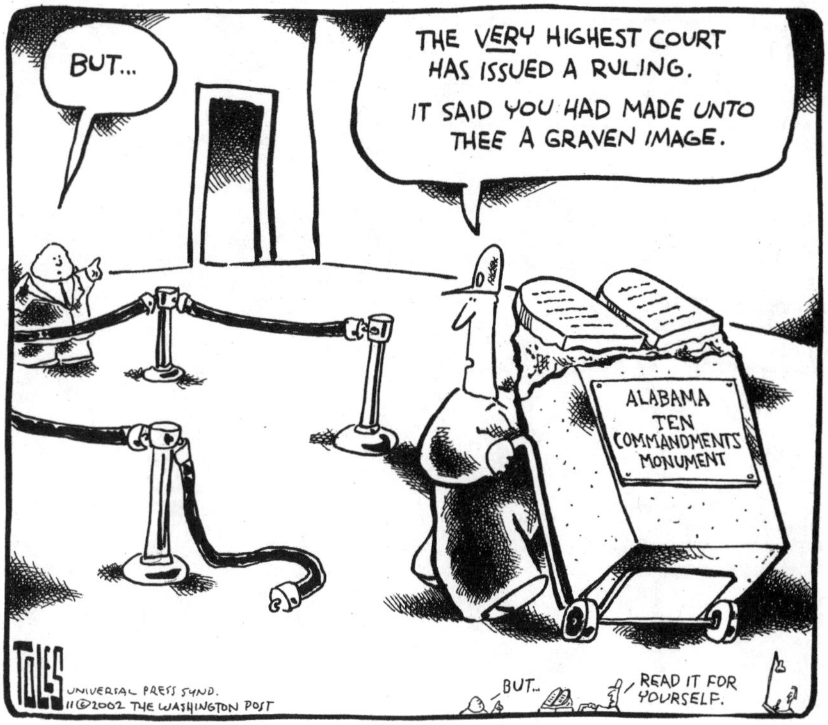
BUT...
THE VERY HIGHEST COURT HAS ISSUED A RULING.
IT SAID YOU HAD MADE UNTO THEE A GRAVEN IMAGE.
ALABAMA TEN COMMANDMENTS MONUMENT
TOLES
UNIVERSAL PRESS SYND.
11©2002 THE WASHINGTON POST
BUT...
READ IT FOR YOURSELF.

11-20-02

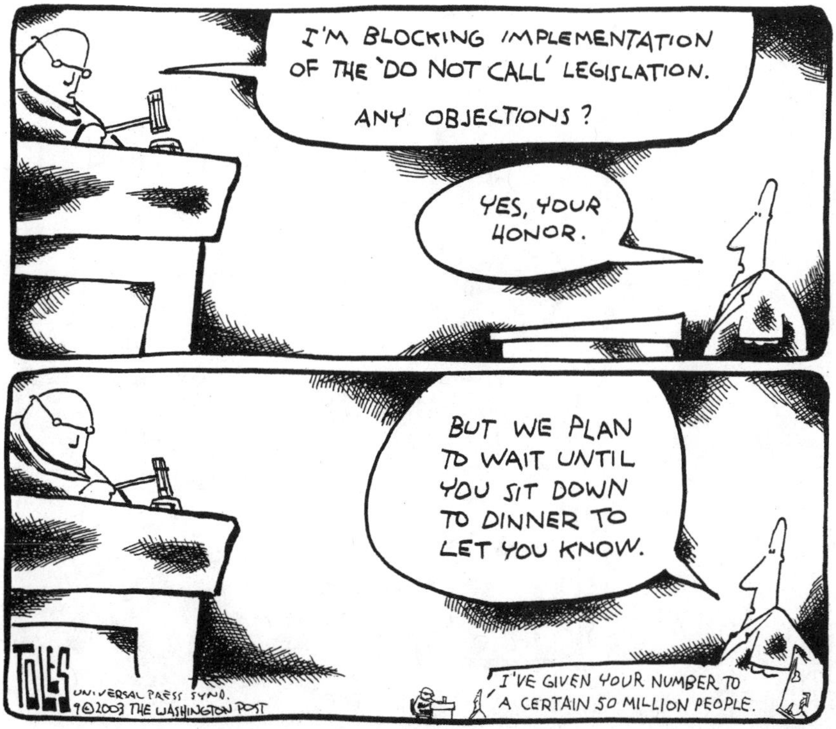
I'M BLOCKING IMPLEMENTATION OF THE 'DO NOT CALL' LEGISLATION.
ANY OBJECTIONS?
YES, YOUR HONOR.
BUT WE PLAN TO WAIT UNTIL YOU SIT DOWN TO DINNER TO LET YOU KNOW.
TOLES
UNIVERSAL PRESS SYND.
9©2003 THE WASHINGTON POST
I'VE GIVEN YOUR NUMBER TO A CERTAIN 50 MILLION PEOPLE.

9-26-03

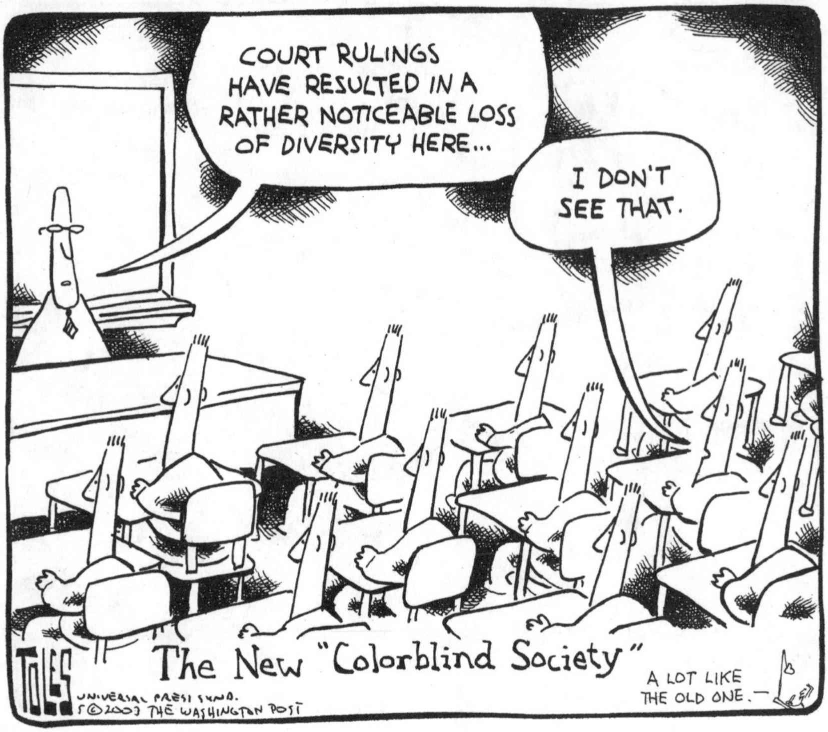
COURT RULINGS HAVE RESULTED IN A RATHER NOTICEABLE LOSS OF DIVERSITY HERE...
I DON'T SEE THAT.
The New "Colorblind Society"
A LOT LIKE THE OLD ONE.
TOLES
UNIVERSAL PRESS SYND.
5 © 2003 THE WASHINGTON POST

5-22-03

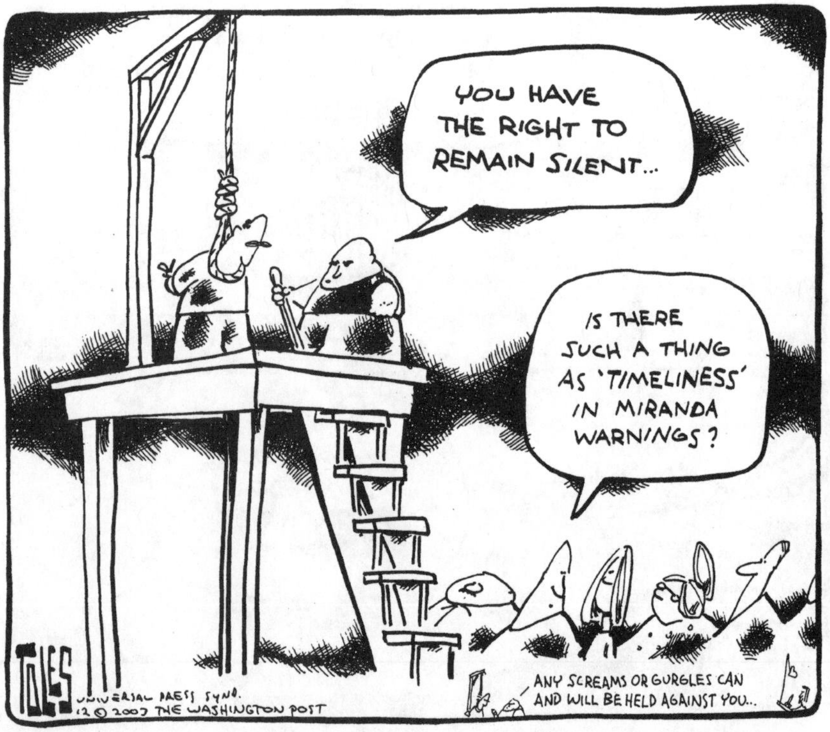
YOU HAVE THE RIGHT TO REMAIN SILENT...
IS THERE SUCH A THING AS 'TIMELINESS' IN MIRANDA WARNINGS?
ANY SCREAMS OR GURGLES CAN AND WILL BE HELD AGAINST YOU...
TOLES
UNIVERSAL PRESS SYND.
12 © 2003 THE WASHINGTON POST

12-11-03

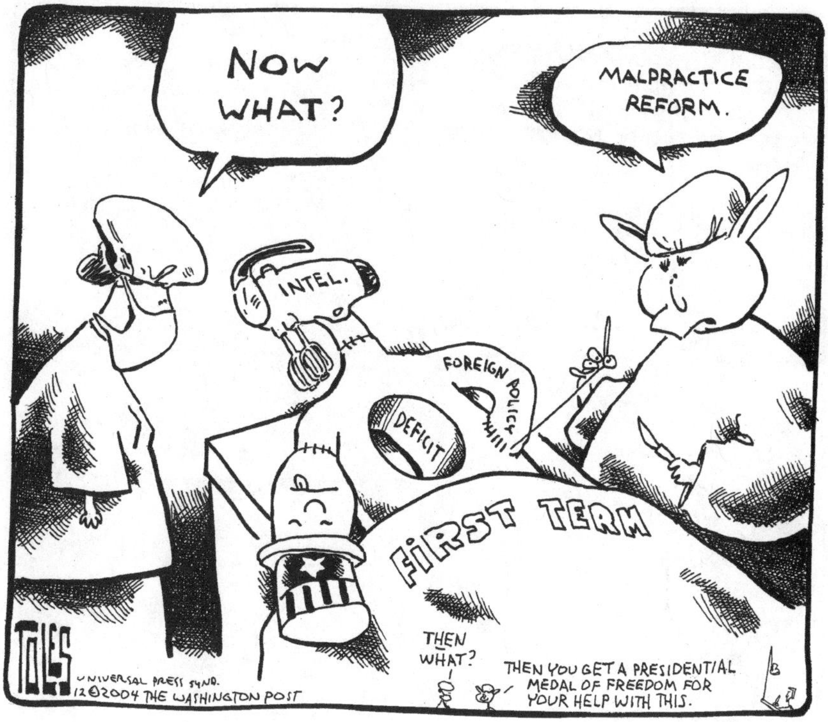
NOW WHAT?
MALPRACTICE REFORM.
INTEL.
FOREIGN POLICY
DEFICIT
FIRST TERM
TOLES
UNIVERSAL PRESS SYND.
12 © 2004 THE WASHINGTON POST
THEN WHAT?
THEN YOU GET A PRESIDENTIAL MEDAL OF FREEDOM FOR YOUR HELP WITH THIS.

12-17-04

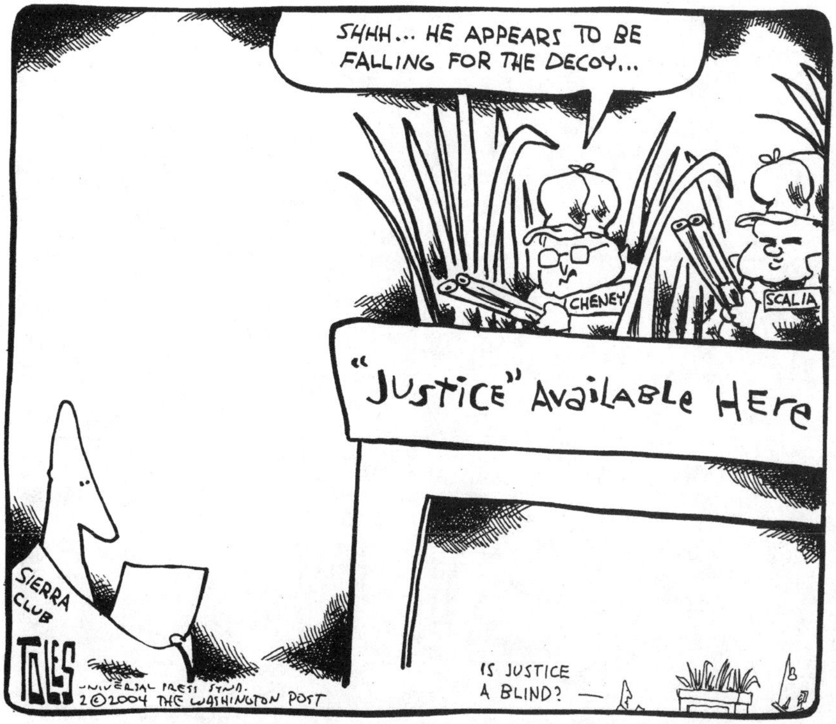
SHHH... HE APPEARS TO BE FALLING FOR THE DECOY...
CHENEY
SCALIA
"JUSTICE" AvaiLaBLe HEre
SIERRA CLUB
TOLES
UNIVERSAL PRESS SYND.
2 © 2004 THE WASHINGTON POST
IS JUSTICE A BLIND?

2-25-04

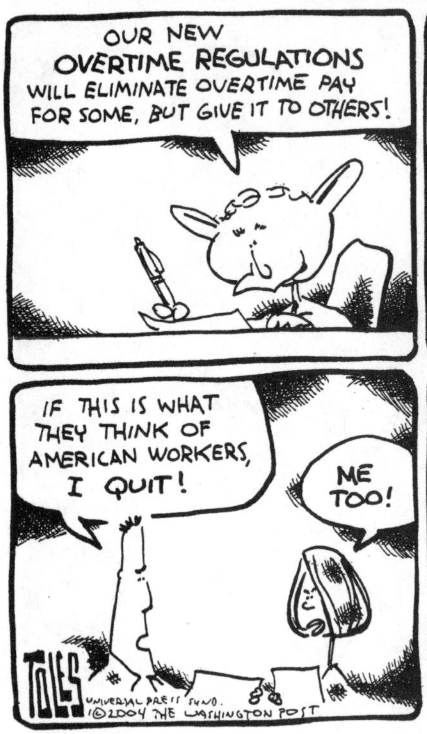
OUR NEW OVERTIME REGULATIONS WILL ELIMINATE OVERTIME PAY FOR SOME, BUT GIVE IT TO OTHERS!
WELL, I DON'T GET OVERTIME PAY ANYMORE, BUT I GUESS YOU DO NOW.
EXCEPT THE GUIDELINES SUGGEST CUTTING MY BASE PAY SO I HAVE TO WORK OVERTIME TO GET BACK TO MY ORIGINAL PAY.
IF THIS IS WHAT THEY THINK OF AMERICAN WORKERS, I QUIT!
ME TOO!
OUR NEW IMMIGRATION POLICY WILL PROVIDE WORKERS FOR THE JOBS AMERICANS WON'T TAKE.
SOME STAFFER MUST HAVE WORKED OVERTIME ON THIS PLAN. HE DESERVES A PAT ON THE BACK.
TOLES
UNIVERSAL PRESS SYND. ©2004 THE WASHINGTON POST

1-8-04

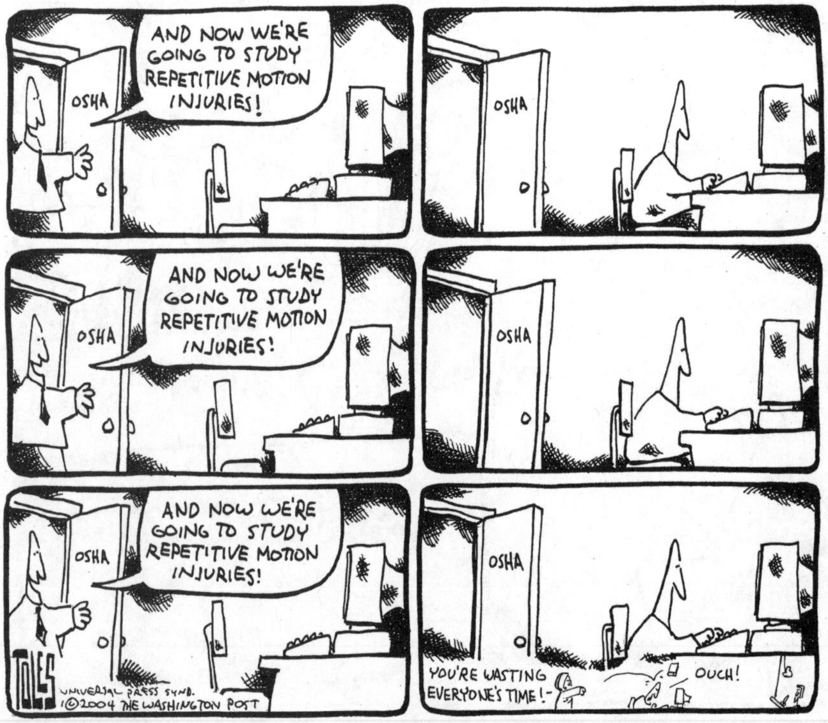
AND NOW WE'RE GOING TO STUDY REPETITIVE MOTION INJURIES!
OSHA
OSHA
AND NOW WE'RE GOING TO STUDY REPETITIVE MOTION INJURIES!
OSHA
OSHA
AND NOW WE'RE GOING TO STUDY REPETITIVE MOTION INJURIES!
OSHA
TOLES
UNIVERSAL PRESS SYND. ©2004 THE WASHINGTON POST
OSHA
YOU'RE WASTING EVERYONE'S TIME!
OUCH!

1-28-04

The argument against sensible redistricting.
The other SIDE Started it
WHO's going to vote for THAT?
THE districts ARE plenty COMPETITIVE as IT IS
IT'S LEGAL if we say IT is.
It's always BEEN like THIS.
Just try and MAKE us.
IT'S A SAFE ARGUMENT—
TOLES
UNIVERSAL PRESS SYND.
2 ©2005 THE WASHINGTON POST

2-28-05

WAIT. THIS IS THE SAME JUDICIAL NOMINEE I SENT BACK TO THE KITCHEN.
NOT EXACTLY. THE CHEF SPIT ON THE PLATE.
I BELIEVE YOU ORDERED THE GAME OF CHICKEN—
TOLES
UNIVERSAL PRESS SYND.
2©2005 THE WASHINGTON POST

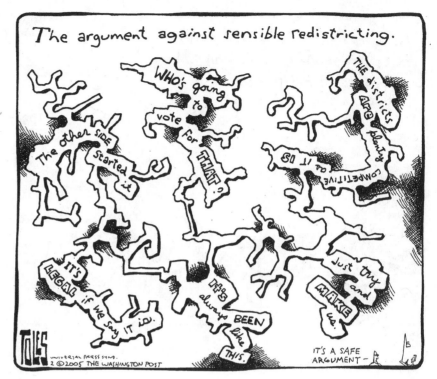

2-16-05

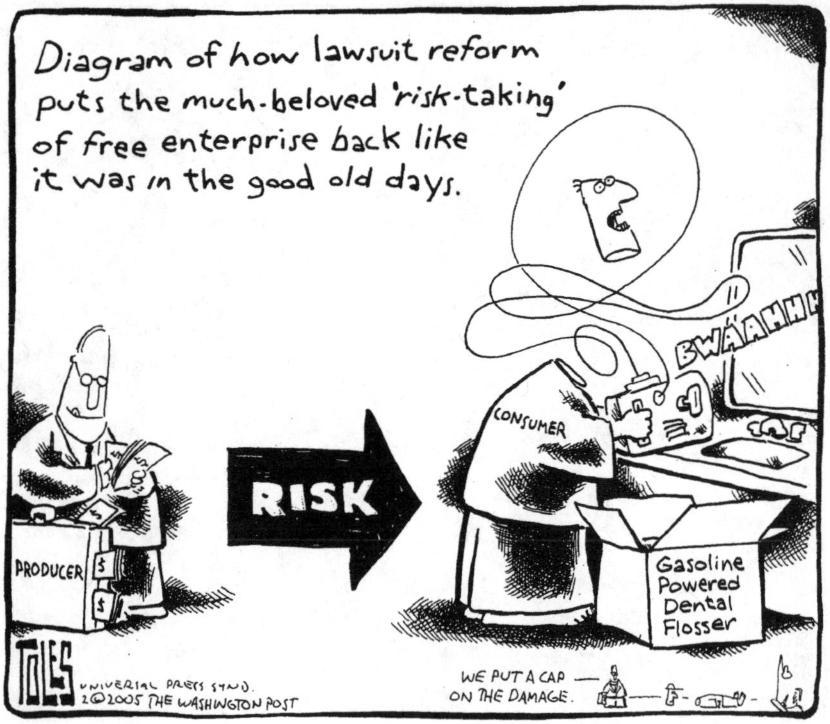
Diagram of how lawsuit reform puts the much-beloved 'risk-taking' of free enterprise back like it was in the good old days.
PRODUCER
RISK
CONSUMER
BWAAHHH
Gasoline Powered Dental Flosser
WE PUT A CAP ON THE DAMAGE.
TOLES
UNIVERSAL PRESS SYND.
2 © 2005 THE WASHINGTON POST

2-14-05

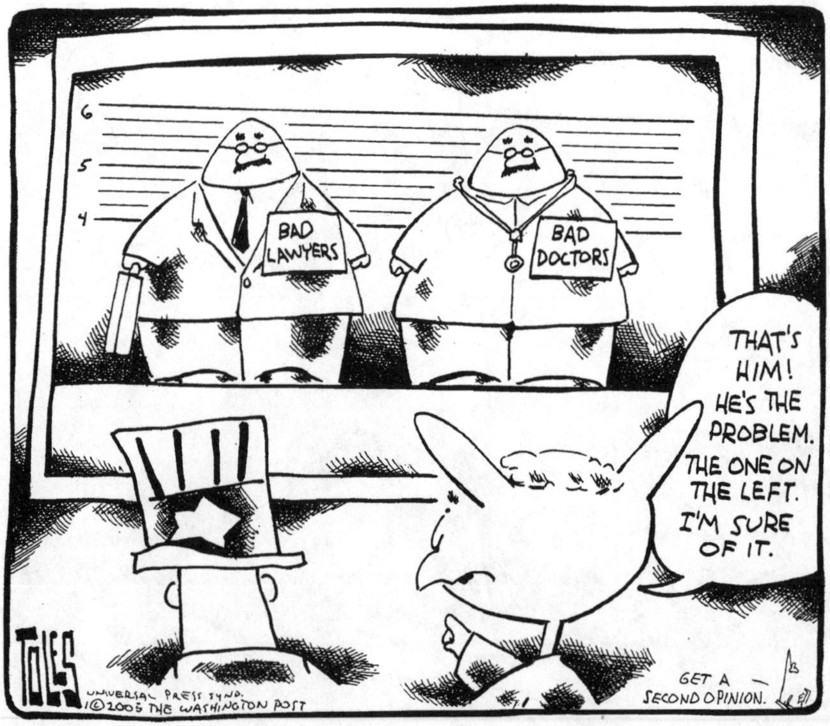
6
5
4
BAD LAWYERS
BAD DOCTORS
THAT'S HIM! HE'S THE PROBLEM. THE ONE ON THE LEFT. I'M SURE OF IT.
GET A SECOND OPINION.
TOLES
UNIVERSAL PRESS SYND.
1 © 2005 THE WASHINGTON POST

1-7-05

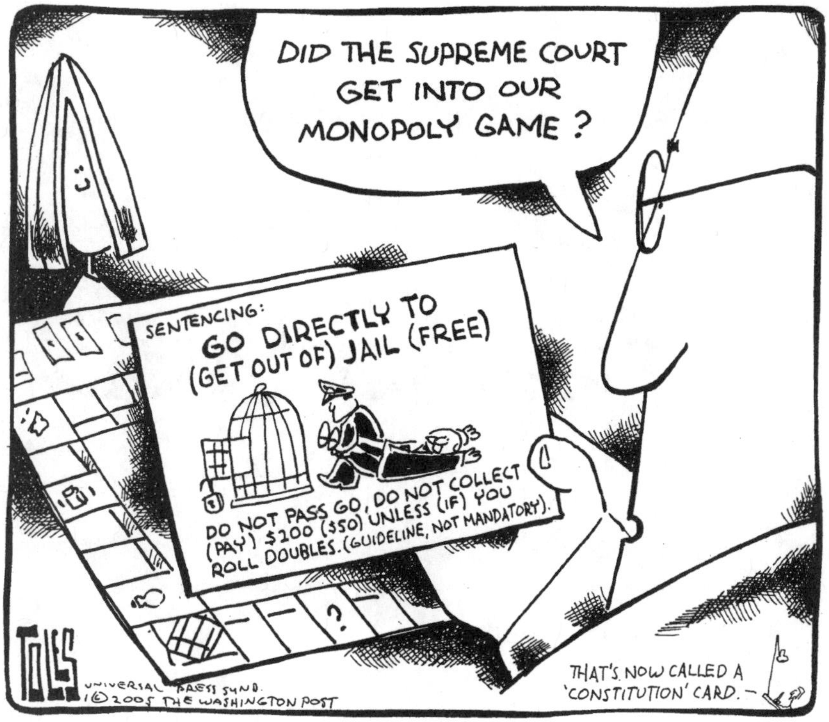
DID THE SUPREME COURT GET INTO OUR MONOPOLY GAME ?
SENTENCING:
GO DIRECTLY TO (GET OUT OF) JAIL (FREE)
DO NOT PASS GO, DO NOT COLLECT (PAY) $200 ($50) UNLESS (IF) YOU ROLL DOUBLES. (GUIDELINE, NOT MANDATORY).
TOLES
UNIVERSAL PRESS SYND.
1 © 2005 THE WASHINGTON POST
THAT'S NOW CALLED A 'CONSTITUTION' CARD.

1-17-05

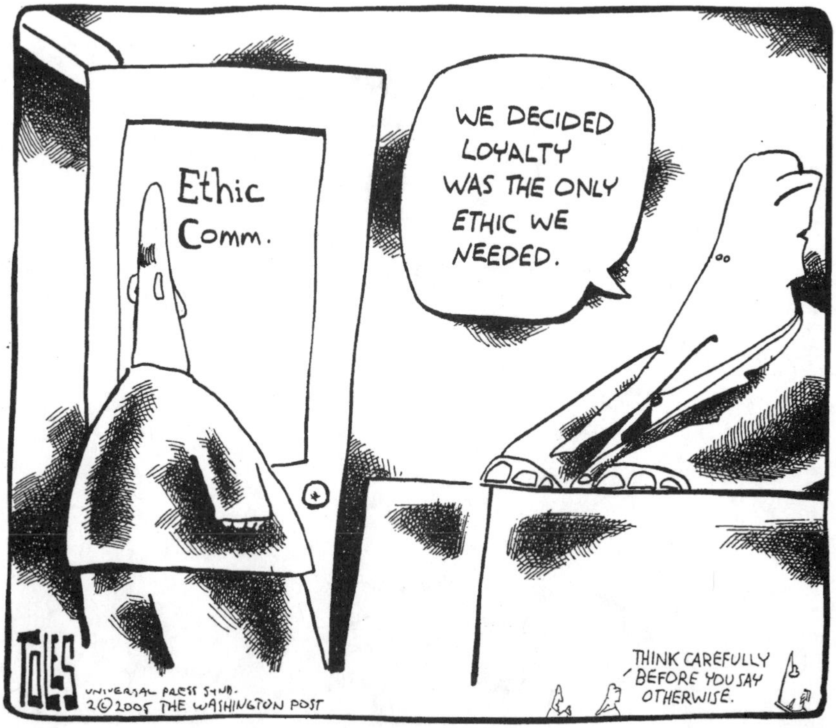
Ethic Comm.
WE DECIDED LOYALTY WAS THE ONLY ETHIC WE NEEDED.
TOLES
UNIVERSAL PRESS SYND.
2 © 2005 THE WASHINGTON POST
THINK CAREFULLY BEFORE YOU SAY OTHERWISE.

2-7-05

PRESS AND MEDIA

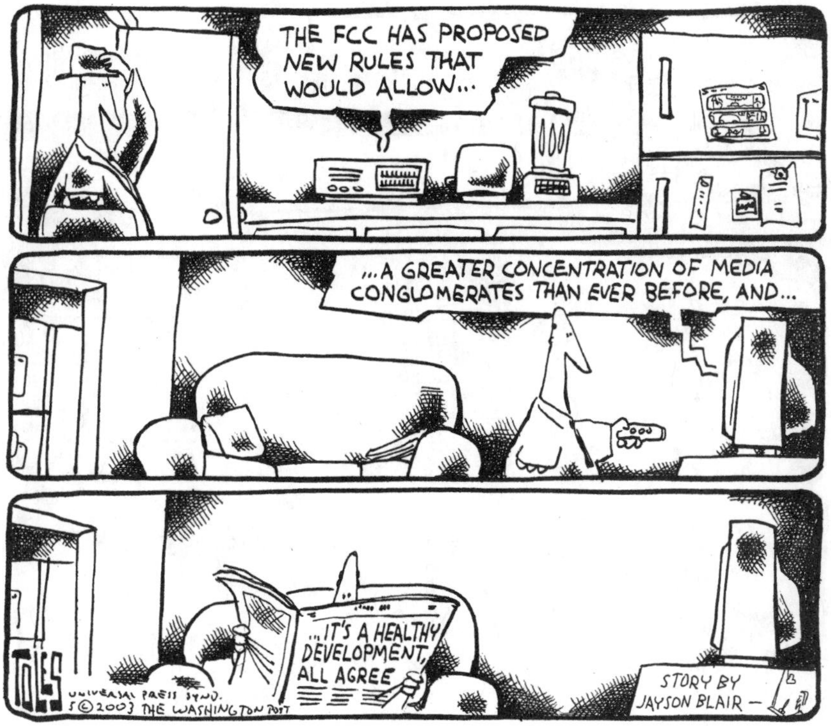
THE FCC HAS PROPOSED NEW RULES THAT WOULD ALLOW...
...A GREATER CONCENTRATION OF MEDIA CONGLOMERATES THAN EVER BEFORE, AND...
...IT'S A HEALTHY DEVELOPMENT, ALL AGREE
STORY BY JAYSON BLAIR —
TOLES
UNIVERSAL PRESS SYND.
5 © 2003 THE WASHINGTON POST

5-14-03

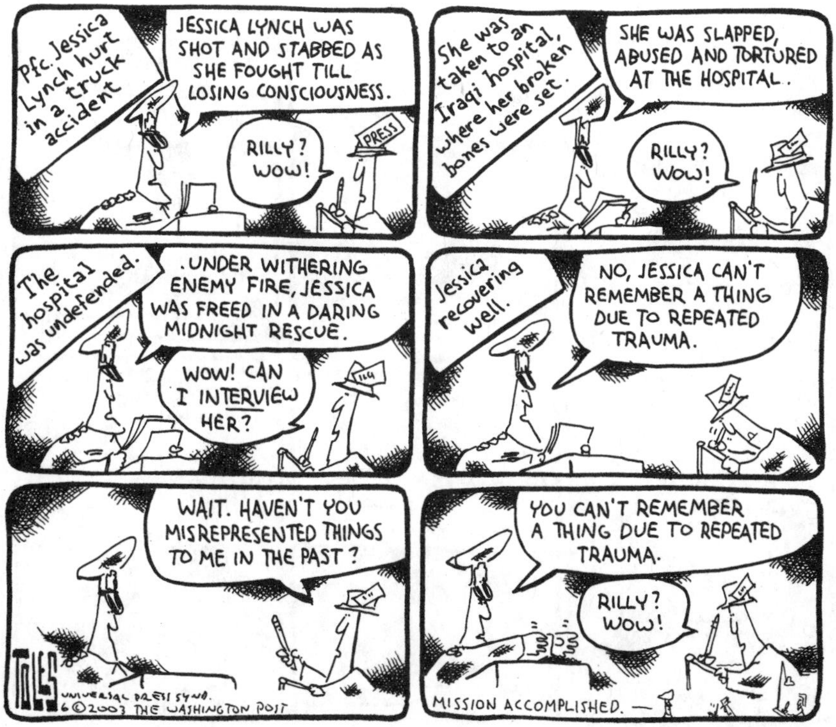
Pfc. Jessica Lynch hurt in a truck accident
JESSICA LYNCH WAS SHOT AND STABBED AS SHE FOUGHT TILL LOSING CONSCIOUSNESS.
RILLY? WOW!
PRESS
She was taken to an Iraqi hospital, where her broken bones were set.
SHE WAS SLAPPED, ABUSED AND TORTURED AT THE HOSPITAL.
RILLY? WOW!
The hospital was undefended.
.UNDER WITHERING ENEMY FIRE, JESSICA WAS FREED IN A DARING MIDNIGHT RESCUE.
WOW! CAN I INTERVIEW HER?
Jessica recovering well.
NO, JESSICA CAN'T REMEMBER A THING DUE TO REPEATED TRAUMA.
WAIT. HAVEN'T YOU MISREPRESENTED THINGS TO ME IN THE PAST?
YOU CAN'T REMEMBER A THING DUE TO REPEATED TRAUMA.
RILLY? WOW!
MISSION ACCOMPLISHED. —
TOLES
UNIVERSAL PRESS SYND.
6 © 2003 THE WASHINGTON POST

6-1-03

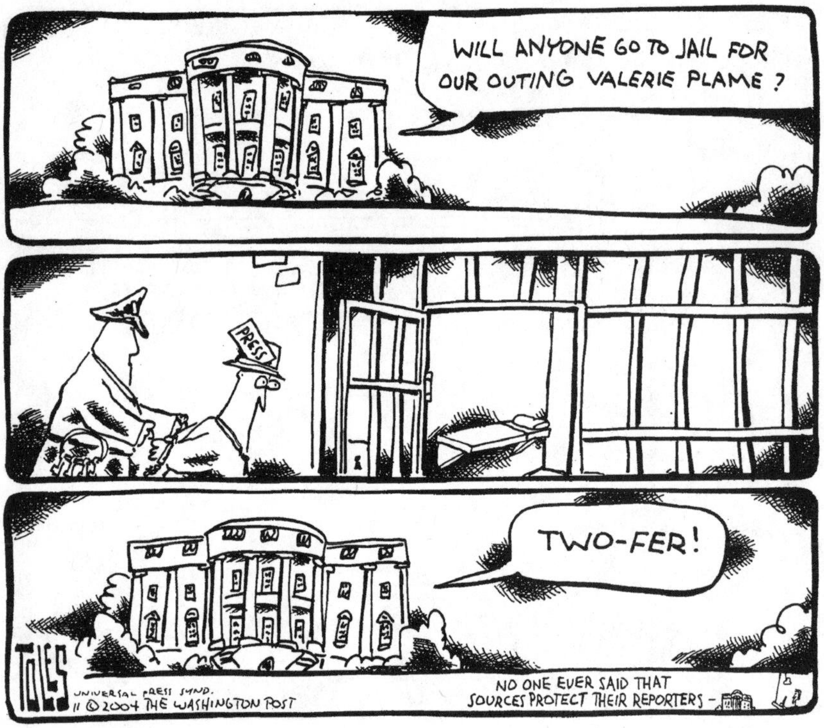
WILL ANYONE GO TO JAIL FOR OUR OUTING VALERIE PLAME ?
PRESS
TWO-FER!
TOLES
UNIVERSAL PRESS SYND.
11 ©2004 THE WASHINGTON POST
NO ONE EVER SAID THAT SOURCES PROTECT THEIR REPORTERS -

11-30-04

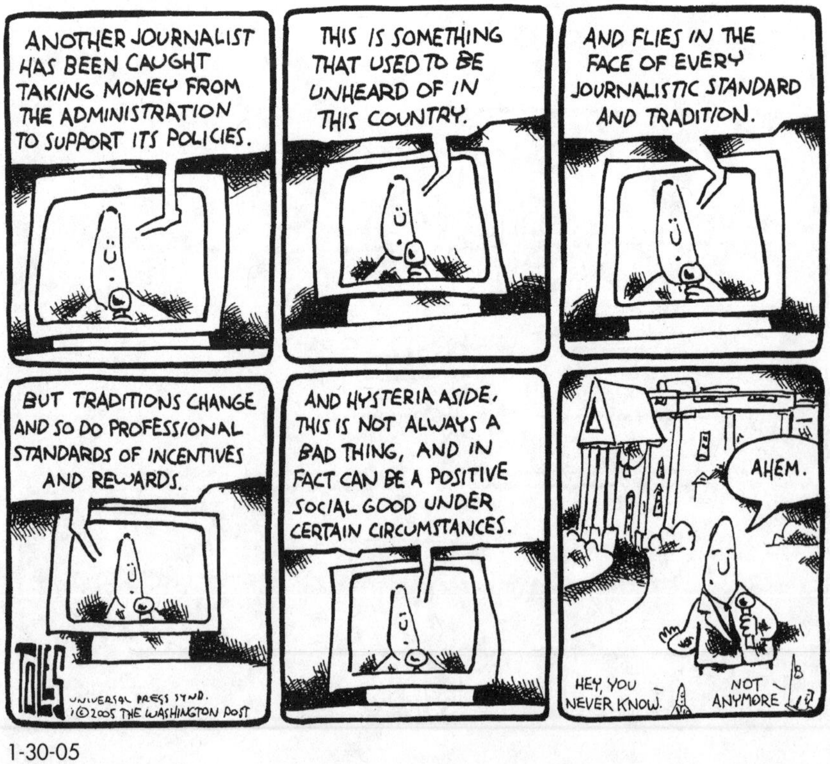
ANOTHER JOURNALIST HAS BEEN CAUGHT TAKING MONEY FROM THE ADMINISTRATION TO SUPPORT ITS POLICIES.
THIS IS SOMETHING THAT USED TO BE UNHEARD OF IN THIS COUNTRY.
AND FLIES IN THE FACE OF EVERY JOURNALISTIC STANDARD AND TRADITION.
BUT TRADITIONS CHANGE AND SO DO PROFESSIONAL STANDARDS OF INCENTIVES AND REWARDS.
AND HYSTERIA ASIDE, THIS IS NOT ALWAYS A BAD THING, AND IN FACT CAN BE A POSITIVE SOCIAL GOOD UNDER CERTAIN CIRCUMSTANCES.
AHEM.
TOLES
UNIVERSAL PRESS SYND.
1 ©2005 THE WASHINGTON POST
HEY, YOU NEVER KNOW.
NOT ANYMORE

1-30-05

THERE WERE PROBLEMS WITH THE DOCUMENTS. WE MADE A MISTAKE. I'M SORRY.
CBS
WHAT A WEIRD THING TO SAY.
IRAQ-AL QAEDA LINKS
WMDs
YELLOW CAKE
WAR PLANS
TOLES
UNIVERSAL PRESS SYND. 9©2004 THE WASHINGTON POST
MOM NEVER ALLOWED US TO USE THAT WORD AT HOME.

9-22-04

JEFF, HERE. IT'S NOT MY REAL NAME, BUT I'D LIKE TO ASK JUST HOW MUCH YOU LOVE FREEDOM.
A TOUGH QUESTION, BUT AN EXCELLENT ONE. VERY, VERY MUCH.
TOLES
UNIVERSAL PRESS SYND. 3©2005 THE WASHINGTON POST
THE PRESIDENT, UNDER SHARP QUESTIONING, DEMONSTRATED ONCE AGAIN TODAY HIS LOVE OF FREEDOM. THIS IS JOSH REPORTING FOR WHAT APPEARS TO BE AN INDEPENDENTLY PRODUCED NEWS REPORT...
...THAT IS NOT DESIGNED TO MISLEAD YOU IN ANY WAY.
AND I THOUGHT DAN RATHER WAS WEIRD.
I DO NOT CONDONE UNAUTHORIZED MONEY I PAID MYSELF TO PRODUCE THIS REPORT, IF ANY.

3-16-05

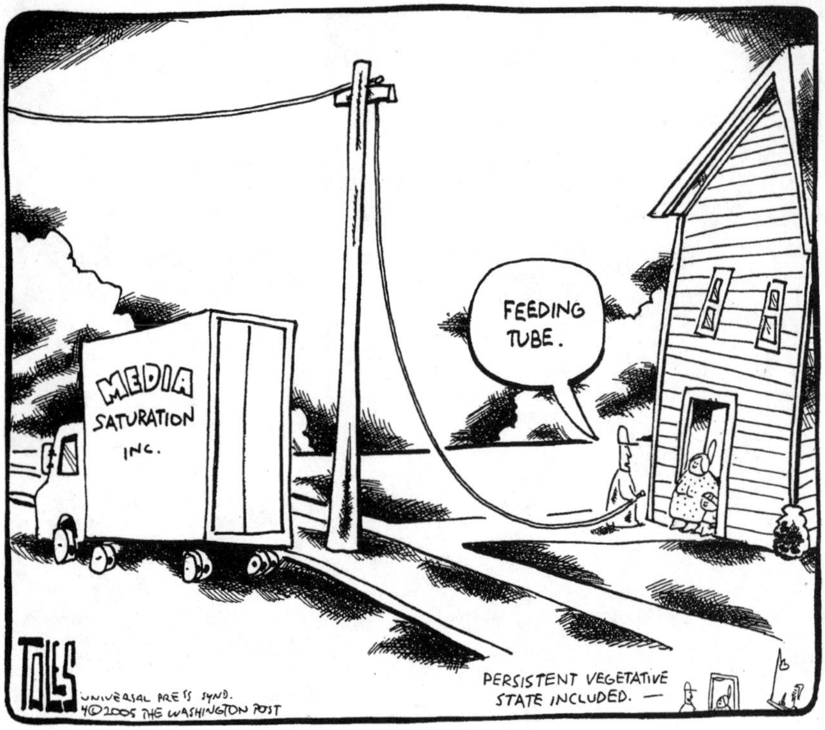
MEDIA
SATURATION
INC.
FEEDING
TUBE.
PERSISTENT VEGETATIVE
STATE INCLUDED. —
TOLES
UNIVERSAL PRESS SYND.
4©2005 THE WASHINGTON POST

4-1-05

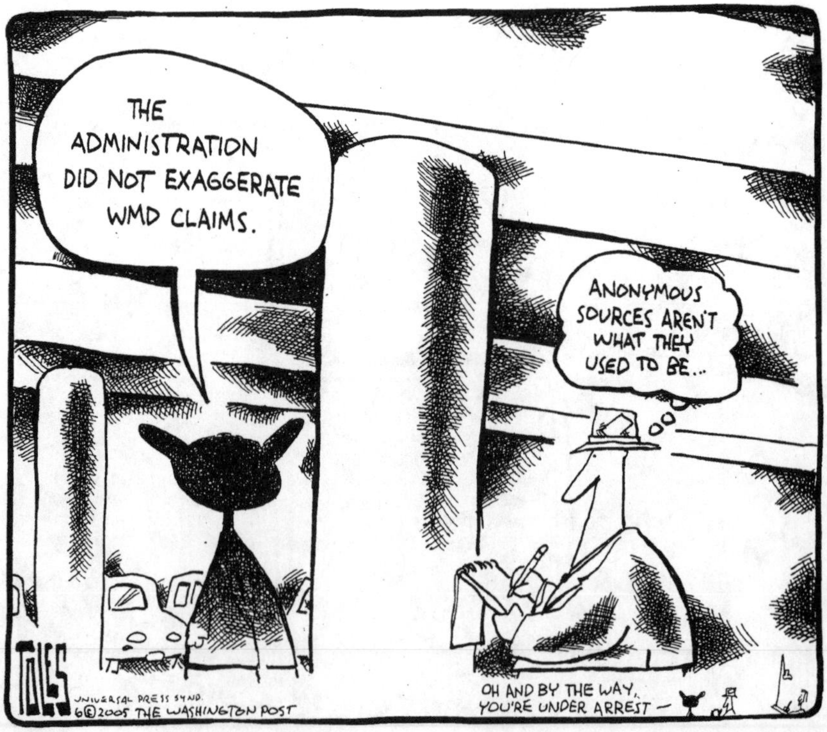
THE
ADMINISTRATION
DID NOT EXAGGERATE
WMD CLAIMS.
ANONYMOUS
SOURCES AREN'T
WHAT THEY
USED TO BE...
OH AND BY THE WAY,
YOU'RE UNDER ARREST —
TOLES
UNIVERSAL PRESS SYND.
6©2005 THE WASHINGTON POST

6-2-05

HEALTH AND EDUCATION

LEFT HAND
-BLUE.
MEDICARE REFORM
ANYBODY
STILL IN?
TOLES
UNIVERSAL PRESS SYND.
3 © 2003 THE WASHINGTON POST

3-13-03

YOU'RE IN GOOD HEALTH
BUT YOU MAY BE ABOUT TO DEVELOP A CONDITION THAT'S NOT COVERED BY YOUR HEALTH INSURANCE.
THEN I'LL GET COVERAGE.
YOU CAN'T AFFORD THAT COVERAGE.
THEN I'LL MAKE MY EMPLOYER PAY FOR IT.
THEN HE'LL DROP YOUR INSURANCE ALTOGETHER.
THEN I'LL GET THE GOVERNMENT TO PAY FOR IT.
THAT WILL CAUSE TAXES TO GO UP AND PUT YOUR EMPLOYER OUT OF BUSINESS.
THEN I'LL JUST WAIT TILL THEY FIND A CURE.
OH, THEY FOUND ONE. BUT YOU CAN'T AFFORD THE PRESCRIPTION.
STOP! YOU'RE MAKING ME CRAZY!
THAT'S THE CONDITION NOT COVERED.
I'M JUST NOT GOING TO THINK ABOUT IT.—
THAT'S HOW EVERYBODY ELSE IS HANDLING IT.
TOLES
UNIVERSAL PRESS SYND.
12 © 2002 THE WASHINGTON POST

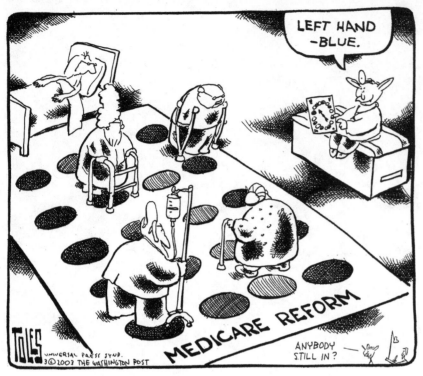

12-29-02

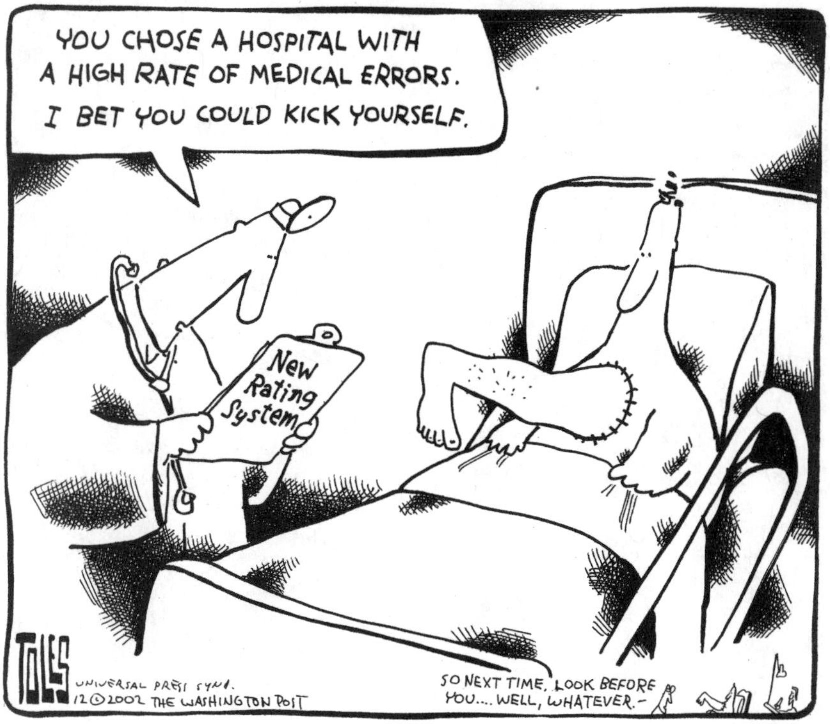
YOU CHOSE A HOSPITAL WITH A HIGH RATE OF MEDICAL ERRORS. I BET YOU COULD KICK YOURSELF.
New Rating System
TOLES
UNIVERSAL PRESS SYND.
12 © 2002 THE WASHINGTON POST
SO NEXT TIME, LOOK BEFORE YOU.... WELL, WHATEVER.

12-16-02

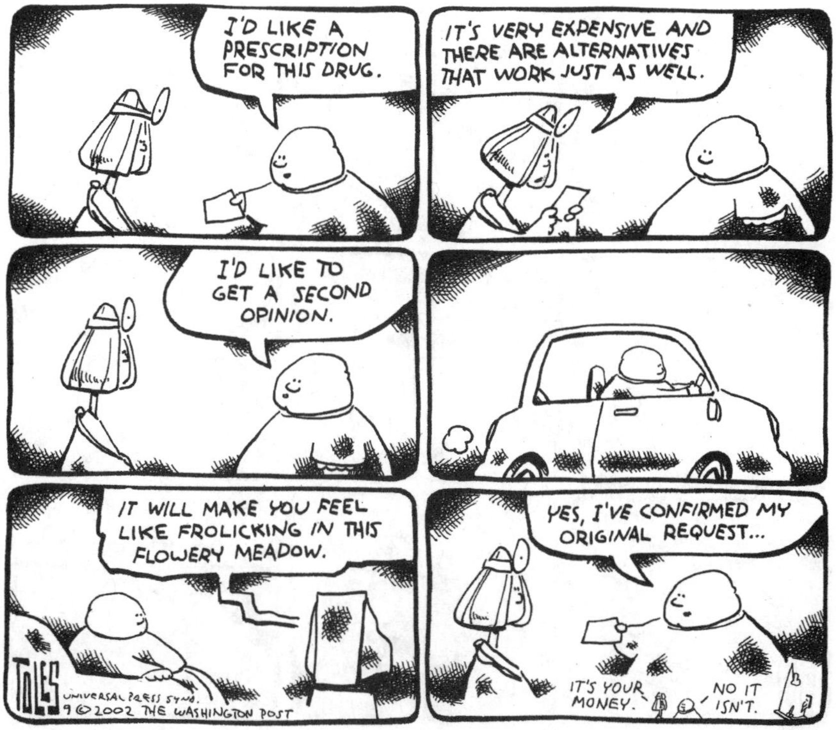
I'D LIKE A PRESCRIPTION FOR THIS DRUG.
IT'S VERY EXPENSIVE AND THERE ARE ALTERNATIVES THAT WORK JUST AS WELL.
I'D LIKE TO GET A SECOND OPINION.
IT WILL MAKE YOU FEEL LIKE FROLICKING IN THIS FLOWERY MEADOW.
TOLES
UNIVERSAL PRESS SYND.
9 © 2002 THE WASHINGTON POST
YES, I'VE CONFIRMED MY ORIGINAL REQUEST...
IT'S YOUR MONEY.
NO IT ISN'T.

9-3-02

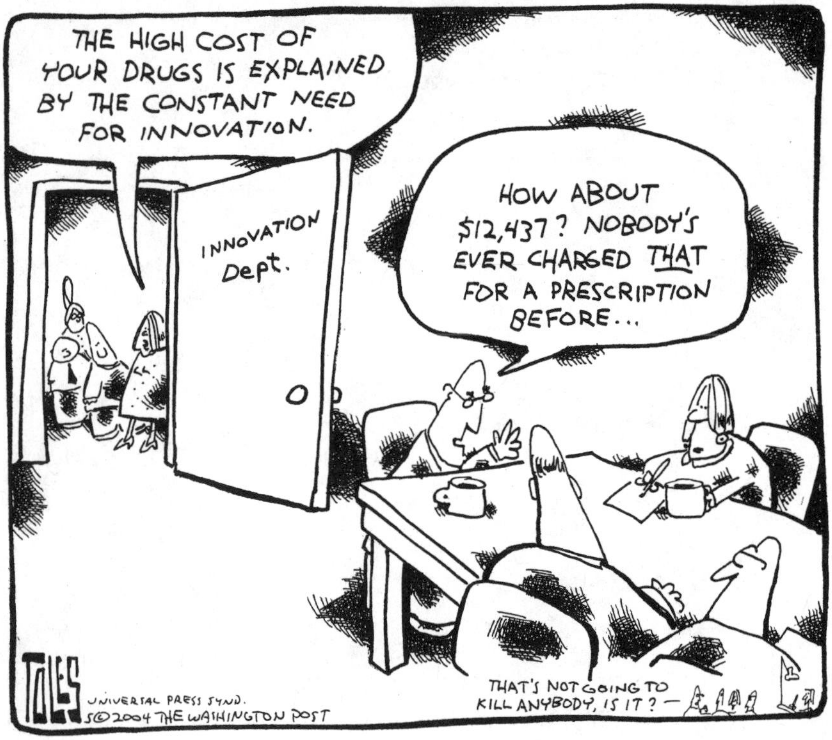
THE HIGH COST OF YOUR DRUGS IS EXPLAINED BY THE CONSTANT NEED FOR INNOVATION.
INNOVATION Dept.
HOW ABOUT $12,437? NOBODY'S EVER CHARGED THAT FOR A PRESCRIPTION BEFORE...
THAT'S NOT GOING TO KILL ANYBODY, IS IT? —
TOLES UNIVERSAL PRESS SYND. ©2004 THE WASHINGTON POST

5-27-04

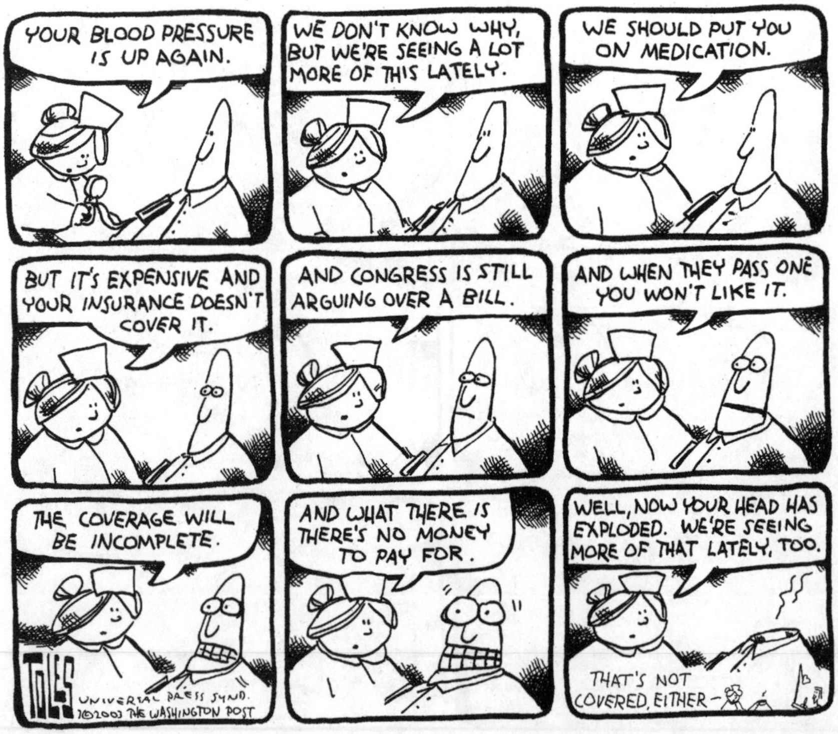
YOUR BLOOD PRESSURE IS UP AGAIN.
WE DON'T KNOW WHY, BUT WE'RE SEEING A LOT MORE OF THIS LATELY.
WE SHOULD PUT YOU ON MEDICATION.
BUT IT'S EXPENSIVE AND YOUR INSURANCE DOESN'T COVER IT.
AND CONGRESS IS STILL ARGUING OVER A BILL.
AND WHEN THEY PASS ONE YOU WON'T LIKE IT.
THE COVERAGE WILL BE INCOMPLETE.
AND WHAT THERE IS THERE'S NO MONEY TO PAY FOR.
WELL, NOW YOUR HEAD HAS EXPLODED. WE'RE SEEING MORE OF THAT LATELY, TOO.
THAT'S NOT COVERED, EITHER —
TOLES UNIVERSAL PRESS SYND. ©2003 THE WASHINGTON POST

7-14-03

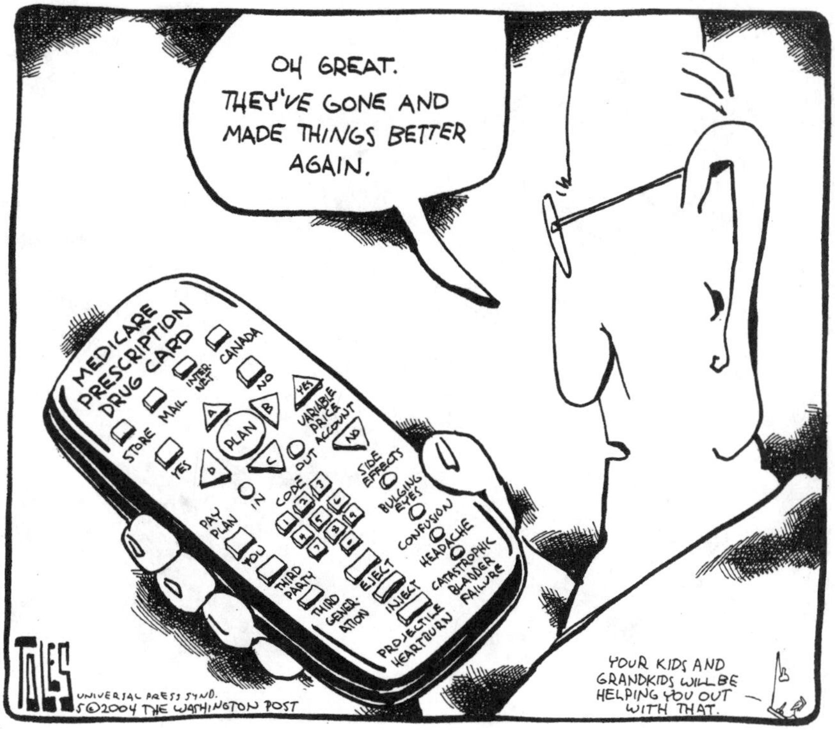
OH GREAT. THEY'VE GONE AND MADE THINGS BETTER AGAIN.
MEDICARE PRESCRIPTION DRUG CARD
STORE
MAIL
INTER-NET
CANADA
YES
NO
YES
PLAN
VARIABLE PRICE ACCOUNT
NO
IN
OUT
CODE
SIDE EFFECTS
BULGING EYES
CONFUSION
HEADACHE
CATASTROPHIC BLADDER FAILURE
PAY PLAN
YOU
THIRD PARTY
THIRD GENER-ATION
EJECT
INJECT
PROJECTILE HEARTBURN
TOLES
UNIVERSAL PRESS SYND. 5©2004 THE WASHINGTON POST
YOUR KIDS AND GRANDKIDS WILL BE HELPING YOU OUT WITH THAT.

5-10-04

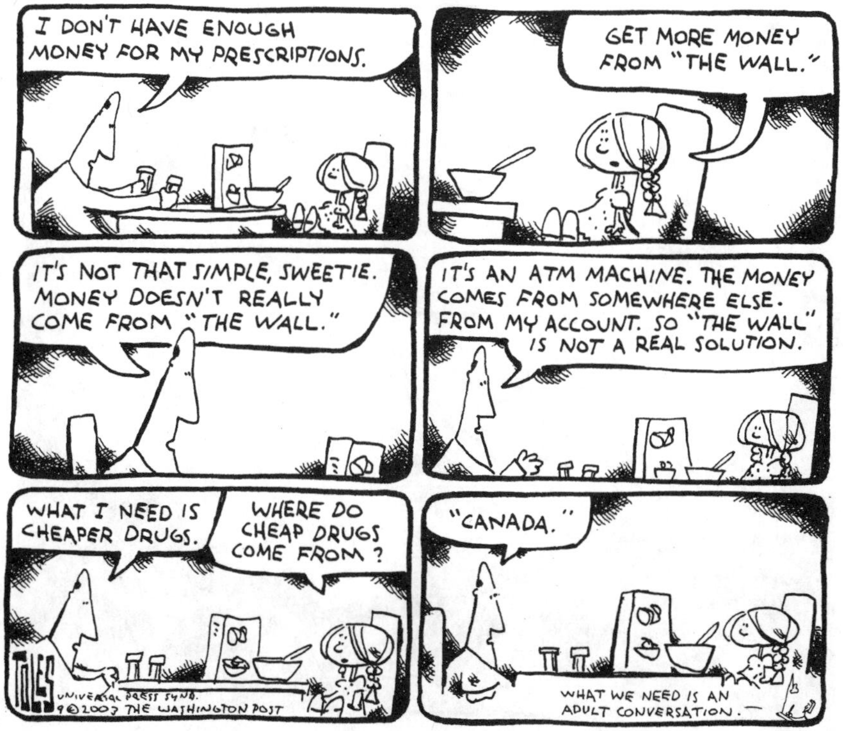
I DON'T HAVE ENOUGH MONEY FOR MY PRESCRIPTIONS.
GET MORE MONEY FROM "THE WALL."
IT'S NOT THAT SIMPLE, SWEETIE. MONEY DOESN'T REALLY COME FROM "THE WALL."
IT'S AN ATM MACHINE. THE MONEY COMES FROM SOMEWHERE ELSE. FROM MY ACCOUNT. SO "THE WALL" IS NOT A REAL SOLUTION.
WHAT I NEED IS CHEAPER DRUGS.
WHERE DO CHEAP DRUGS COME FROM ?
"CANADA."
TOLES
UNIVERSAL PRESS SYND. 9©2003 THE WASHINGTON POST
WHAT WE NEED IS AN ADULT CONVERSATION.

9-29-03

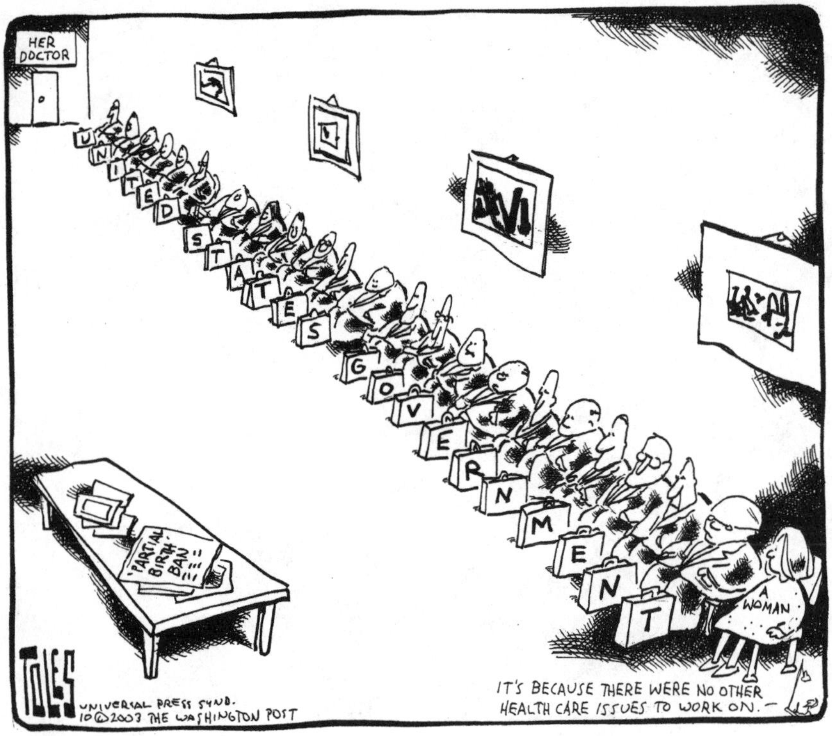
HER DOCTOR
UNITED STATES GOVERNMENT
"PARTIAL BIRTH BAN"
A WOMAN
TOLES
UNIVERSAL PRESS SYND.
10 © 2003 THE WASHINGTON POST
IT'S BECAUSE THERE WERE NO OTHER HEALTH CARE ISSUES TO WORK ON. —

10-23-03

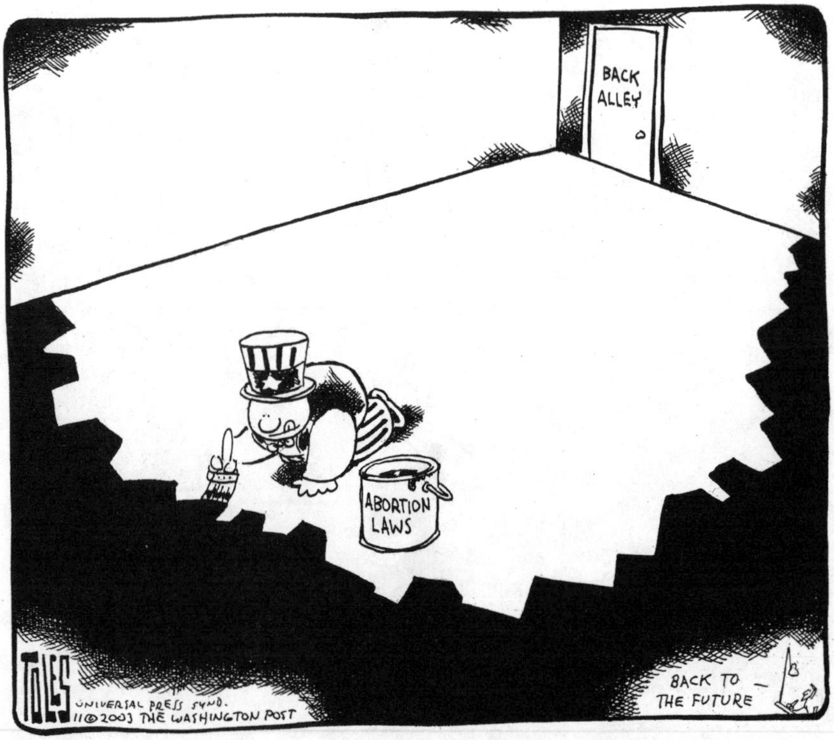
BACK ALLEY
ABORTION LAWS
TOLES
UNIVERSAL PRESS SYND.
11 © 2003 THE WASHINGTON POST
BACK TO THE FUTURE —

11-9-03

ALL HE DOES IS WATCH TV.
HE NEVER READS.
AND ALL HE EVER EATS IS JUNK FOOD.
IT'S MAKING HIM FAT.
NOW THEY'RE TALKING ABOUT BETTER FOOD LABELING.
DO YOU THINK THAT WOULD HELP?
REFER BACK TO PANEL #2
TOLES
UNIVERSAL PRESS SYND.
11©2003 THE WASHINGTON POST
THEN SHOULD HE GET UP AND TURN OFF THE TV?
HE CAN'T GET UP.

11-28-03

I DON'T SEE WHY I SHOULD SUFFER NOW FOR THINGS I DID DECADES AGO...
SUBPOENA
BIG TOBACCO
OXYGEN
LUNG DISEASE
TOLES
UNIVERSAL PRESS SYND.
9©2004 THE WASHINGTON POST
BUT NO LEGISLATION. SO YOU CAN BREATHE EASIER.

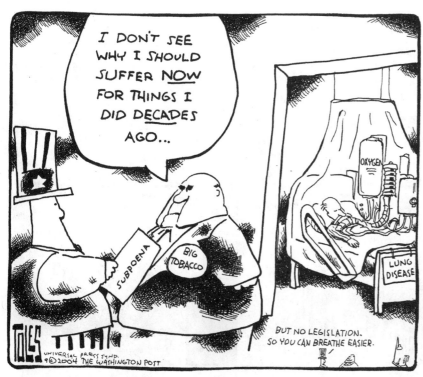

9-24-04

Researchers investigate why Americans don't get enough sleep.
THREE JOBS IS A LONG DAY. THAT ONLY LEAVES 5½ HOURS FOR UNINTERRUPTED WORRYING ABOUT MY DEBTS AND NO HEALTH INSURANCE.
CAN I GET BACK TO THAT NOW PLEASE?
TOLES
UNIVERSAL PRESS SYND. 3 ©2005 THE WASHINGTON POST

3-30-05

KIDS TODAY ARE ENGAGING IN LESS RISKY BEHAVIOR.
Childhood Well-being Report
BUT THEY ARE ALSO INCREASINGLY OBESE.
OF COURSE THE TWO THINGS MAY BE RELATED.
TOLES
UNIVERSAL PRESS SYND. 3 ©2005 THE WASHINGTON POST
AND NOT COUNTING THE RISK OF EXPLOSION.

3-31-05

SCIENCE AND THE ENVIRONMENT

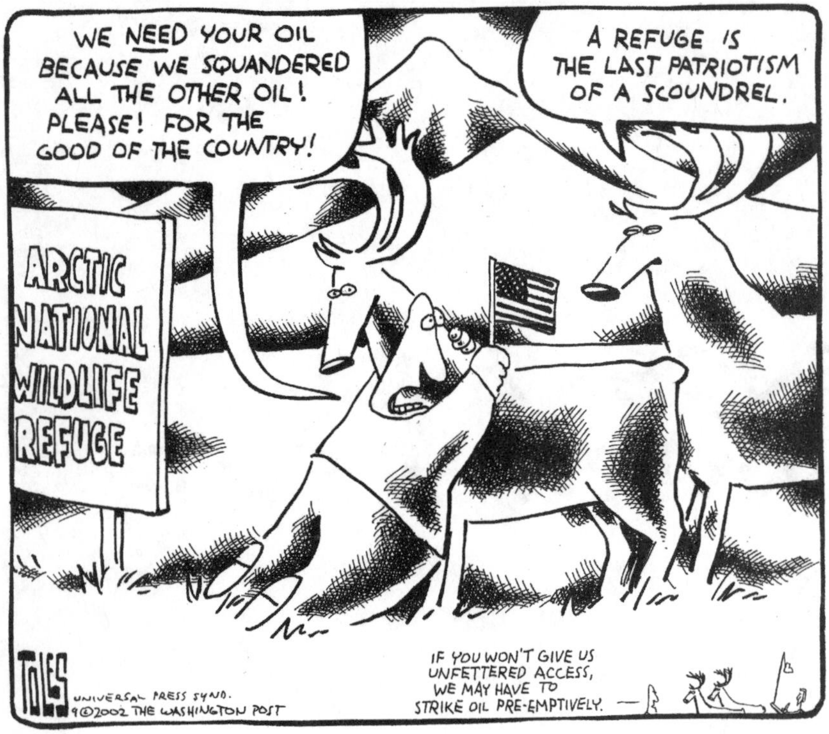
WE NEED YOUR OIL BECAUSE WE SQUANDERED ALL THE OTHER OIL! PLEASE! FOR THE GOOD OF THE COUNTRY!
A REFUGE IS THE LAST PATRIOTISM OF A SCOUNDREL.
ARCTIC NATIONAL WILDLIFE REFUGE
TOLES
UNIVERSAL PRESS SYND.
9 ©2002 THE WASHINGTON POST
IF YOU WON'T GIVE US UNFETTERED ACCESS, WE MAY HAVE TO STRIKE OIL PRE-EMPTIVELY.

9-29-02

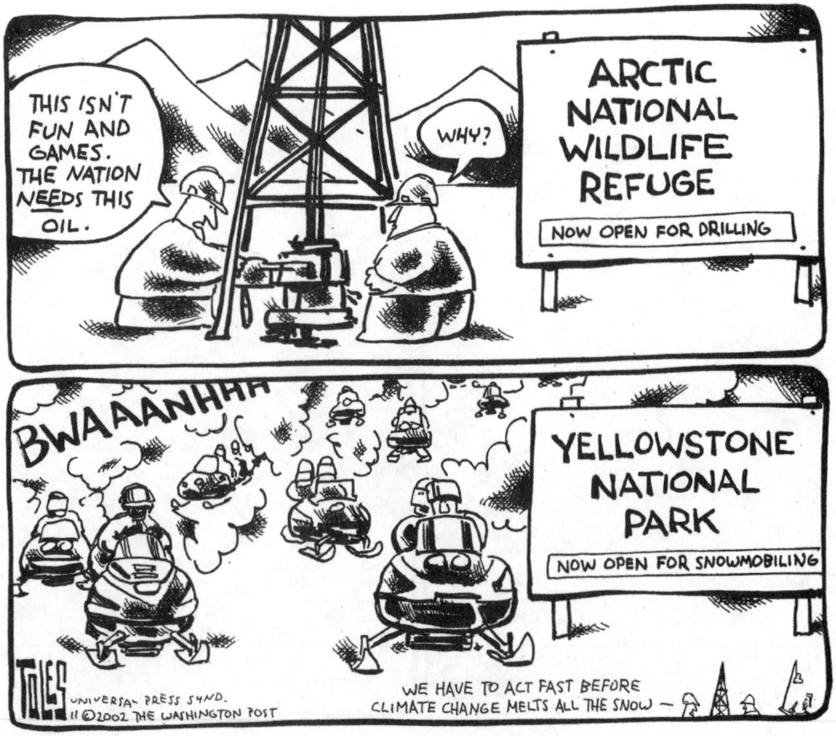
THIS ISN'T FUN AND GAMES. THE NATION NEEDS THIS OIL.
WHY?
ARCTIC NATIONAL WILDLIFE REFUGE
NOW OPEN FOR DRILLING
BWAAANHHH
YELLOWSTONE NATIONAL PARK
NOW OPEN FOR SNOWMOBILING
TOLES
UNIVERSAL PRESS SYND.
11 ©2002 THE WASHINGTON POST
WE HAVE TO ACT FAST BEFORE CLIMATE CHANGE MELTS ALL THE SNOW —

11-14-02

THE PROBLEM IS YOU JUST DON'T UNDERSTAND THE VALUE OF OUR NATION'S NATURAL TREASURES.
I DO SO.
YOU DON'T UNDERSTAND THE VALUE OF OUR NATIONAL FORESTS.
I DO SO.
YOU DON'T UNDERSTAND THE VALUE OF OUR NATION'S UNDEVELOPED WILDLIFE HABITAT.
I DO SO.
YOU DON'T UNDERSTAND THE VALUE OF OUR REMAINING AREAS OF ECOLOGICAL BOUNTY.
I DO SO.
THEN WHY DON'T YOU ACT LIKE YOU APPRECIATE THEM?
WHO SAID I APPRECIATE THEM?
I JUST UNDERSTAND THEIR VALUE.
TOLES
UNIVERSAL PRESS SYND.
12 ©2002 THE WASHINGTON POST
THESE CAMPAIGN CONTRIBUTIONS, ...THEY SPEAK TO ME.

12-1-02

I SHALL PAINT A BEAUTIFUL FOREST.
BUT FIRST I MUST 'THIN THE BRUSH.'
Plink Plink
IF THE BRUSH IS TOO THICK, IT MIGHT CATCH FIRE AND BURN UP.
Plink P-plink plink
THERE! ALL THINNED.
THERE'S NO 'BRUSH' LEFT. HOW ARE YOU GOING TO PAINT THE FOREST?
TOLES
UNIVERSAL PRESS SYND.
12©2002 THE WASHINGTON POST
DOES HE HAVE TO PAINT A PICTURE?

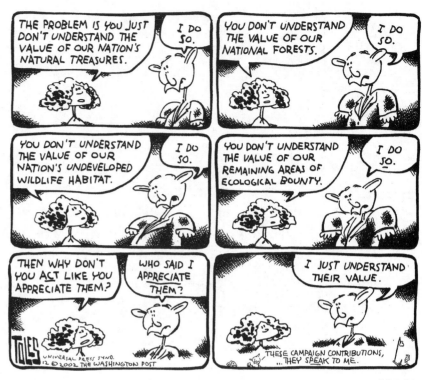

12-13-02

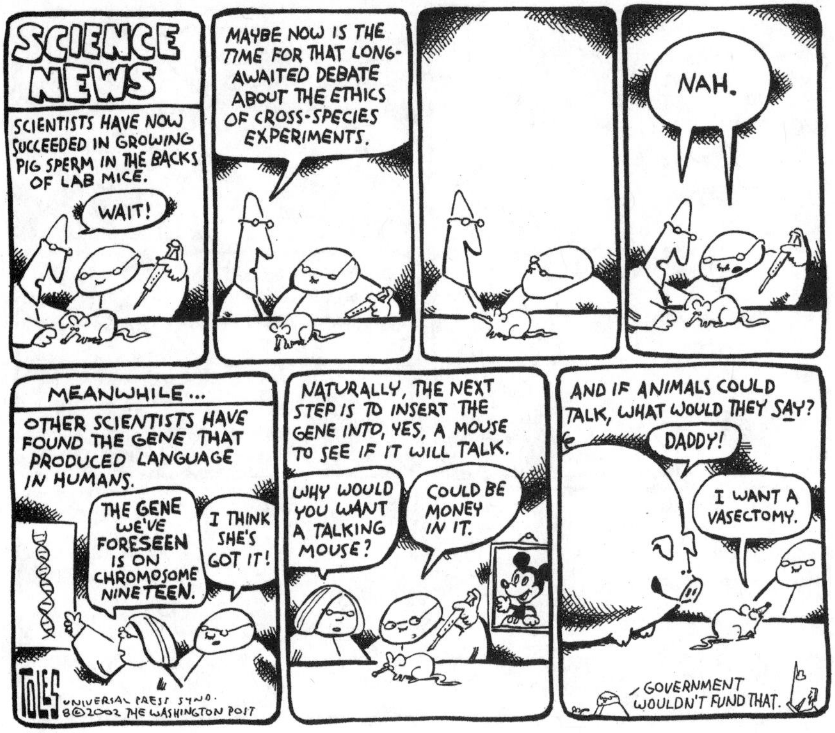
SCIENCE NEWS
SCIENTISTS HAVE NOW SUCCEEDED IN GROWING PIG SPERM IN THE BACKS OF LAB MICE.
WAIT!
MAYBE NOW IS THE TIME FOR THAT LONG-AWAITED DEBATE ABOUT THE ETHICS OF CROSS-SPECIES EXPERIMENTS.
NAH.
MEANWHILE...
OTHER SCIENTISTS HAVE FOUND THE GENE THAT PRODUCED LANGUAGE IN HUMANS.
THE GENE WE'VE FORESEEN IS ON CHROMOSOME NINETEEN.
I THINK SHE'S GOT IT!
NATURALLY, THE NEXT STEP IS TO INSERT THE GENE INTO, YES, A MOUSE TO SEE IF IT WILL TALK.
WHY WOULD YOU WANT A TALKING MOUSE?
COULD BE MONEY IN IT.
AND IF ANIMALS COULD TALK, WHAT WOULD THEY SAY?
DADDY!
I WANT A VASECTOMY.
GOVERNMENT WOULDN'T FUND THAT.
TOLES UNIVERSAL PRESS SYND. 8 © 2002 THE WASHINGTON POST

8-18-02

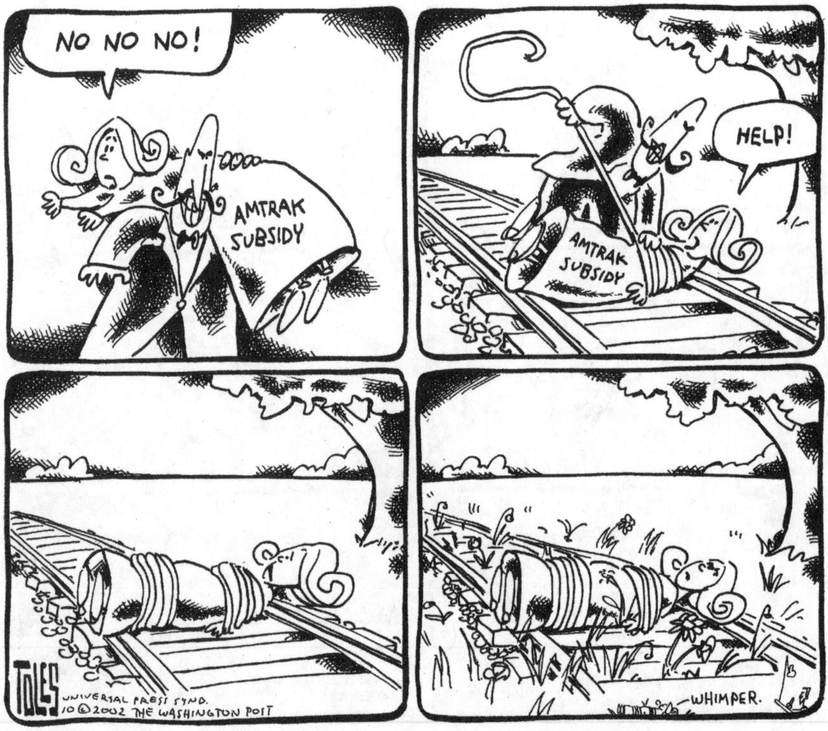
NO NO NO!
AMTRAK SUBSIDY
HELP!
AMTRAK SUBSIDY
TOLES UNIVERSAL PRESS SYND. 10 © 2002 THE WASHINGTON POST
WHIMPER.

10-1-02

TUCKING YOU IN USED TO BE ONE OF THE THINGS I LOOKED FORWARD TO.
DUST AND DIRT FIGHT ALLERGIES
TOLES
UNIVERSAL PRESS SYND.
9©2002 THE WASHINGTON POST
HOW ABOUT A LIVE -BUNNY?

9-23-02

HUMAN SPACE FLIGHT...
...IS NECESSARY BECAUSE IT'S THE ONLY WAY TO DO THE RESEARCH...
...ON THE EFFECTS OF SPACE ON THE HUMAN BODY...
...WHICH IF WE DON'T UNDERSTAND, WE WON'T BE ABLE TO HAVE...
Circular Argument
TOLES
UNIVERSAL PRESS SYND
3 © 2003 THE WASHINGTON POST
BUT CIRCULAR ARGUMENTS HAVE SPINOFF USES IN MANY DISCUSSIONS.

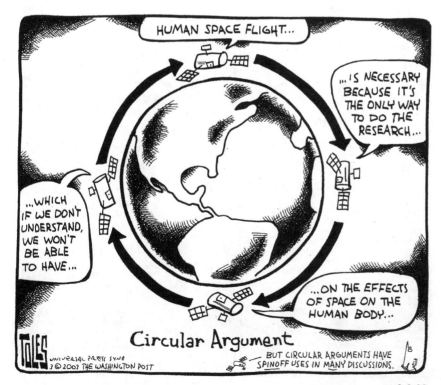

3-3-03

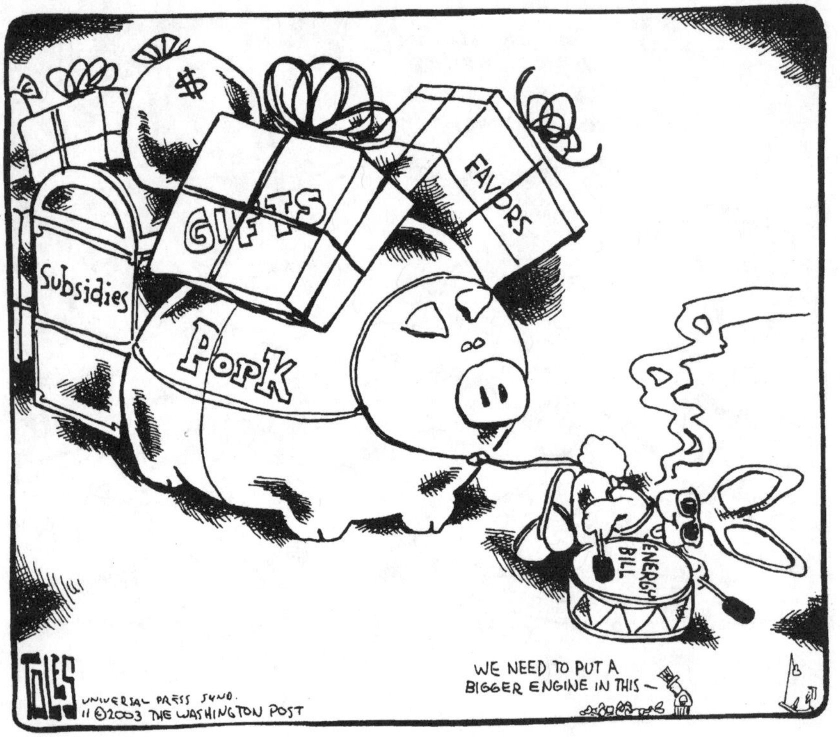
Subsidies
GIFTS
FAVORS
PorK
ENERGY BILL
WE NEED TO PUT A BIGGER ENGINE IN THIS
TOLES
UNIVERSAL PRESS SYND.
11 ©2003 THE WASHINGTON POST

11-26-03

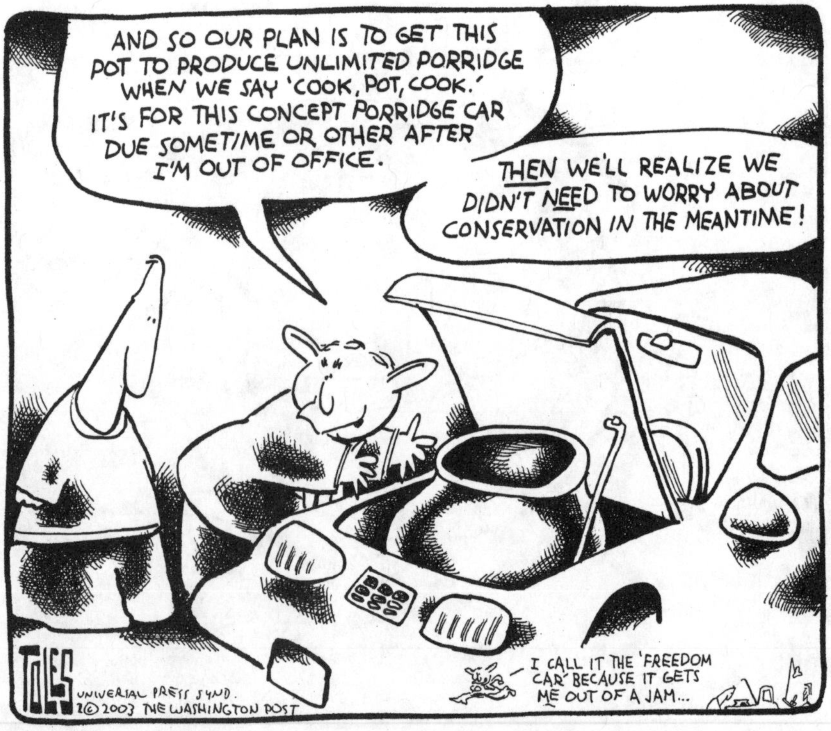
AND SO OUR PLAN IS TO GET THIS POT TO PRODUCE UNLIMITED PORRIDGE WHEN WE SAY 'COOK, POT, COOK.' IT'S FOR THIS CONCEPT PORRIDGE CAR DUE SOMETIME OR OTHER AFTER I'M OUT OF OFFICE.
THEN WE'LL REALIZE WE DIDN'T NEED TO WORRY ABOUT CONSERVATION IN THE MEANTIME!
I CALL IT THE 'FREEDOM CAR' BECAUSE IT GETS ME OUT OF A JAM...
TOLES
UNIVERSAL PRESS SYND.
2© 2003 THE WASHINGTON POST

2-3-03

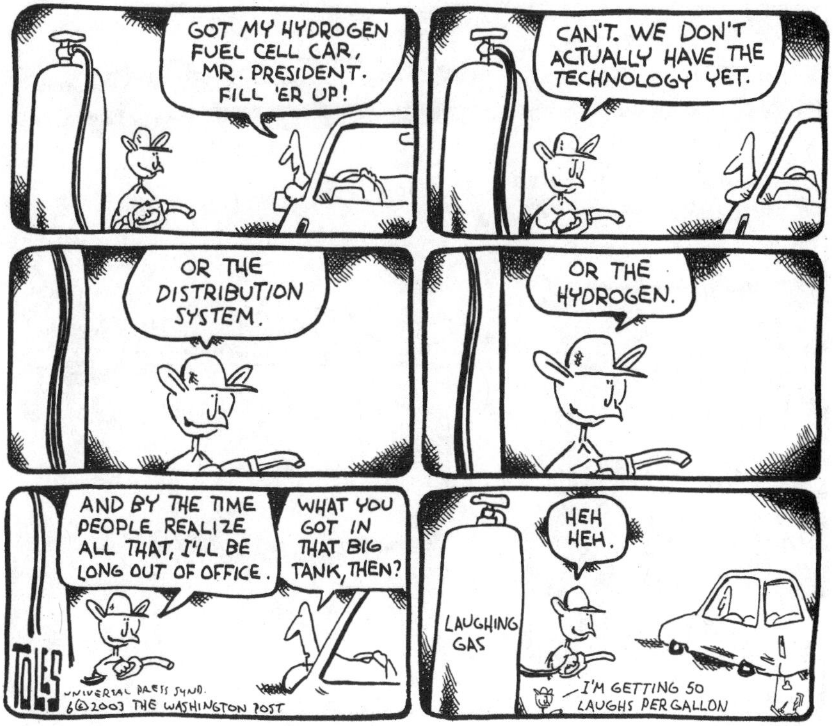
GOT MY HYDROGEN FUEL CELL CAR, MR. PRESIDENT. FILL 'ER UP!
CAN'T. WE DON'T ACTUALLY HAVE THE TECHNOLOGY YET.
OR THE DISTRIBUTION SYSTEM.
OR THE HYDROGEN.
AND BY THE TIME PEOPLE REALIZE ALL THAT, I'LL BE LONG OUT OF OFFICE.
WHAT YOU GOT IN THAT BIG TANK, THEN?
HEH HEH.
LAUGHING GAS
I'M GETTING 50 LAUGHS PER GALLON
TOLES
UNIVERSAL PRESS SYND.
6 © 2003 THE WASHINGTON POST

6-22-03

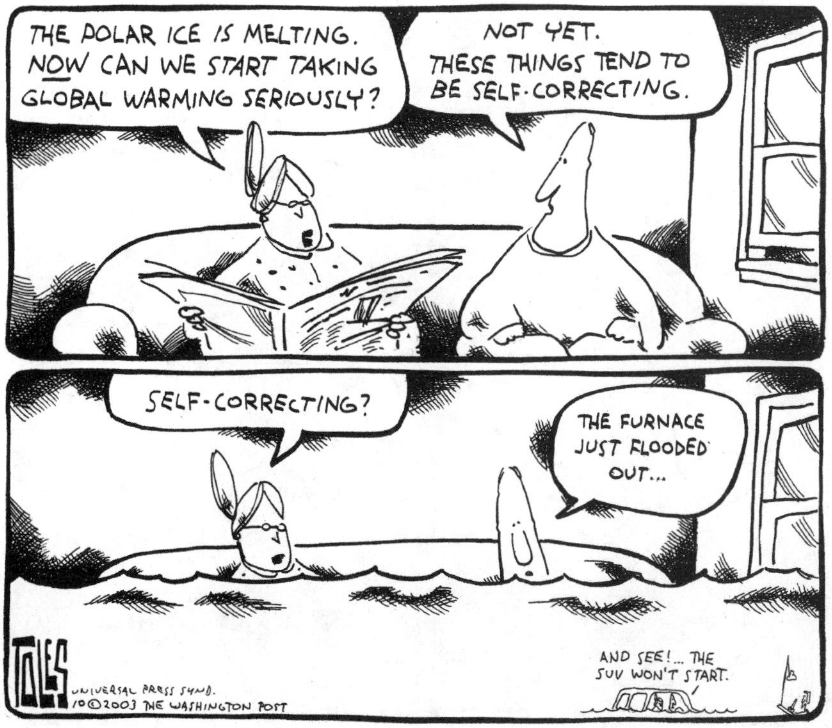
THE POLAR ICE IS MELTING. NOW CAN WE START TAKING GLOBAL WARMING SERIOUSLY?
NOT YET. THESE THINGS TEND TO BE SELF-CORRECTING.
SELF-CORRECTING?
THE FURNACE JUST FLOODED OUT...
AND SEE!... THE SUV WON'T START.
TOLES
UNIVERSAL PRESS SYND.
10 © 2003 THE WASHINGTON POST

10-31-03

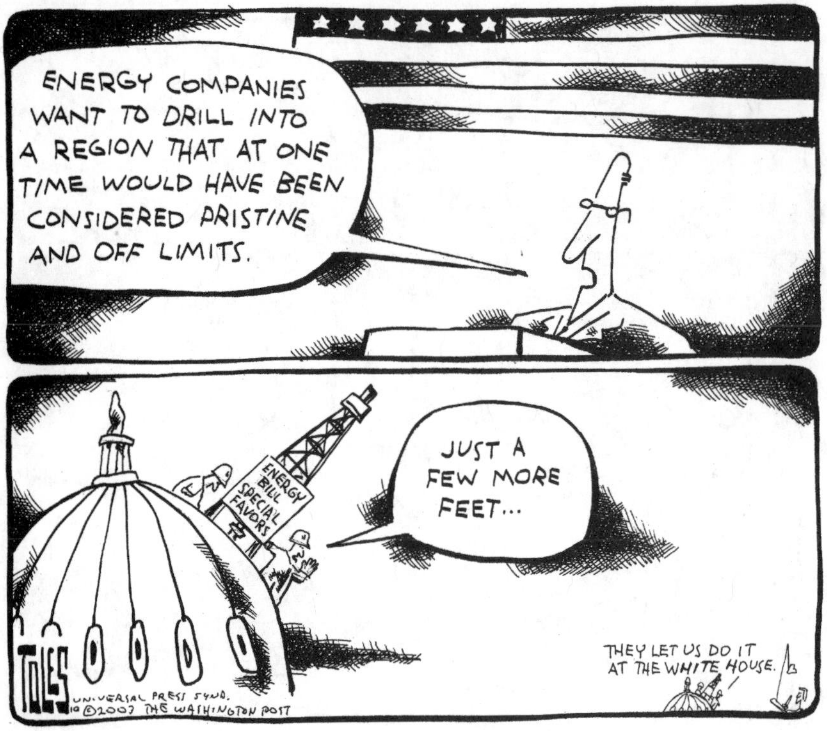
ENERGY COMPANIES WANT TO DRILL INTO A REGION THAT AT ONE TIME WOULD HAVE BEEN CONSIDERED PRISTINE AND OFF LIMITS.
ENERGY BILL SPECIAL FAVORS
JUST A FEW MORE FEET...
TOLES
UNIVERSAL PRESS SYND.
©2003 THE WASHINGTON POST
THEY LET US DO IT AT THE WHITE HOUSE.

10-13-03

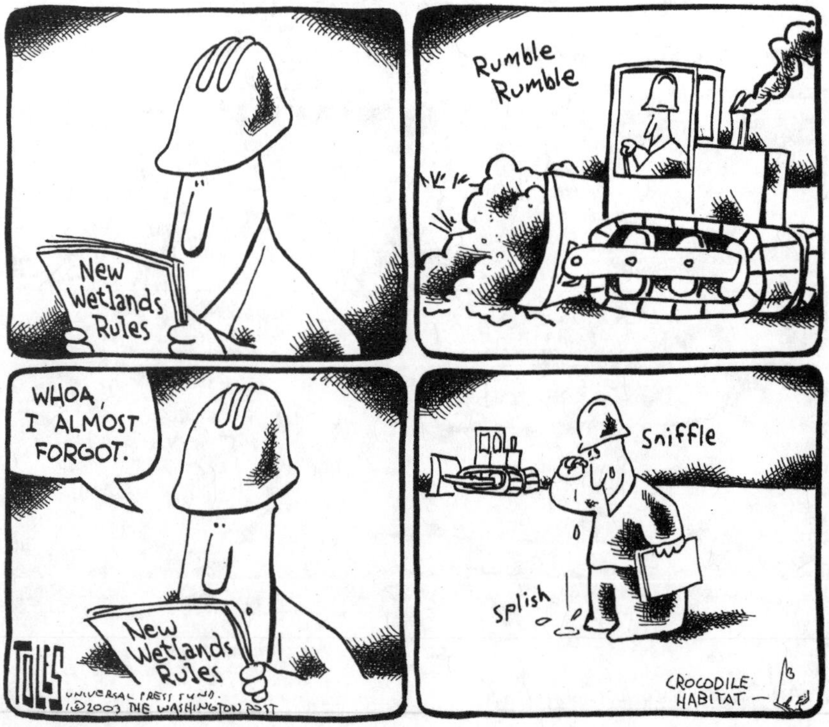
New Wetlands Rules
Rumble Rumble
WHOA, I ALMOST FORGOT.
New Wetlands Rules
TOLES
UNIVERSAL PRESS SYND.
©2003 THE WASHINGTON POST
Sniffle
Splish
CROCODILE HABITAT

1-14-03

I PROMISED TO LOVE YOU UNTIL THE MOUNTAINS CRUMBLED INTO THE VALLEYS AND I MEANT IT.
THE ENVIRONMENT
MOUNTAIN-TOP REMOVAL MINING OPERATION #347
TOLES
UNIVERSAL PRESS SYND.
6 © 2003 THE WASHINGTON POST
...UNTIL ALL THE OCEANS ARE OVERFISHED...

6-10-03

GLOBAL WARMING
one more study
TOLES
UNIVERSAL PRESS SYND.
7 © 2003 THE WASHINGTON POST
HINT ON FINDINGS: "TOO LATE."

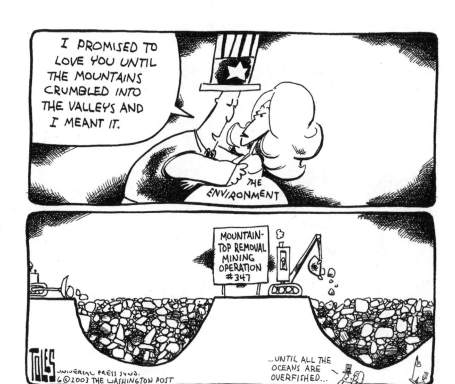

7-27-03

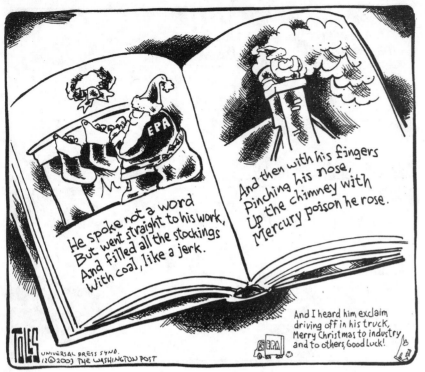

He spoke not a word
But went straight to his work,
And filled all the stockings
With coal, like a jerk.

And then with his fingers
Pinching his nose,
Up the chimney with
Mercury poison he rose.

And I heard him exclaim
driving off in his truck,
Merry Christmas to industry
and to others, Good Luck!

TOLES
UNIVERSAL PRESS SYND.
12©2003 THE WASHINGTON POST

12-8-03

I'M HERE TO DEBUNK ALL THE GLOBAL WARMING SCIENCE.

EXCELLENT!

INDUSTRY

I'M NOT A CLIMATE SCIENTIST BUT I PLAY ONE ON TV.

TOO MUCH CANDOR.

UM... THIS LAB COAT IS TOO BIG BECAUSE IT ISN'T REALLY MINE. THEY GAVE IT TO ME TO WEAR.

DON'T TELL THEM THAT!

IT...UH... COVERS THE ENERGY COMPANIES' CASH BULGING IN MY POCKETS.

NO!

BUT YOU SAID I DON'T HAVE TO CONVINCE SCIENTISTS, ONLY JOURNALISTS, AND THEY'RE REALLY EASY.

YOU HAVE TO PLAY THE GAME!

IS IT GETTING WARM IN HERE OR IS IT JUST ME?

NEVER LET THEM SEE YOU SWEAT!

NOW WE NEED A SCIENTIST WHO'LL SAY IT'S NOT SWEAT

TOLES
UNIVERSAL PRESS SYND
11©2003 THE WASHINGTON POST

11-30-03

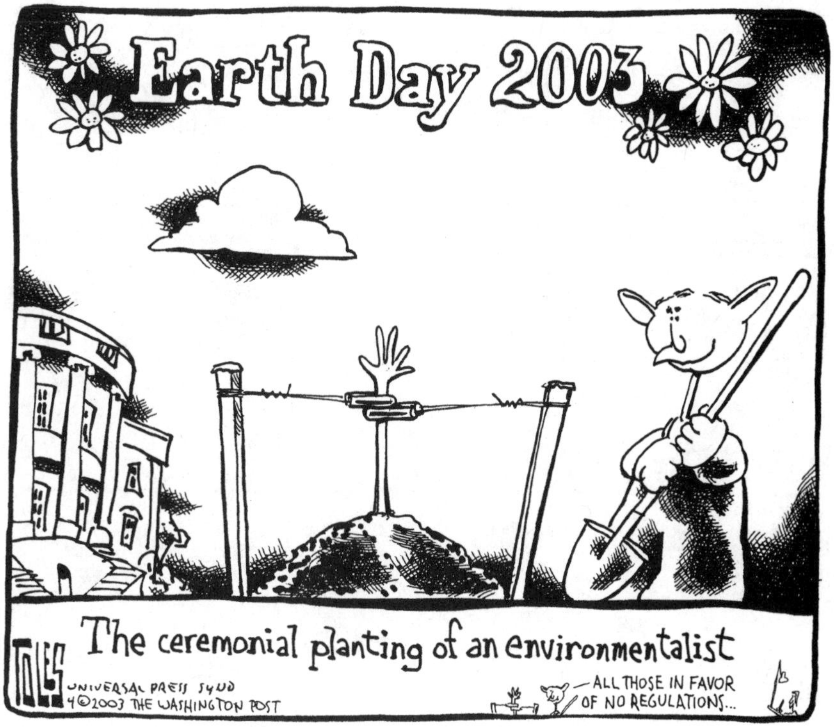
Earth Day 2003
The ceremonial planting of an environmentalist
TOLES
UNIVERSAL PRESS SYND
4©2003 THE WASHINGTON POST
ALL THOSE IN FAVOR OF NO REGULATIONS...

4-22-03

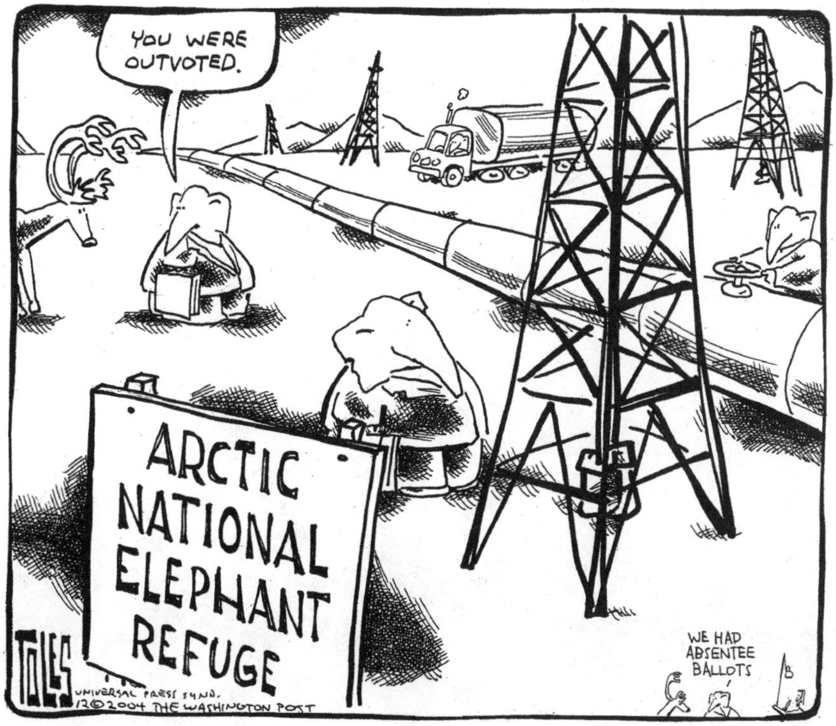
YOU WERE OUTVOTED.
ARCTIC NATIONAL ELEPHANT REFUGE
WE HAD ABSENTEE BALLOTS
TOLES
UNIVERSAL PRESS SYND.
12©2004 THE WASHINGTON POST

12-20-04

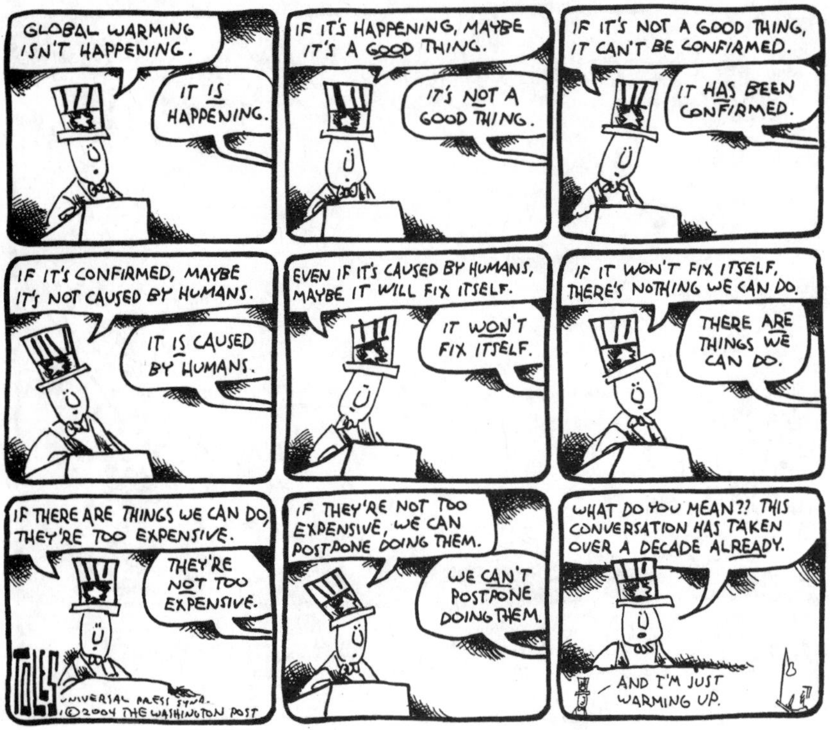

GLOBAL WARMING ISN'T HAPPENING.
IT IS HAPPENING.
IF IT'S HAPPENING, MAYBE IT'S A GOOD THING.
IT'S NOT A GOOD THING.
IF IT'S NOT A GOOD THING, IT CAN'T BE CONFIRMED.
IT HAS BEEN CONFIRMED.
IF IT'S CONFIRMED, MAYBE IT'S NOT CAUSED BY HUMANS.
IT IS CAUSED BY HUMANS.
EVEN IF IT'S CAUSED BY HUMANS, MAYBE IT WILL FIX ITSELF.
IT WON'T FIX ITSELF.
IF IT WON'T FIX ITSELF, THERE'S NOTHING WE CAN DO.
THERE ARE THINGS WE CAN DO.
IF THERE ARE THINGS WE CAN DO, THEY'RE TOO EXPENSIVE.
THEY'RE NOT TOO EXPENSIVE.
IF THEY'RE NOT TOO EXPENSIVE, WE CAN POSTPONE DOING THEM.
WE CAN'T POSTPONE DOING THEM.
WHAT DO YOU MEAN?? THIS CONVERSATION HAS TAKEN OVER A DECADE ALREADY.
AND I'M JUST WARMING UP.
TOLES
UNIVERSAL PRESS SYND.
©2004 THE WASHINGTON POST

1-2-04

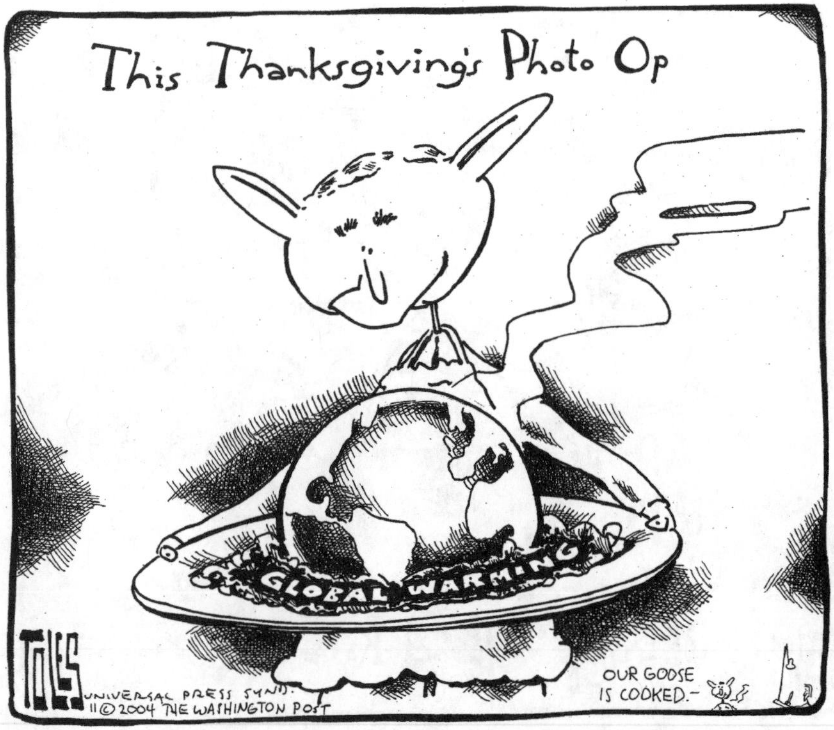

This Thanksgiving's Photo Op
GLOBAL WARMING
TOLES
UNIVERSAL PRESS SYND.
©2004 THE WASHINGTON POST
OUR GOOSE IS COOKED.

11-25-04

A NASA satellite, used to study global warming and to track hurricanes, will be sent to a watery grave.

SPLASH

And the Hubble telescope, which has provided unprecedented views of the universe, will be going dark.

CLICK

WE'RE GOING TO USE OUR SPACE BUDGET FOR REAL SCIENCE!

TOLES
UNIVERSAL PRESS SYND.
© 2004 THE WASHINGTON POST

NOW WATCH THIS DRIVE.

Golfing on Mars.

DARN! I WAS HOPING THE HUBBLE WOULD GET A SHOT OF THIS.

7-20-04

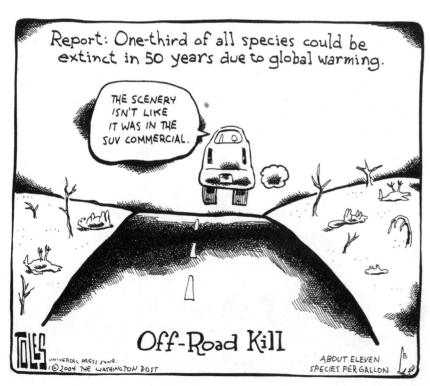

Report: One-third of all species could be extinct in 50 years due to global warming.

THE SCENERY ISN'T LIKE IT WAS IN THE SUV COMMERCIAL.

Off-Road Kill

TOLES
UNIVERSAL PRESS SYND.
© 2004 THE WASHINGTON POST

ABOUT ELEVEN SPECIES PER GALLON

1-12-04

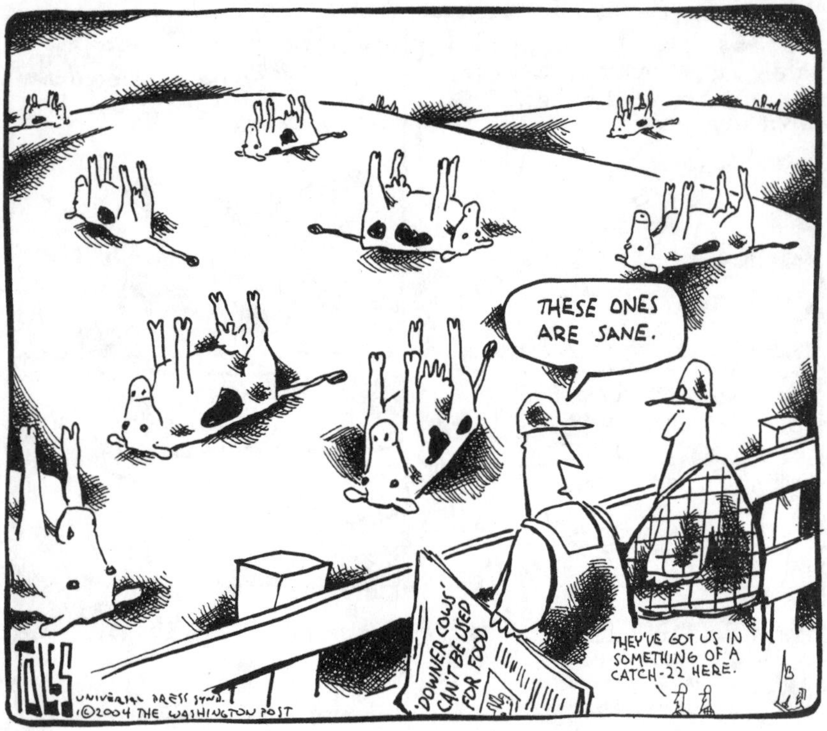
THESE ONES ARE SANE.
'DOWNER COWS' CAN'T BE USED FOR FOOD
THEY'VE GOT US IN SOMETHING OF A CATCH-22 HERE.
UNIVERSAL PRESS SYND. ©2004 THE WASHINGTON POST

1-1-04

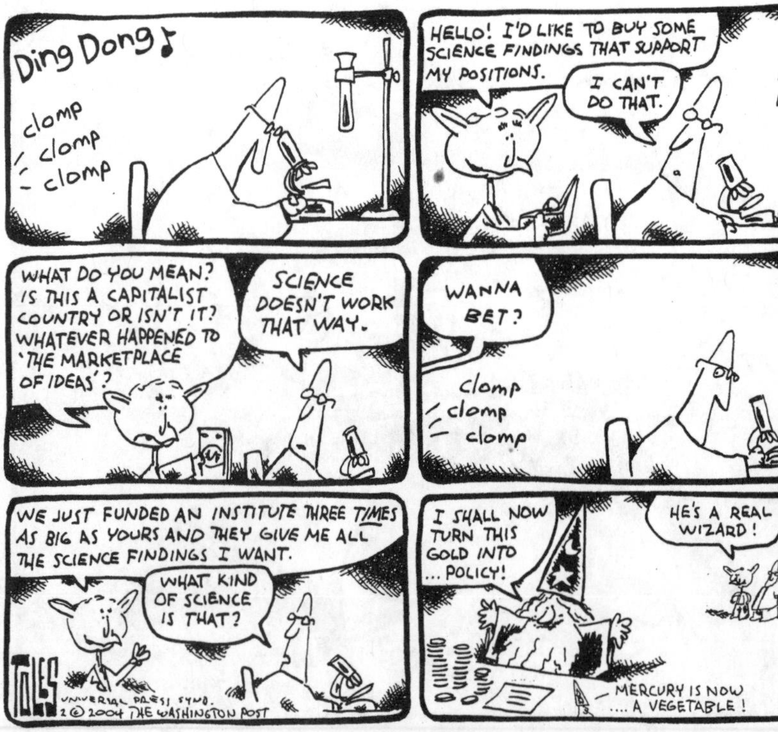
Ding Dong
clomp clomp clomp
HELLO! I'D LIKE TO BUY SOME SCIENCE FINDINGS THAT SUPPORT MY POSITIONS.
I CAN'T DO THAT.
WHAT DO YOU MEAN? IS THIS A CAPITALIST COUNTRY OR ISN'T IT? WHATEVER HAPPENED TO 'THE MARKETPLACE OF IDEAS'?
SCIENCE DOESN'T WORK THAT WAY.
WANNA BET?
clomp clomp clomp
WE JUST FUNDED AN INSTITUTE THREE TIMES AS BIG AS YOURS AND THEY GIVE ME ALL THE SCIENCE FINDINGS I WANT.
WHAT KIND OF SCIENCE IS THAT?
UNIVERSAL PRESS SYND. ©2004 THE WASHINGTON POST
I SHALL NOW TURN THIS GOLD INTO ... POLICY!
HE'S A REAL WIZARD!
MERCURY IS NOW .... A VEGETABLE!

2-20-04

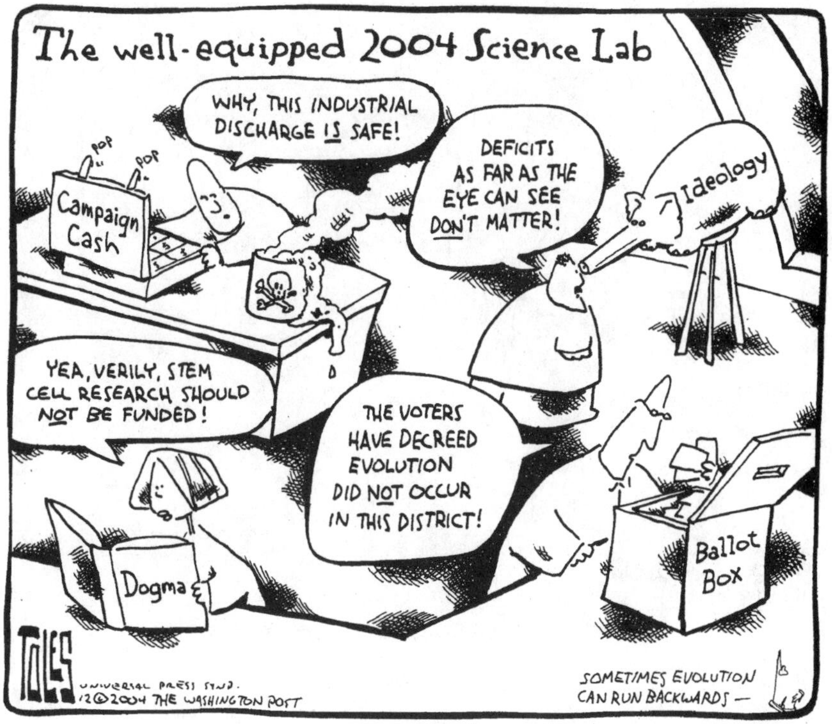
The well-equipped 2004 Science Lab
WHY, THIS INDUSTRIAL DISCHARGE IS SAFE!
POP
POP
Campaign Cash
DEFICITS AS FAR AS THE EYE CAN SEE DON'T MATTER!
Ideology
YEA, VERILY, STEM CELL RESEARCH SHOULD NOT BE FUNDED!
THE VOTERS HAVE DECREED EVOLUTION DID NOT OCCUR IN THIS DISTRICT!
Dogma
Ballot Box
TOLES
UNIVERSAL PRESS SYND.
12 © 2004 THE WASHINGTON POST
SOMETIMES EVOLUTION CAN RUN BACKWARDS —

12-6-04

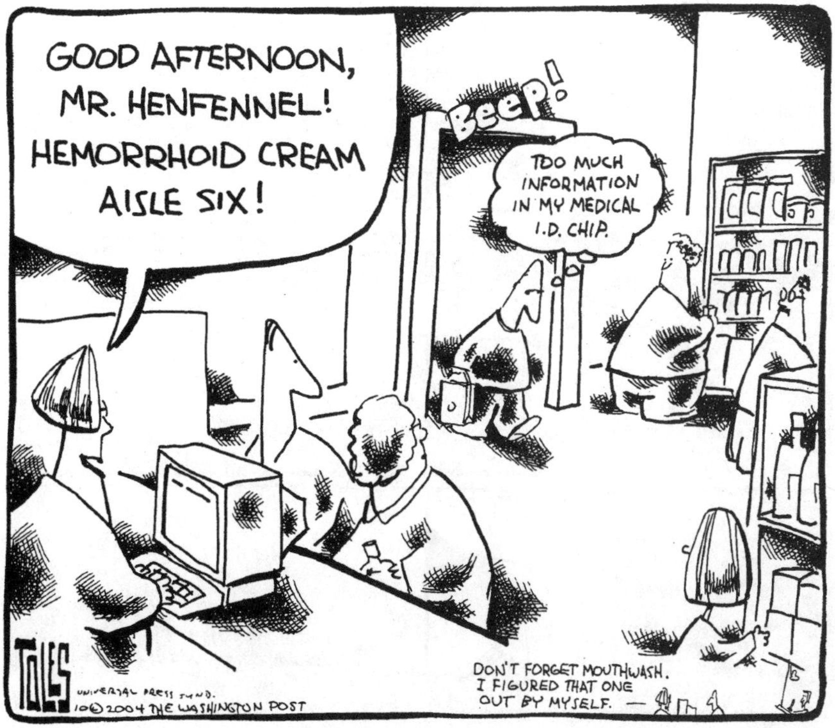
GOOD AFTERNOON, MR. HENFENNEL! HEMORRHOID CREAM AISLE SIX!
Beep!
TOO MUCH INFORMATION IN MY MEDICAL I.D. CHIP.
TOLES
UNIVERSAL PRESS SYND.
10 © 2004 THE WASHINGTON POST
DON'T FORGET MOUTHWASH. I FIGURED THAT ONE OUT BY MYSELF. —

10-17-04

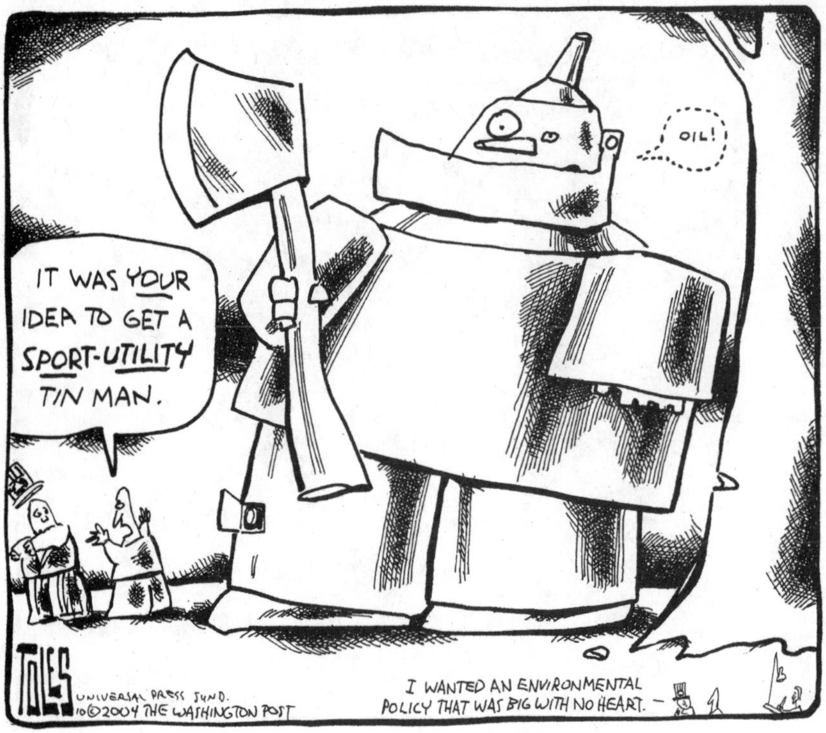
OIL!
IT WAS YOUR IDEA TO GET A SPORT-UTILITY TIN MAN.
I WANTED AN ENVIRONMENTAL POLICY THAT WAS BIG WITH NO HEART.
TOLES
UNIVERSAL PRESS SYND.
10 © 2004 THE WASHINGTON POST

10-4-04

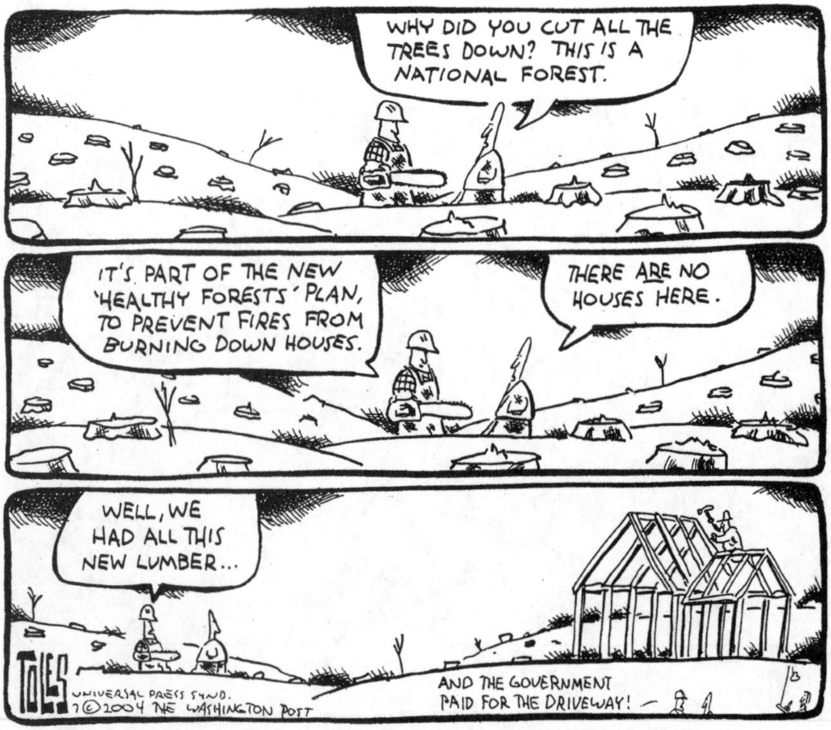
WHY DID YOU CUT ALL THE TREES DOWN? THIS IS A NATIONAL FOREST.
IT'S PART OF THE NEW 'HEALTHY FORESTS' PLAN, TO PREVENT FIRES FROM BURNING DOWN HOUSES.
THERE ARE NO HOUSES HERE.
WELL, WE HAD ALL THIS NEW LUMBER...
AND THE GOVERNMENT PAID FOR THE DRIVEWAY!
TOLES
UNIVERSAL PRESS SYND.
7 © 2004 THE WASHINGTON POST

7-4-04

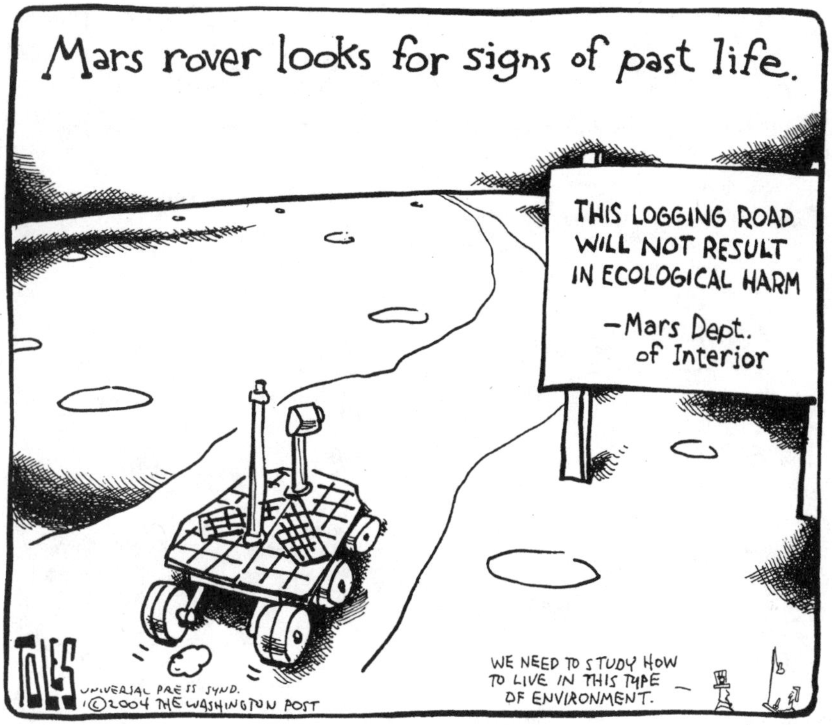
Mars rover looks for signs of past life.
THIS LOGGING ROAD WILL NOT RESULT IN ECOLOGICAL HARM
—Mars Dept. of Interior
TOLES
UNIVERSAL PRESS SYND.
©2004 THE WASHINGTON POST
WE NEED TO STUDY HOW TO LIVE IN THIS TYPE OF ENVIRONMENT.

1-6-04

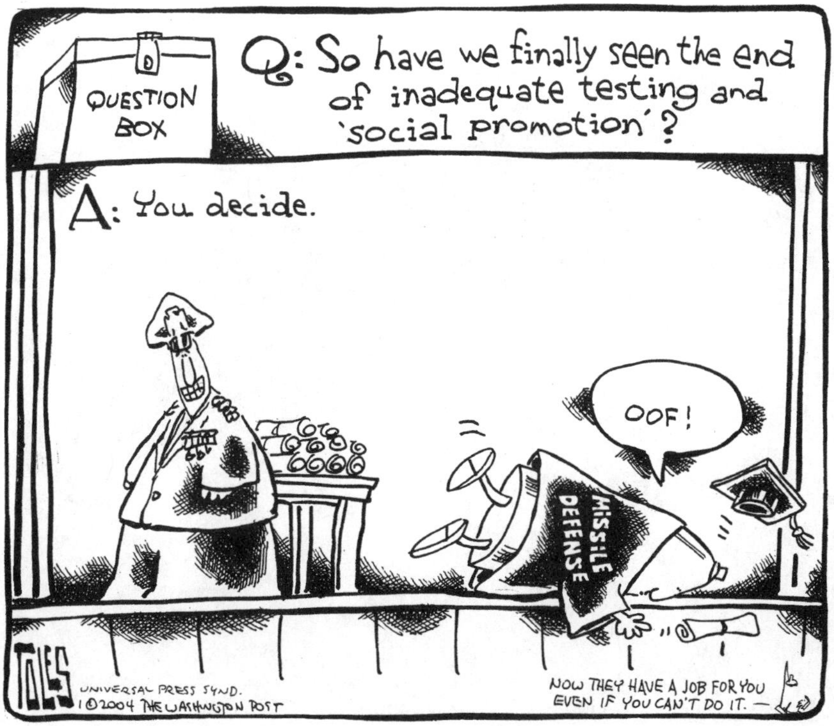
QUESTION BOX
Q: So have we finally seen the end of inadequate testing and 'social promotion'?
A: You decide.
OOF!
MISSILE DEFENSE
TOLES
UNIVERSAL PRESS SYND.
©2004 THE WASHINGTON POST
NOW THEY HAVE A JOB FOR YOU EVEN IF YOU CAN'T DO IT.

1-26-04

SUVs Explained!
DRIVING CAUSES OBESITY
THE MORE YOU DRIVE, THE BIGGER YOU GET. -STUDY
The Enabler
Relaxed Fit
TOLES
UNIVERSAL PRESS SYND.
6©2004 THE WASHINGTON POST
PERHAPS IT'S TIME TO REDEFINE FOSSIL FUELS AS A CARB. —

6-2-04

NATIONAL PARK SMOG
OH, SAY, CAN YOU SEE?
TOLES
UNIVERSAL PRESS SYND.
4©2004 THE WASHINGTON POST
THIS ALWAYS CHOKES ME UP. —

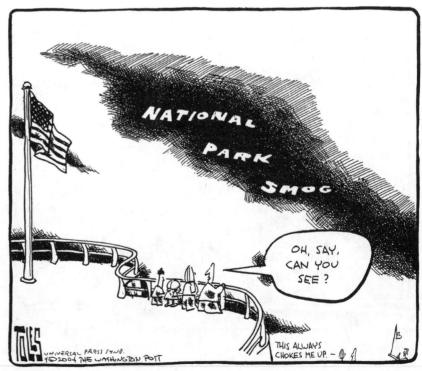

4-26-04

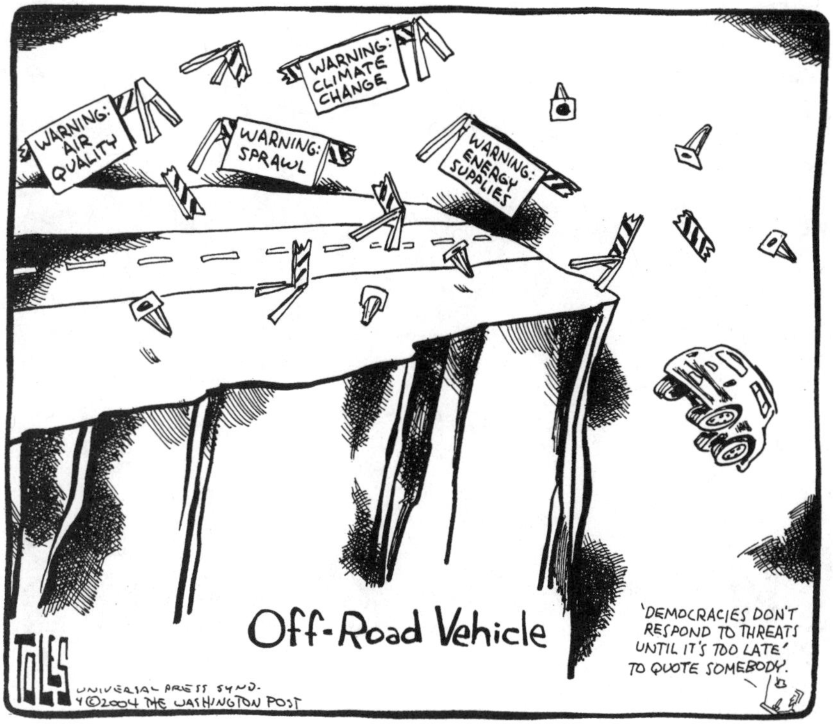
WARNING: AIR QUALITY
WARNING: CLIMATE CHANGE
WARNING: SPRAWL
WARNING: ENERGY SUPPLIES
Off-Road Vehicle
'DEMOCRACIES DON'T RESPOND TO THREATS UNTIL IT'S TOO LATE' TO QUOTE SOMEBODY.
TOLES
UNIVERSAL PRESS SYND.
©2004 THE WASHINGTON POST

4-12-04

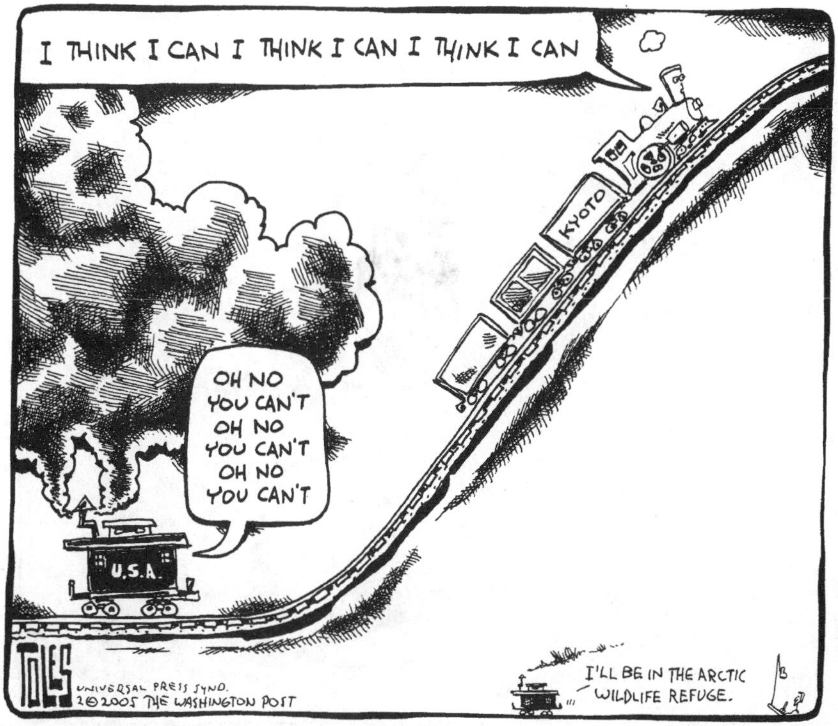
I THINK I CAN I THINK I CAN I THINK I CAN
KYOTO
OH NO YOU CAN'T OH NO YOU CAN'T OH NO YOU CAN'T
U.S.A.
I'LL BE IN THE ARCTIC WILDLIFE REFUGE.
TOLES
UNIVERSAL PRESS SYND.
©2005 THE WASHINGTON POST

2-17-05

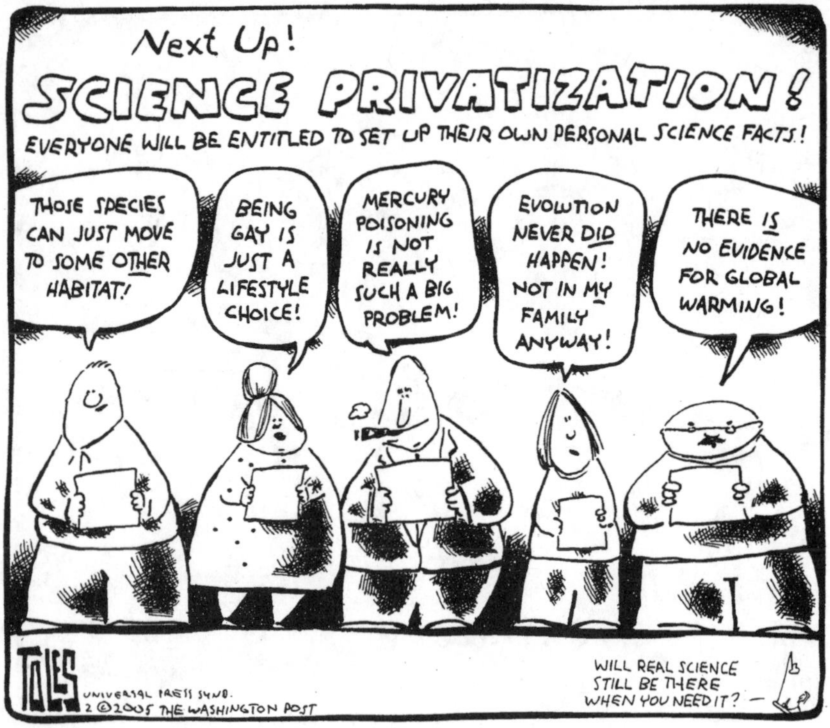
Next Up!
SCIENCE PRIVATIZATION!
EVERYONE WILL BE ENTITLED TO SET UP THEIR OWN PERSONAL SCIENCE FACTS!
THOSE SPECIES CAN JUST MOVE TO SOME OTHER HABITAT!
BEING GAY IS JUST A LIFESTYLE CHOICE!
MERCURY POISONING IS NOT REALLY SUCH A BIG PROBLEM!
EVOLUTION NEVER DID HAPPEN! NOT IN MY FAMILY ANYWAY!
THERE IS NO EVIDENCE FOR GLOBAL WARMING!
TOLES
UNIVERSAL PRESS SYND.
2 ©2005 THE WASHINGTON POST
WILL REAL SCIENCE STILL BE THERE WHEN YOU NEED IT?

2-2-05

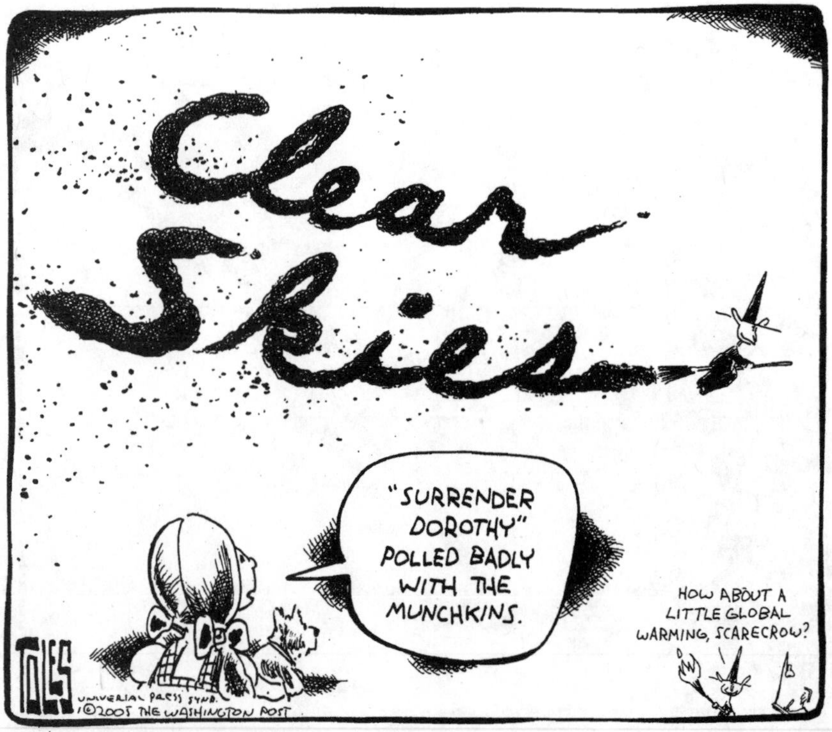
Clear Skies
"SURRENDER DOROTHY" POLLED BADLY WITH THE MUNCHKINS.
HOW ABOUT A LITTLE GLOBAL WARMING, SCARECROW?
TOLES
UNIVERSAL PRESS SYND.
1 ©2005 THE WASHINGTON POST

1-31-05

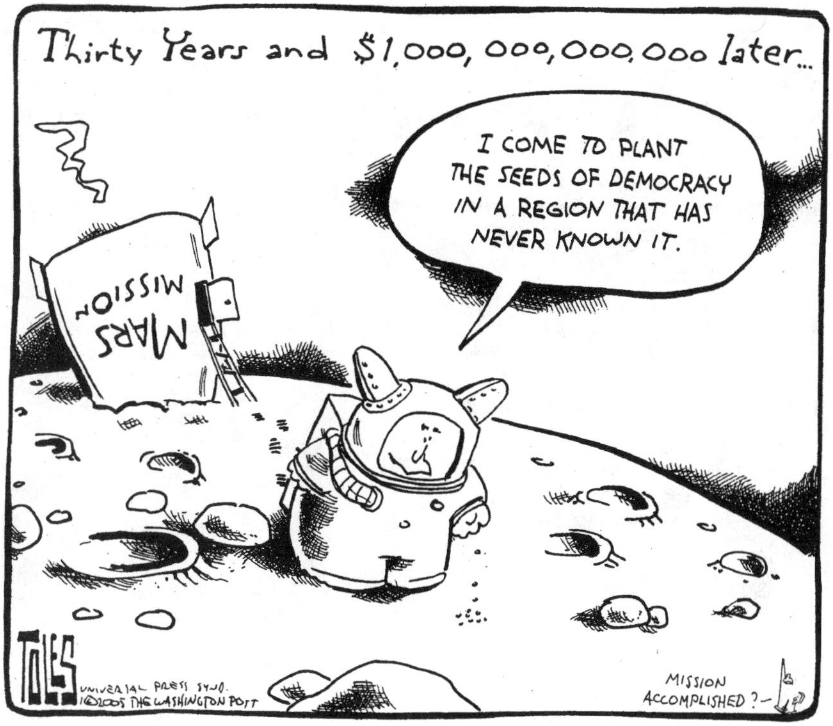
Thirty Years and $1,000,000,000,000 later...
I COME TO PLANT THE SEEDS OF DEMOCRACY IN A REGION THAT HAS NEVER KNOWN IT.
MARS MISSION
TOLES
UNIVERSAL PRESS SYND. ©2005 THE WASHINGTON POST
MISSION ACCOMPLISHED ?

1-3-05

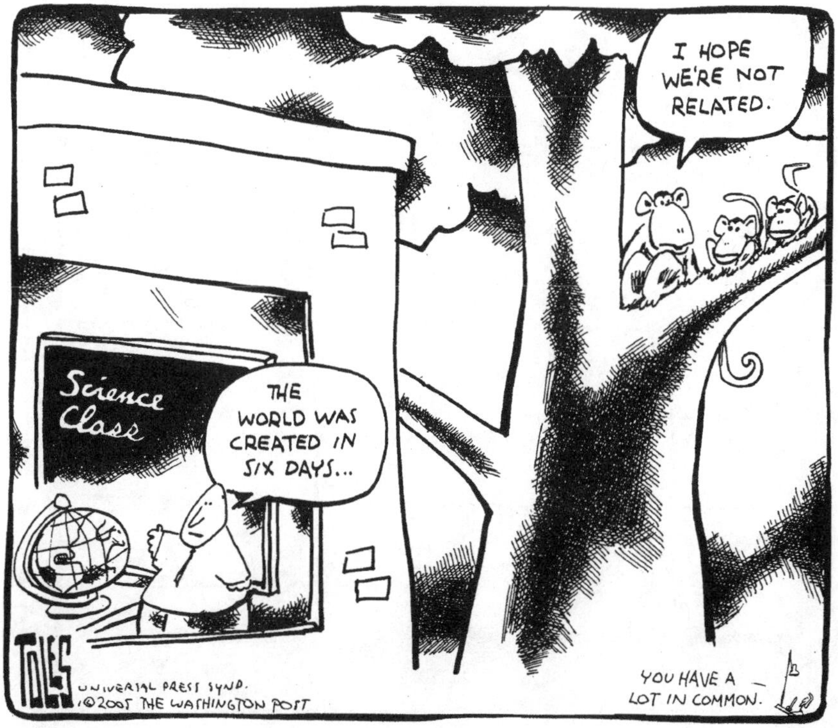
I HOPE WE'RE NOT RELATED.
Science Class
THE WORLD WAS CREATED IN SIX DAYS...
TOLES
UNIVERSAL PRESS SYND. ©2005 THE WASHINGTON POST
YOU HAVE A LOT IN COMMON.

1-24-05

Pawn
Shop
ANWR
OIL
BAR
I CAN ONLY GIVE YOU ENOUGH FOR ONE DRINK.
DEAL! —
TOLES
UNIVERSAL PRESS SYND.
3©2005 THE WASHINGTON POST

3-18-05

GAS PRICES
SUVs
I GET A BETTER VIEW FROM UP HERE
TOLES
UNIVERSAL PRESS SYND.
3©2005 THE WASHINGTON POST

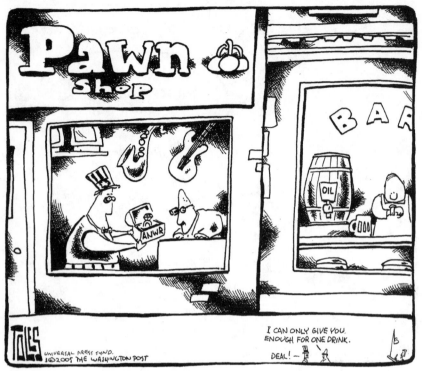

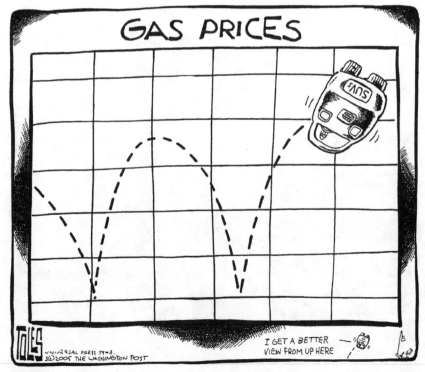

3-28-05

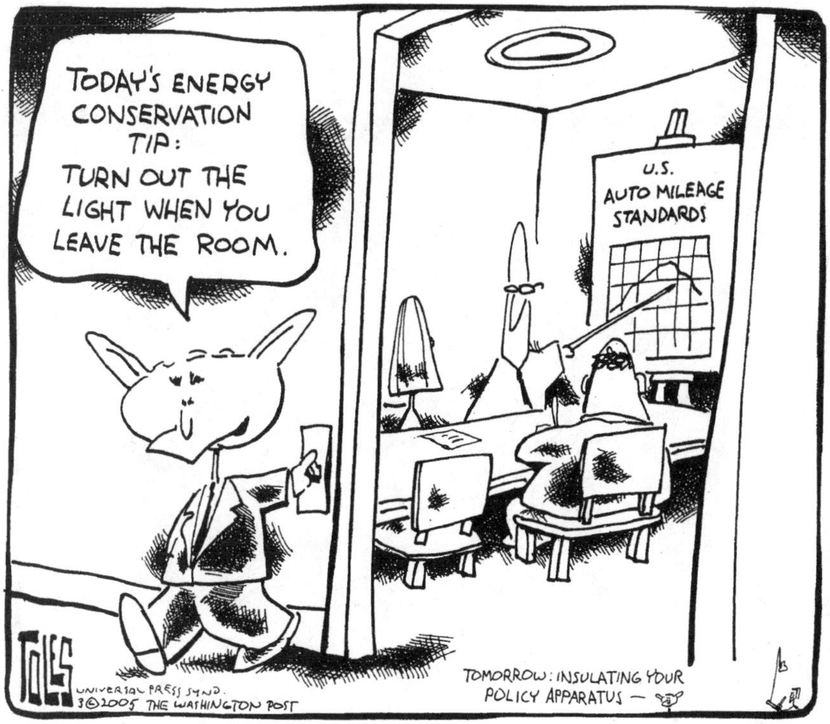
TODAY'S ENERGY CONSERVATION TIP: TURN OUT THE LIGHT WHEN YOU LEAVE THE ROOM.
U.S. AUTO MILEAGE STANDARDS
TOLES
UNIVERSAL PRESS SYND.
3 © 2005 THE WASHINGTON POST
TOMORROW: INSULATING YOUR POLICY APPARATUS —

3-14-05

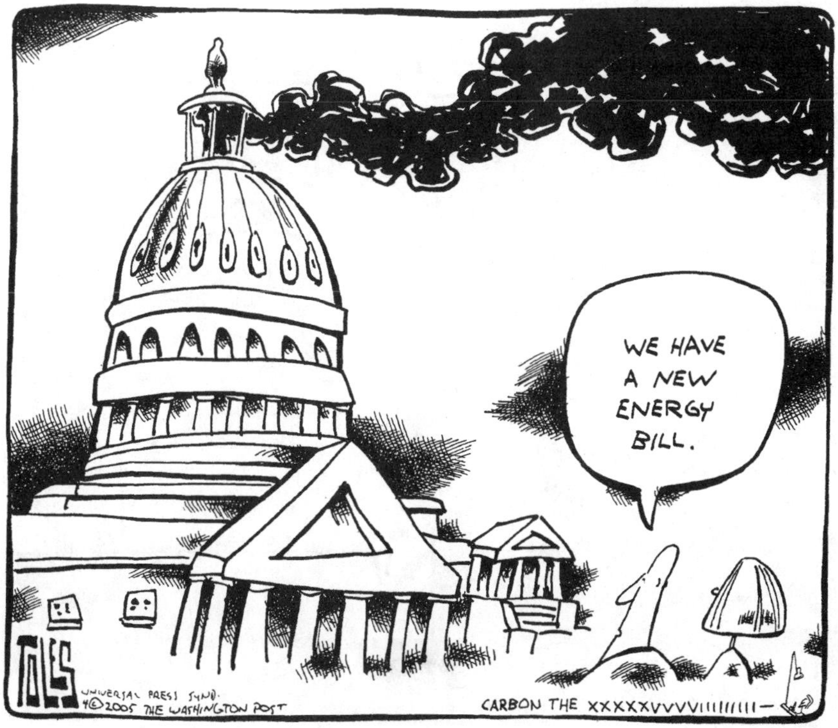
WE HAVE A NEW ENERGY BILL.
TOLES
UNIVERSAL PRESS SYND.
4 © 2005 THE WASHINGTON POST
CARBON THE XXXXXVVVVIIIIIIIII—

4-20-05

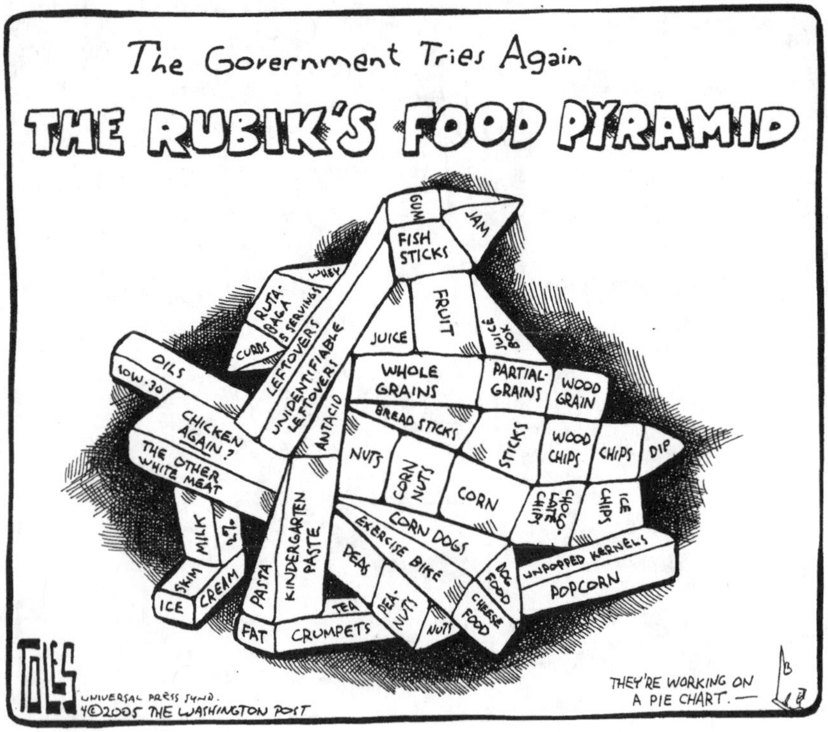
The Government Tries Again
THE RUBIK'S FOOD PYRAMID
GUM
JAM
FISH STICKS
WHEY
RUTA-BAGA
5 SERVINGS
CURDS
FRUIT
JUICE
JUICE BOX
LEFTOVERS
UNIDENTIFIABLE LEFTOVERS
WHOLE GRAINS
PARTIAL-GRAINS
WOOD GRAIN
OILS
10W-30
CHICKEN AGAIN?
THE OTHER WHITE MEAT
ANTACID
BREAD STICKS
NUTS
CORN NUTS
STICKS
WOOD CHIPS
CHIPS
DIP
CORN
CHOCOLATE CHIPS
ICE CHIPS
MILK
ICE
SKIM
CREAM
PASTA
KINDERGARTEN PASTE
CORN DOGS
EXERCISE BIKE
PEAS
PEA-NUTS
DOG FOOD
CHEESE FOOD
UNPOPPED KERNELS
POPCORN
TEA
NUTS
FAT
CRUMPETS
TOLES
UNIVERSAL PRESS SYND.
4©2005 THE WASHINGTON POST
THEY'RE WORKING ON A PIE CHART.

4-21-05

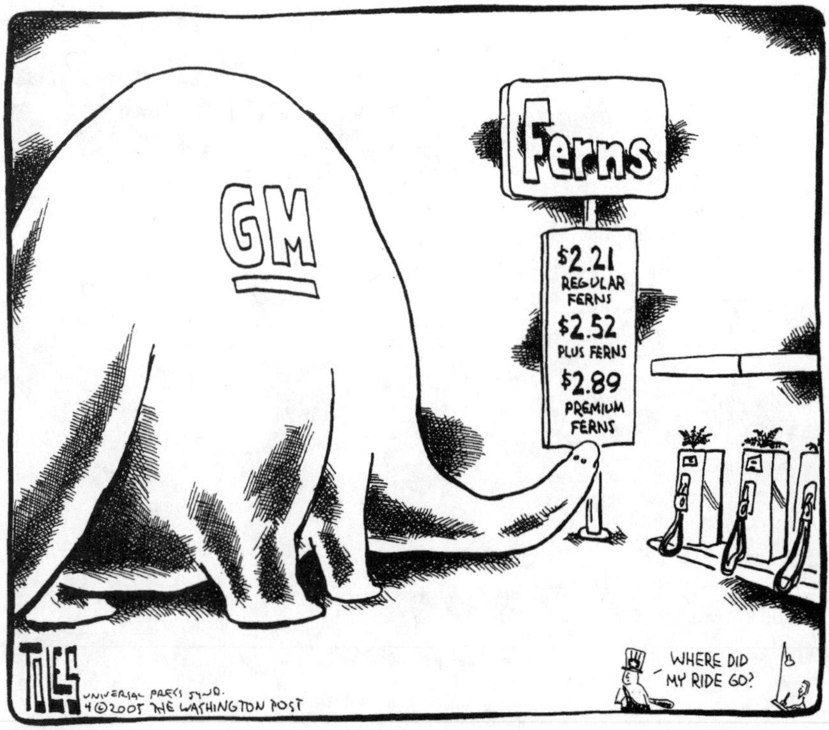
Ferns
GM
$2.21 REGULAR FERNS
$2.52 PLUS FERNS
$2.89 PREMIUM FERNS
TOLES
UNIVERSAL PRESS SYND.
4©2005 THE WASHINGTON POST
WHERE DID MY RIDE GO?

4-25-05

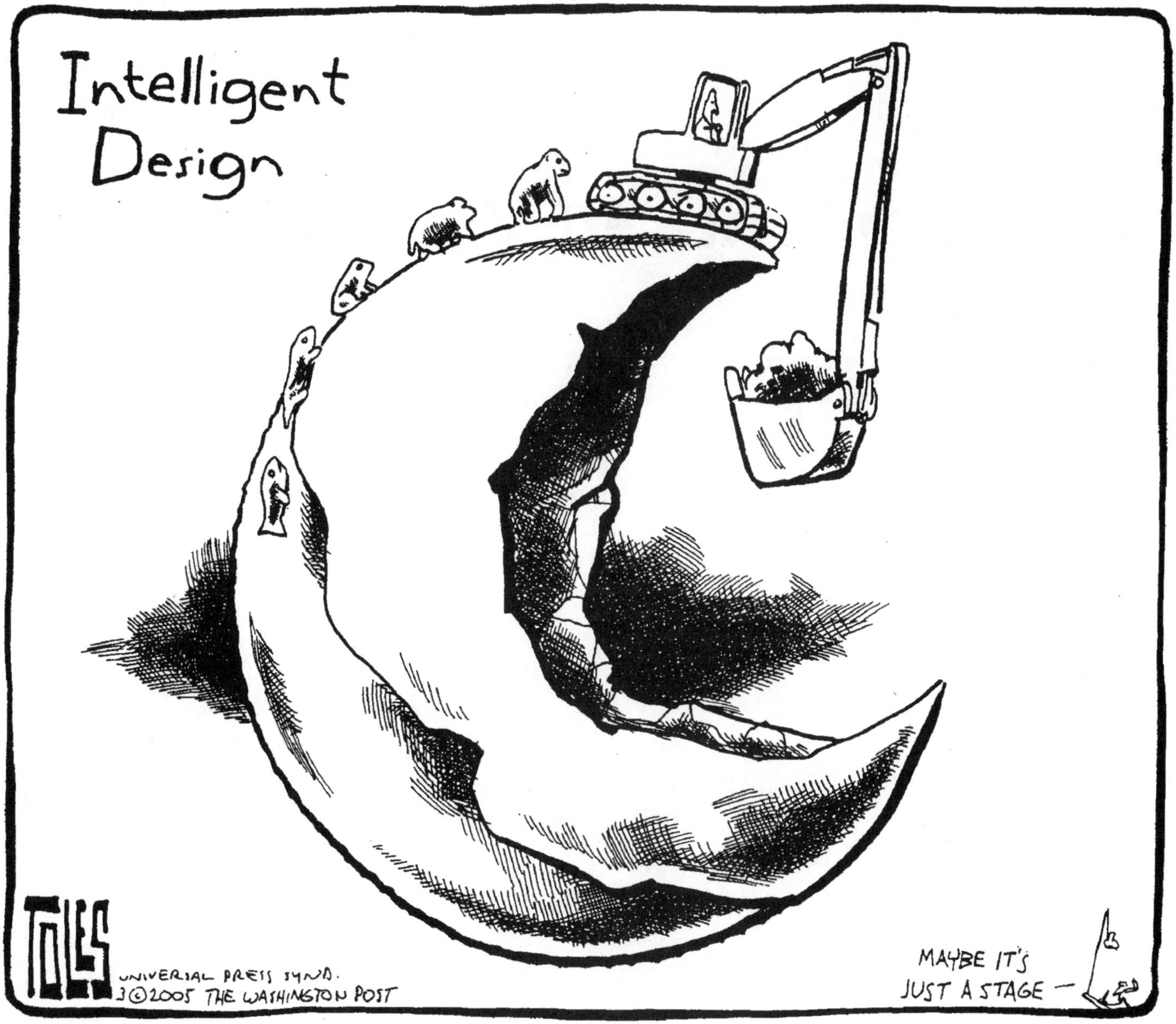
Intelligent Design
TOLES
UNIVERSAL PRESS SYND.
3©2005 THE WASHINGTON POST
MAYBE IT'S JUST A STAGE —

3-29-05

SOCIAL SECURITY

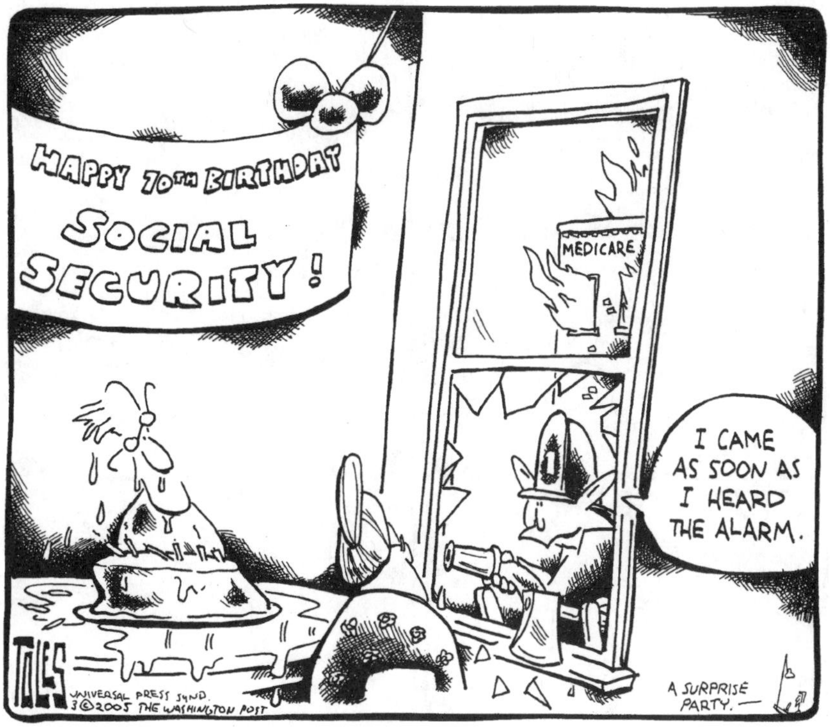
HAPPY 70TH BIRTHDAY
SOCIAL SECURITY!
MEDICARE
I CAME AS SOON AS I HEARD THE ALARM.
A SURPRISE PARTY.
TOLES
UNIVERSAL PRESS SYND.
3 © 2005 THE WASHINGTON POST

3-25-05

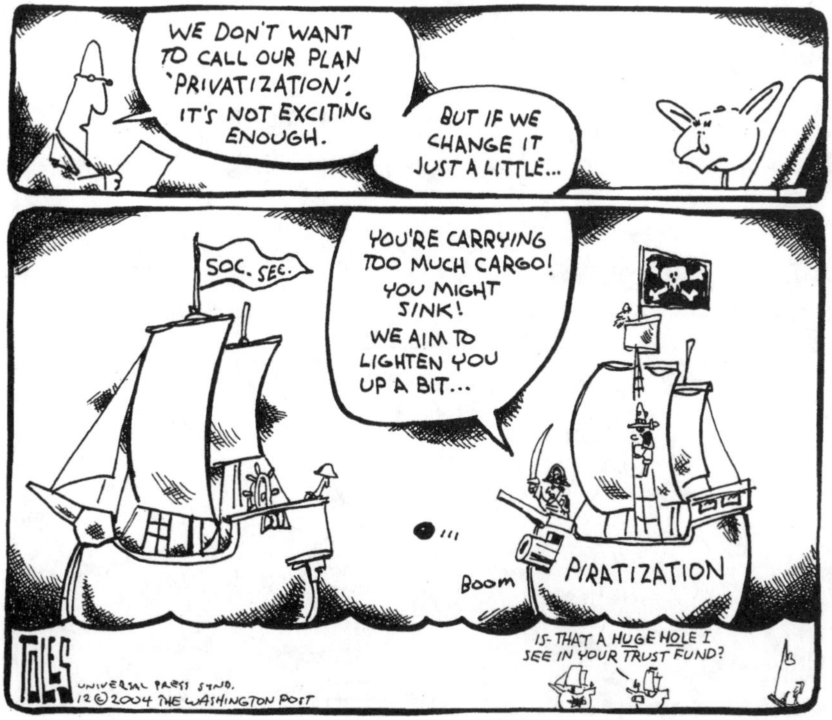
WE DON'T WANT TO CALL OUR PLAN 'PRIVATIZATION'. IT'S NOT EXCITING ENOUGH.
BUT IF WE CHANGE IT JUST A LITTLE...
SOC. SEC.
YOU'RE CARRYING TOO MUCH CARGO! YOU MIGHT SINK!
WE AIM TO LIGHTEN YOU UP A BIT...
Boom
PIRATIZATION
IS THAT A HUGE HOLE I SEE IN YOUR TRUST FUND?
TOLES
UNIVERSAL PRESS SYND.
12 © 2004 THE WASHINGTON POST

12-19-04

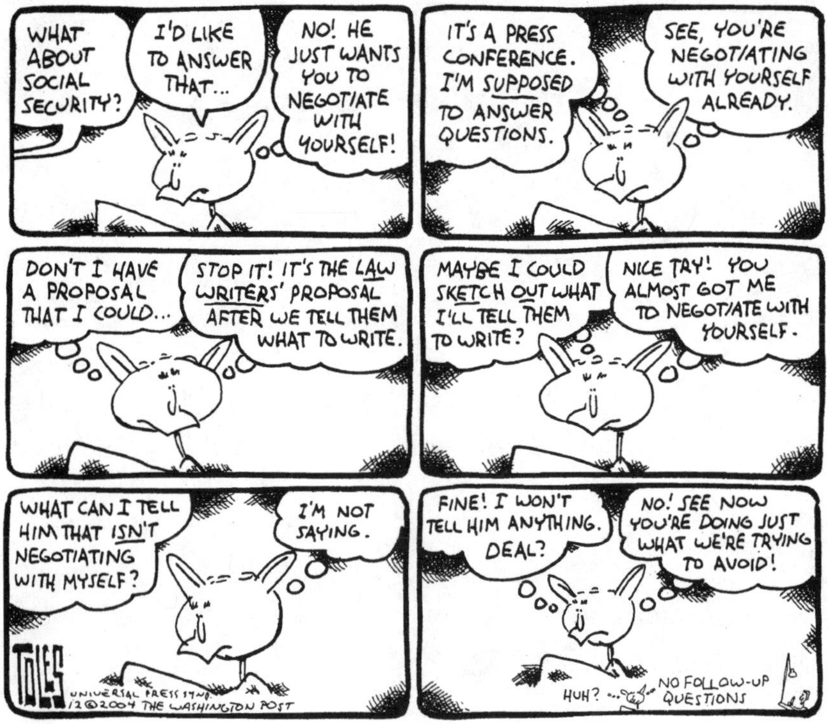

WHAT ABOUT SOCIAL SECURITY?
I'D LIKE TO ANSWER THAT...
NO! HE JUST WANTS YOU TO NEGOTIATE WITH YOURSELF!
IT'S A PRESS CONFERENCE. I'M SUPPOSED TO ANSWER QUESTIONS.
SEE, YOU'RE NEGOTIATING WITH YOURSELF ALREADY.
DON'T I HAVE A PROPOSAL THAT I COULD...
STOP IT! IT'S THE LAW WRITERS' PROPOSAL AFTER WE TELL THEM WHAT TO WRITE.
MAYBE I COULD SKETCH OUT WHAT I'LL TELL THEM TO WRITE?
NICE TRY! YOU ALMOST GOT ME TO NEGOTIATE WITH YOURSELF.
WHAT CAN I TELL HIM THAT ISN'T NEGOTIATING WITH MYSELF?
I'M NOT SAYING.
FINE! I WON'T TELL HIM ANYTHING. DEAL?
NO! SEE NOW YOU'RE DOING JUST WHAT WE'RE TRYING TO AVOID!
TOLES
UNIVERSAL PRESS SYND.
12 ©2004 THE WASHINGTON POST
HUH?
NO FOLLOW-UP QUESTIONS

12-22-04

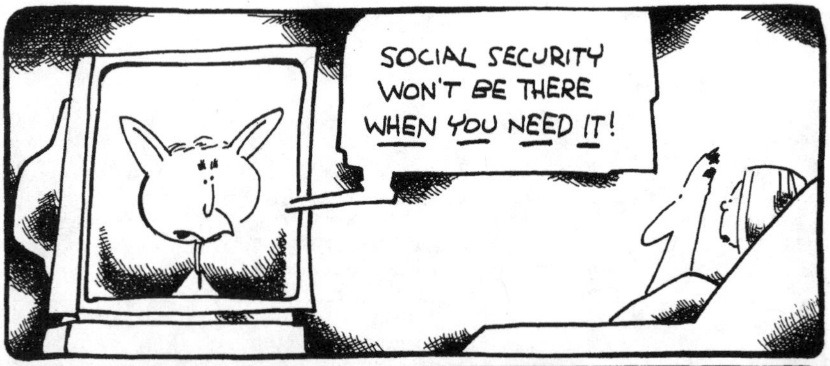

SOCIAL SECURITY WON'T BE THERE WHEN YOU NEED IT!
Later
WE MADE BAD INVESTMENT CHOICES. THEN THE MARKET TANKED. WHAT LITTLE WE HAD WAS EATEN UP BY MANAGEMENT FEES.
OUR PERSONAL ACCOUNT IS EMPTY.
NOW WHAT?
PRESIDENT BUSH WAS RIGHT!
TOLES
UNIVERSAL PRESS SYND.
1 ©2005 THE WASHINGTON POST
YOU JUST PAID HIS BIG MANAGEMENT FEE.

1-10-05

I HAVE A COMMENT ABOUT MY PRIVATE ACCOUNT.
"PERSONAL".
NO, IT'S NOT REALLY A PERSONAL COMMENT.
NO, "PERSONAL" ACCOUNT.
SOC. SEC.
WELL, YES, IT'S MY PERSONAL ACCOUNT OF MY EXPERIENCE WITH PRIVATIZATION.
NO NO, NOT PRIVATIZATION. "PERSONAL" ACCOUNTS IS WHAT WE CALL IT.
CALL WHAT?
YOUR PERSONAL ACCOUNT. WE CALL YOUR PERSONAL ACCOUNT YOUR "PERSONAL" ACCOUNT BECAUSE THE WORD PRIVATE POLLED BADLY.
WHATEVER. IT'S EMPTY.
"UNENCUMBERED".
TOLES
UNIVERSAL PRESS SYND.
1©2005 THE WASHINGTON POST
'DESTITUTION' POLLED BADLY.

1-25-05

I'M ASKING FOR YOUR SUPPORT FOR MY SOCIAL SECURITY REFORM.
NO. WE DON'T LIKE YOUR PLAN.
HOW CAN YOU CRITICIZE IT? THERE ISN'T EVEN A SPECIFIC PROPOSAL YET.
WAIT TO HEAR ALL THE DETAILS BEFORE YOU PASS JUDGMENT.
WHEN DO WE HEAR THE DETAILS?
AFTER I HAVE YOUR SUPPORT.
TOLES
UNIVERSAL PRESS SYND.
3©2005 THE WASHINGTON POST
THEN WE WON'T HAVE TO NEGOTIATE WITH OURSELVES

3-7-05

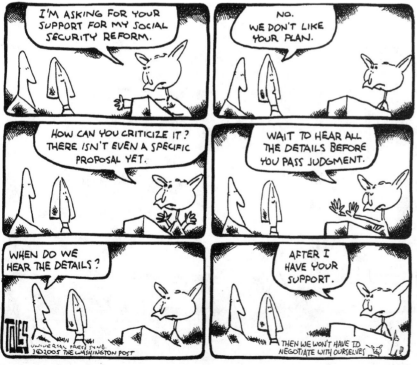

TODAY'S COOKING LESSON: SOCIAL SECURITY REFORM SOUP!
START WITH THE FINEST CUTS OF BENEFITS.
DON'T FORGET THE BORROWING!
MAYBE A FEW REVENUE ENHANCERS...
A DELICIOUS SOLUTION!
OOPS! I ALMOST FORGOT THE STONE!
PERSONAL ACCOUNTS
TOLES
UNIVERSAL PRESS SYND.
2©2005 THE WASHINGTON POST
JUST TRYING TO — FLOAT THE IDEA...

2-22-05

WITHIN FIFTY YEARS, OBESITY WILL CUT U.S. LIFE EXPECTANCY BY TWO TO FIVE YEARS.
THE FOOD INDUSTRY HAS PUT FORWARD ITS PLAN FOR SOLVING SOCIAL SECURITY.
TOLES
UNIVERSAL PRESS SYND.
3©2005 THE WASHINGTON POST
WANT ANYTHING FROM THE 'LOCKBOX'?

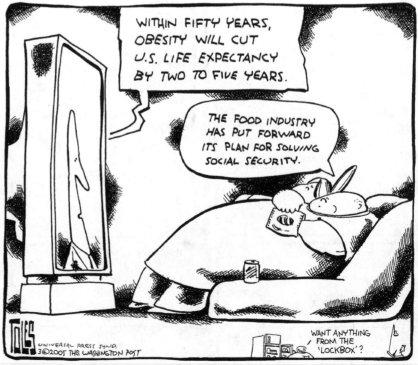

3-21-05

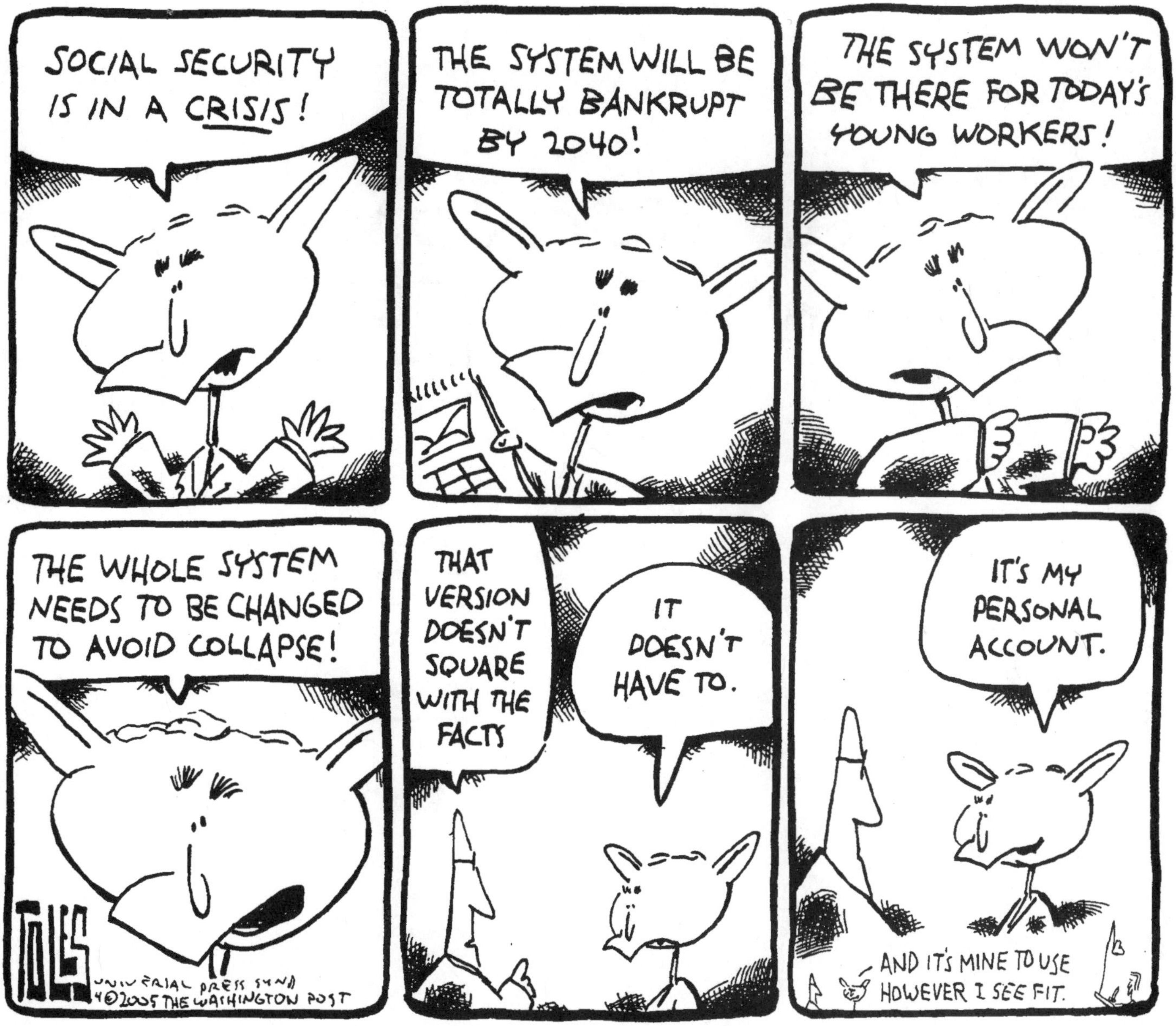
SOCIAL SECURITY IS IN A CRISIS!
THE SYSTEM WILL BE TOTALLY BANKRUPT BY 2040!
THE SYSTEM WON'T BE THERE FOR TODAY'S YOUNG WORKERS!
THE WHOLE SYSTEM NEEDS TO BE CHANGED TO AVOID COLLAPSE!
TOLES
UNIVERSAL PRESS SYND
4 © 2005 THE WASHINGTON POST
THAT VERSION DOESN'T SQUARE WITH THE FACTS
IT DOESN'T HAVE TO.
IT'S MY PERSONAL ACCOUNT.
AND IT'S MINE TO USE HOWEVER I SEE FIT.

4-3-05

THE ECONOMY
AND BUDGET

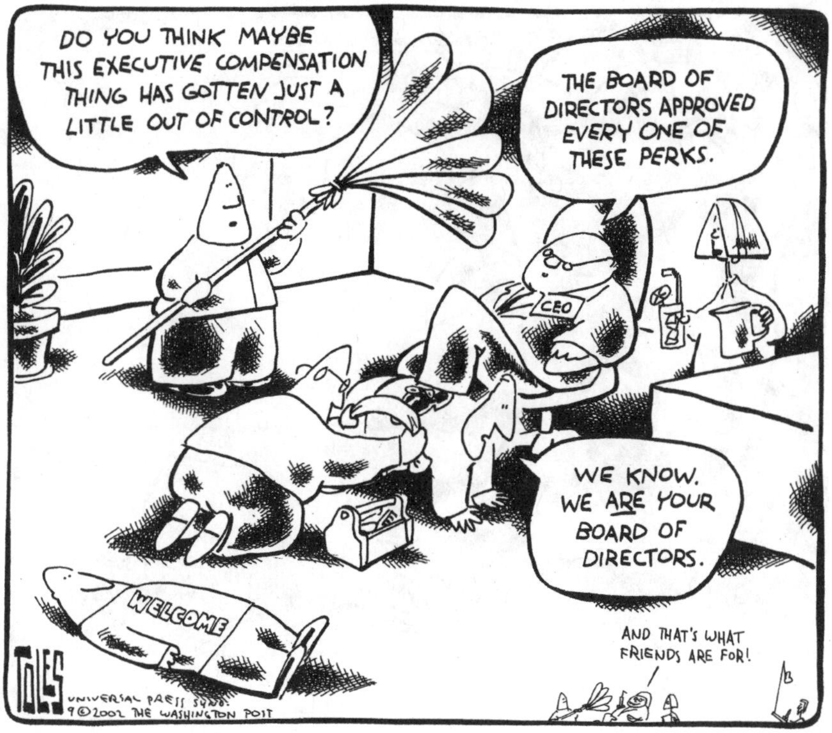
DO YOU THINK MAYBE THIS EXECUTIVE COMPENSATION THING HAS GOTTEN JUST A LITTLE OUT OF CONTROL?
THE BOARD OF DIRECTORS APPROVED EVERY ONE OF THESE PERKS.
WE KNOW. WE ARE YOUR BOARD OF DIRECTORS.
CEO
WELCOME
AND THAT'S WHAT FRIENDS ARE FOR!
TOLES
UNIVERSAL PRESS SYND.
9 © 2002 THE WASHINGTON POST

9-16-02

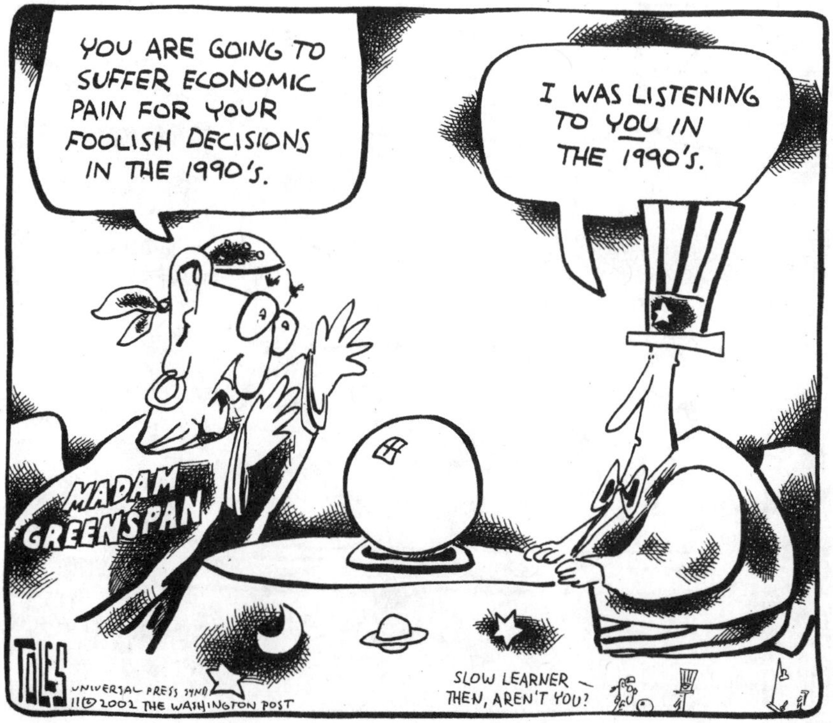
YOU ARE GOING TO SUFFER ECONOMIC PAIN FOR YOUR FOOLISH DECISIONS IN THE 1990'S.
I WAS LISTENING TO YOU IN THE 1990'S.
MADAM GREENSPAN
SLOW LEARNER — THEN, AREN'T YOU?
TOLES
UNIVERSAL PRESS SYND
11 © 2002 THE WASHINGTON POST

11-1-02

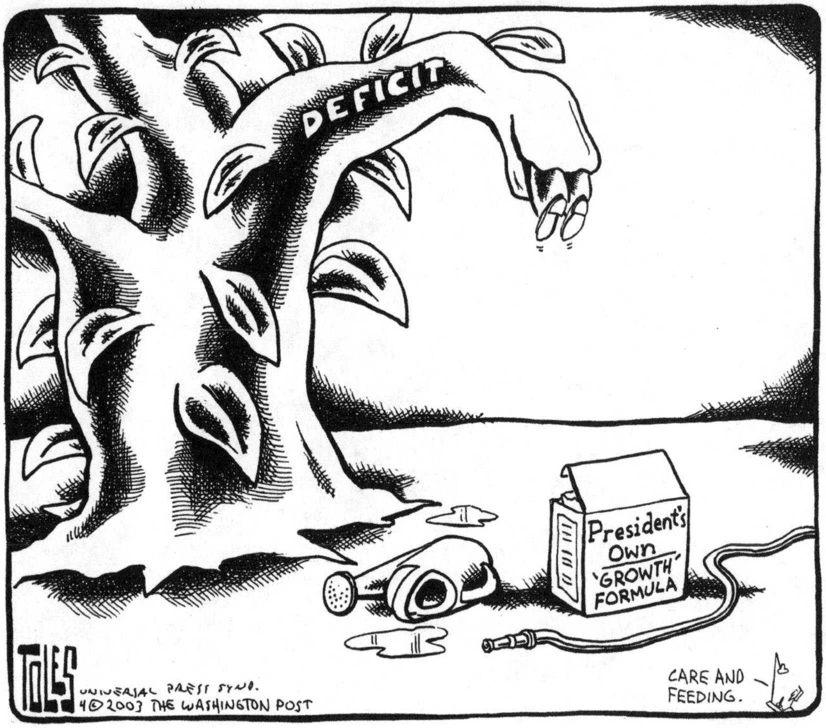
DEFICIT
President's Own 'GROWTH' FORMULA
TOLES
UNIVERSAL PRESS SYND.
4 © 2003 THE WASHINGTON POST
CARE AND FEEDING.

4-2-03

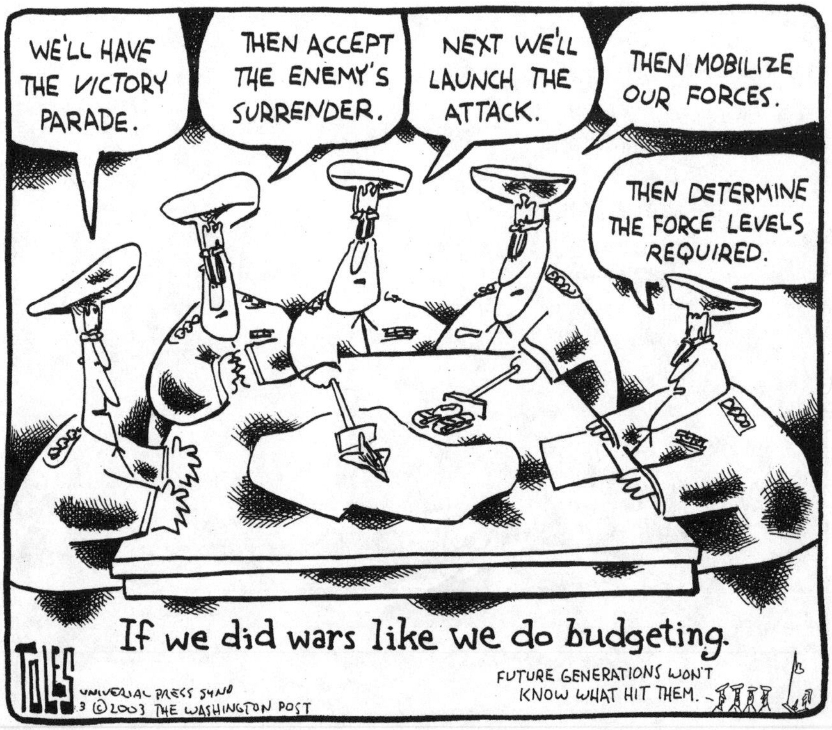
WE'LL HAVE THE VICTORY PARADE.
THEN ACCEPT THE ENEMY'S SURRENDER.
NEXT WE'LL LAUNCH THE ATTACK.
THEN MOBILIZE OUR FORCES.
THEN DETERMINE THE FORCE LEVELS REQUIRED.
If we did wars like we do budgeting.
TOLES
UNIVERSAL PRESS SYND
3 © 2003 THE WASHINGTON POST
FUTURE GENERATIONS WON'T KNOW WHAT HIT THEM.

3-21-03

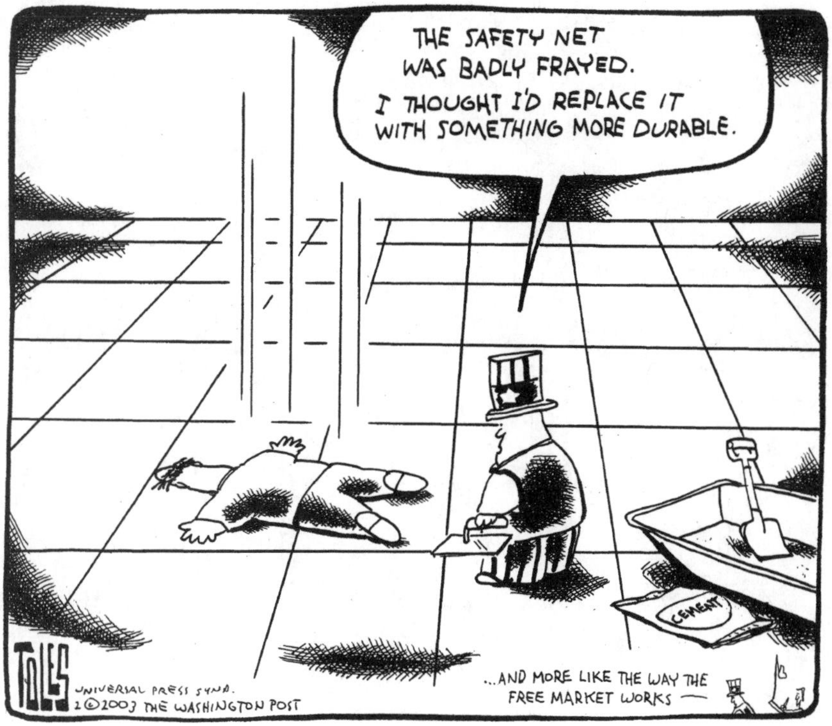
THE SAFETY NET WAS BADLY FRAYED.
I THOUGHT I'D REPLACE IT WITH SOMETHING MORE DURABLE.
CEMENT
TOLES
UNIVERSAL PRESS SYND.
2 © 2003 THE WASHINGTON POST
...AND MORE LIKE THE WAY THE FREE MARKET WORKS —

2-24-03

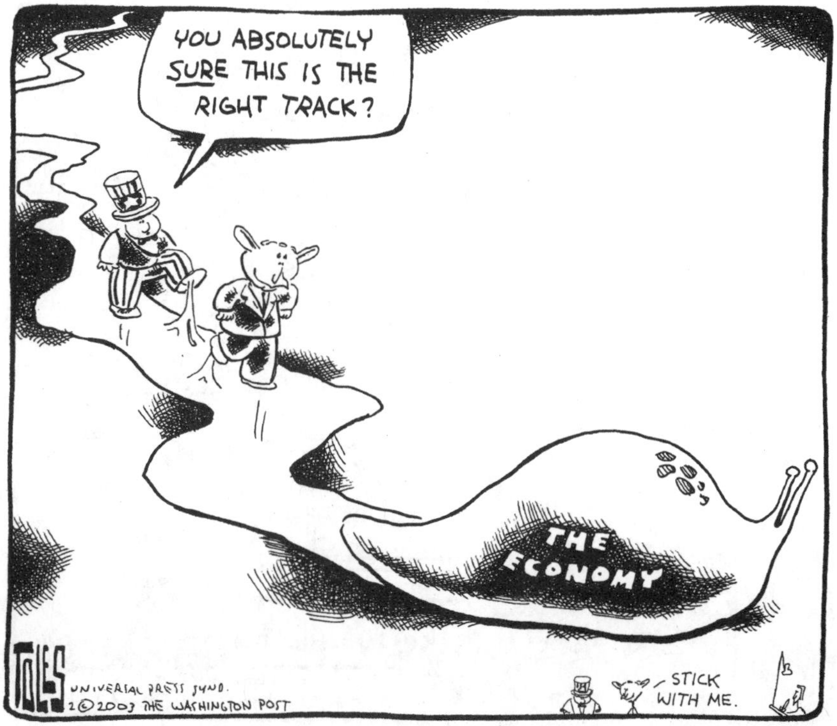
YOU ABSOLUTELY SURE THIS IS THE RIGHT TRACK?
THE ECONOMY
TOLES
UNIVERSAL PRESS SYND.
2 © 2003 THE WASHINGTON POST
— STICK WITH ME.

2-10-03

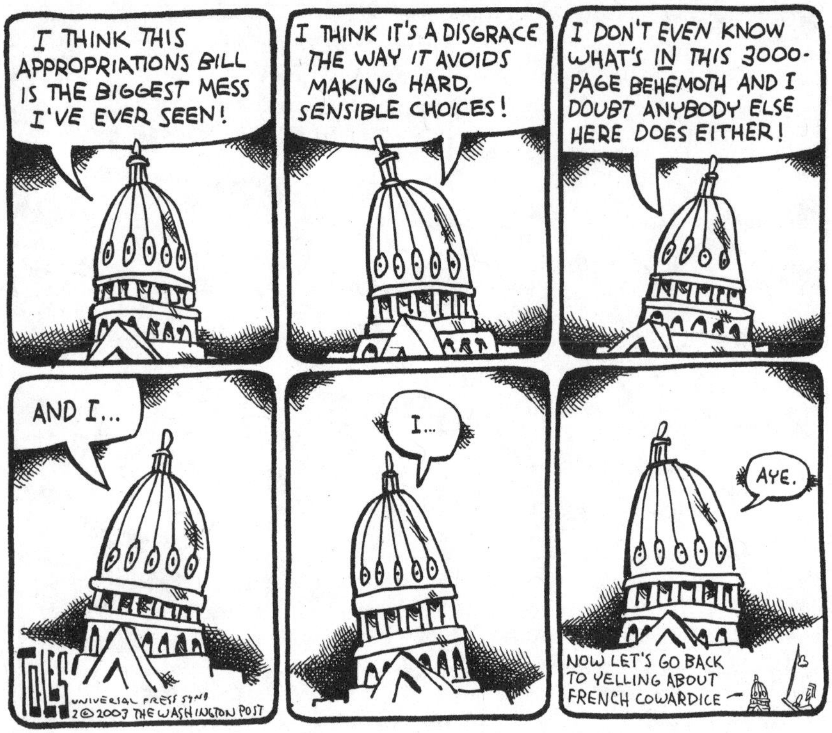
I THINK THIS APPROPRIATIONS BILL IS THE BIGGEST MESS I'VE EVER SEEN!
I THINK IT'S A DISGRACE THE WAY IT AVOIDS MAKING HARD, SENSIBLE CHOICES!
I DON'T EVEN KNOW WHAT'S IN THIS 3000-PAGE BEHEMOTH AND I DOUBT ANYBODY ELSE HERE DOES EITHER!
AND I...
I...
AYE.
NOW LET'S GO BACK TO YELLING ABOUT FRENCH COWARDICE —
TOLES
UNIVERSAL PRESS SYND
2 © 2003 THE WASHINGTON POST

2-18-03

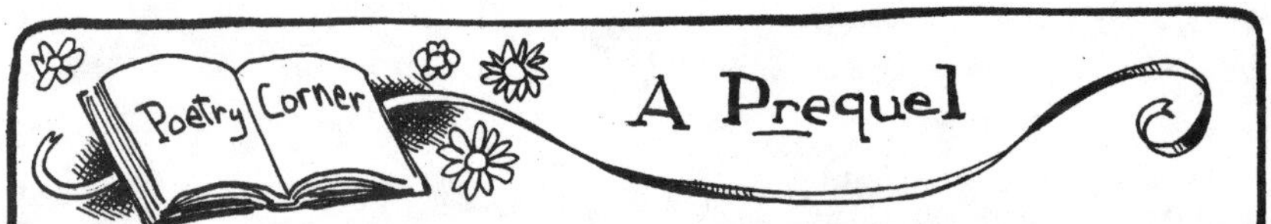
Poetry Corner
A Prequel
Old Father Hubbard
Went to the cupboard
Which was then overflowing with dough.
He succumbed to the itch:
More tax cuts for the rich!
And the rest, well, you already know.
WAIT. HERE'S AN — I.O.U. FOR YOU.
TOLES
UNIVERSAL PRESS SYND.
5 © 2003 THE WASHINGTON POST

5-25-03

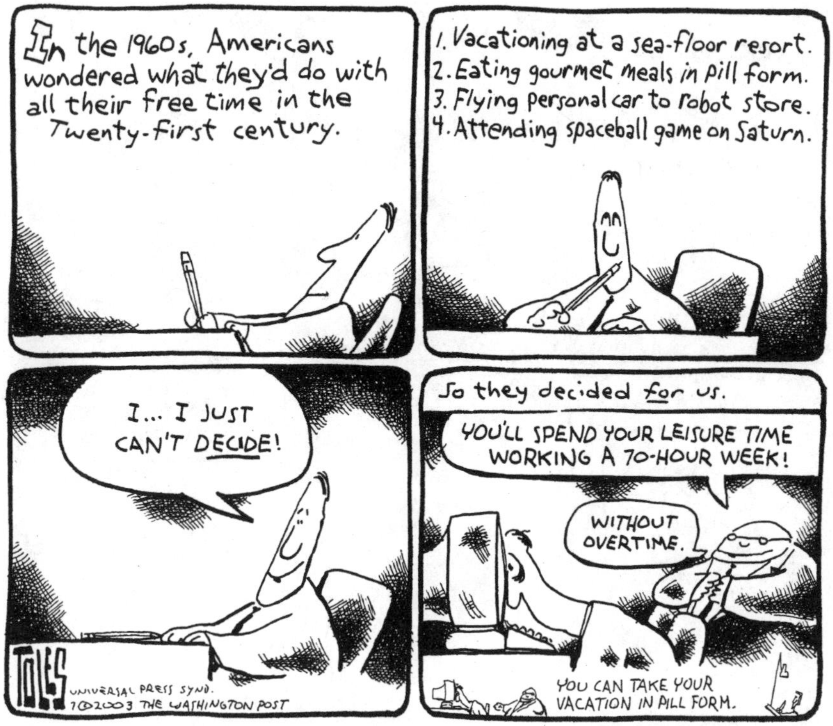
In the 1960s, Americans wondered what they'd do with all their free time in the Twenty-First century.
1. Vacationing at a sea-floor resort.
2. Eating gourmet meals in pill form.
3. Flying personal car to robot store.
4. Attending spaceball game on Saturn.
I... I JUST CAN'T DECIDE!
So they decided for us.
YOU'LL SPEND YOUR LEISURE TIME WORKING A 70-HOUR WEEK!
WITHOUT OVERTIME.
YOU CAN TAKE YOUR VACATION IN PILL FORM.
TOLES
UNIVERSAL PRESS SYND.
7 © 2003 THE WASHINGTON POST

7-30-03

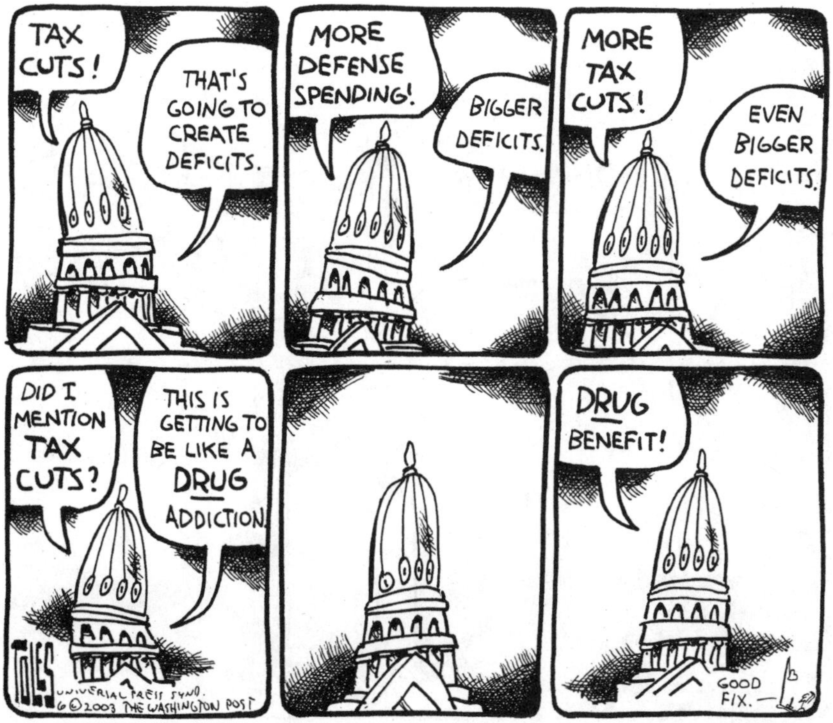
TAX CUTS!
THAT'S GOING TO CREATE DEFICITS.
MORE DEFENSE SPENDING!
BIGGER DEFICITS.
MORE TAX CUTS!
EVEN BIGGER DEFICITS.
DID I MENTION TAX CUTS?
THIS IS GETTING TO BE LIKE A DRUG ADDICTION.
DRUG BENEFIT!
GOOD FIX.
TOLES
UNIVERSAL PRESS SYND.
6 © 2003 THE WASHINGTON POST

6-15-03

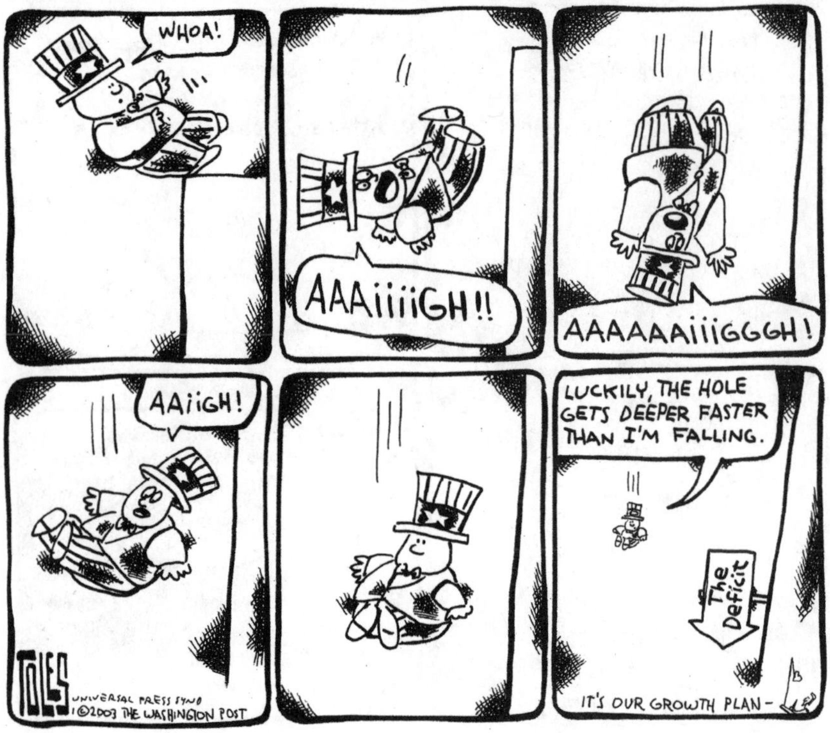
WHOA!
AAAiiiiGH!!
AAAAAAiiiGGGH!
AAiiGH!
LUCKILY, THE HOLE GETS DEEPER FASTER THAN I'M FALLING.
The Deficit
IT'S OUR GROWTH PLAN—
TOLES
UNIVERSAL PRESS SYND
1 ©2003 THE WASHINGTON POST

1-21-03

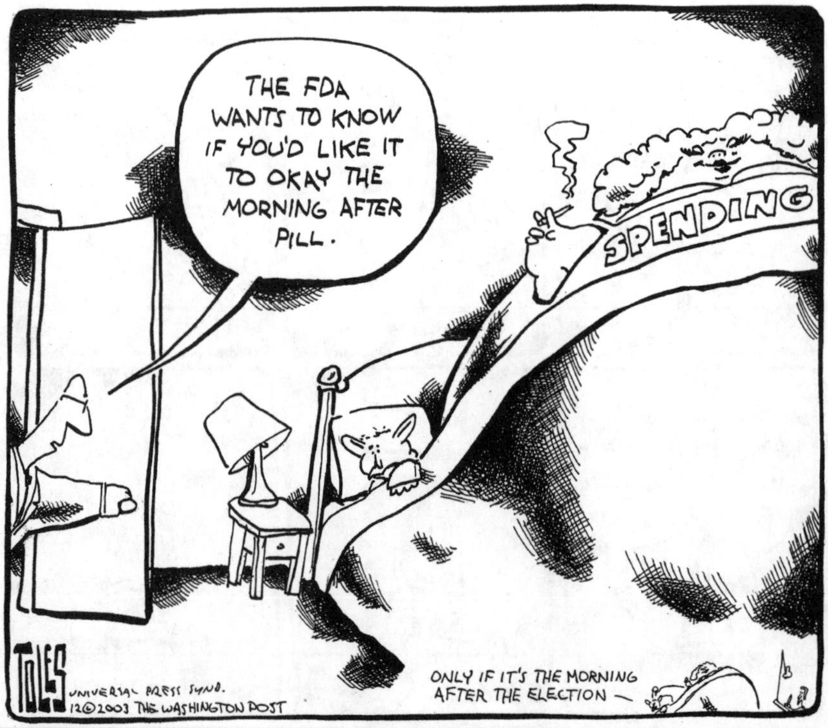
THE FDA WANTS TO KNOW IF YOU'D LIKE IT TO OKAY THE MORNING AFTER PILL.
SPENDING
ONLY IF IT'S THE MORNING AFTER THE ELECTION—
TOLES
UNIVERSAL PRESS SYND.
12 ©2003 THE WASHINGTON POST

12-18-03

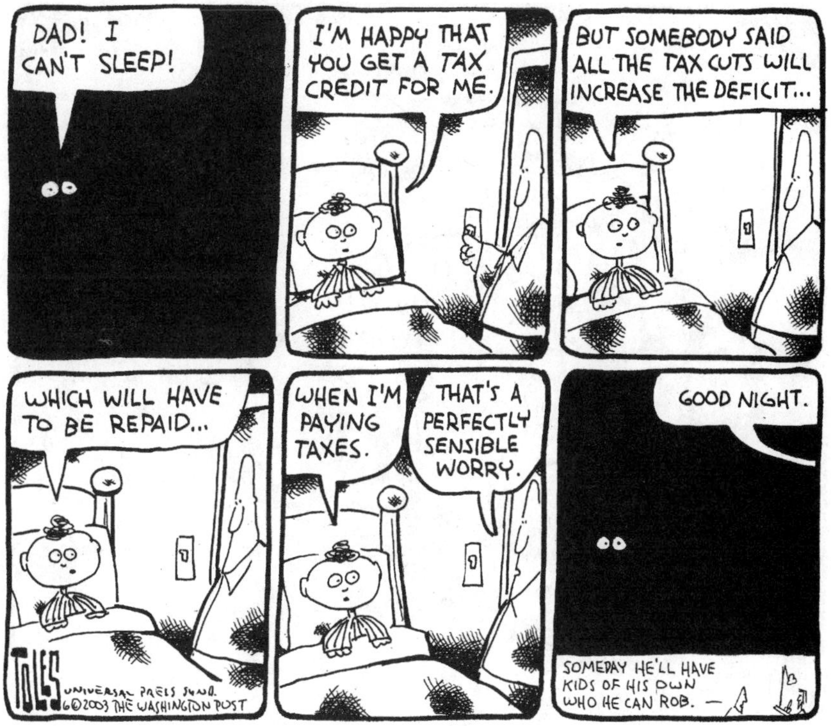
DAD! I CAN'T SLEEP!
I'M HAPPY THAT YOU GET A TAX CREDIT FOR ME.
BUT SOMEBODY SAID ALL THE TAX CUTS WILL INCREASE THE DEFICIT...
WHICH WILL HAVE TO BE REPAID...
WHEN I'M PAYING TAXES.
THAT'S A PERFECTLY SENSIBLE WORRY.
GOOD NIGHT.
TOLES
UNIVERSAL PRESS SYND.
6©2003 THE WASHINGTON POST
SOMEDAY HE'LL HAVE KIDS OF HIS OWN WHO HE CAN ROB.

6-9-03

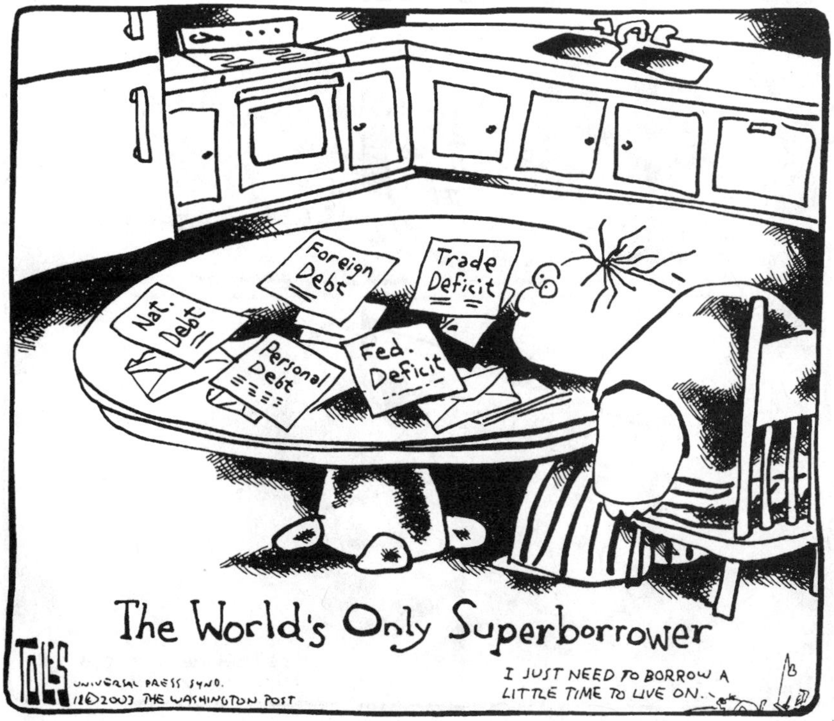
Foreign Debt
Trade Deficit
Nat. Debt
Personal Debt
Fed. Deficit
The World's Only Superborrower
TOLES
UNIVERSAL PRESS SYND.
12©2003 THE WASHINGTON POST
I JUST NEED TO BORROW A LITTLE TIME TO LIVE ON.

12-1-03

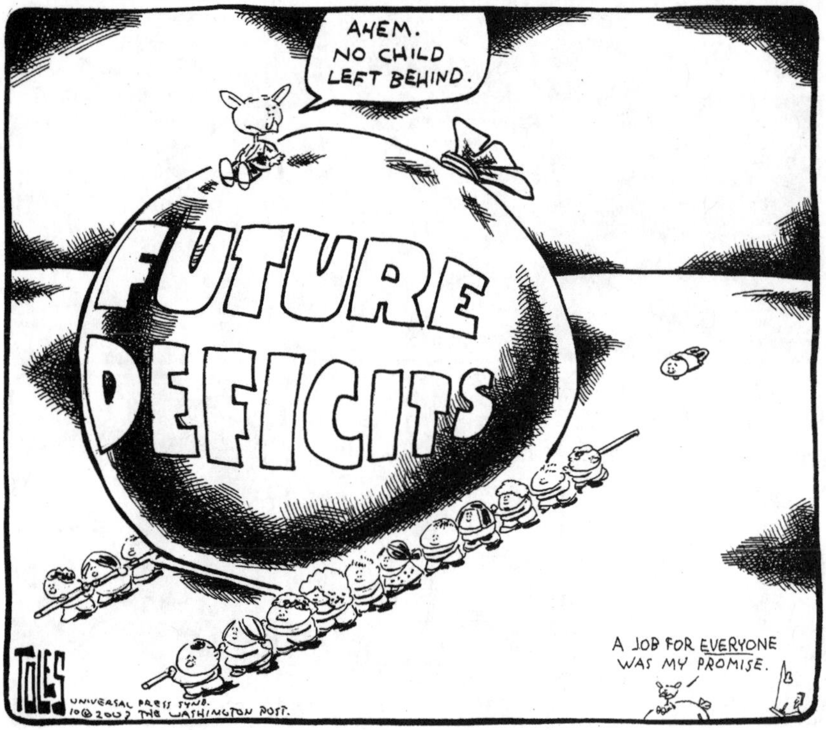
AHEM.
NO CHILD
LEFT BEHIND.
FUTURE
DEFICITS
A JOB FOR EVERYONE
WAS MY PROMISE.
TOLES
UNIVERSAL PRESS SYND.
10 © 2003 THE WASHINGTON POST.

10-14-03

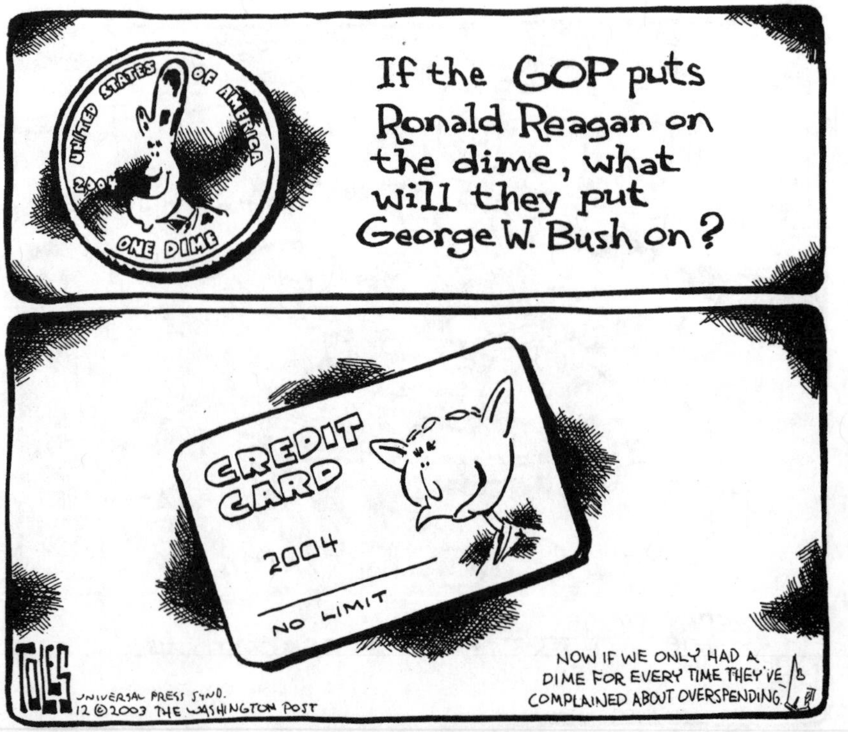
UNITED STATES OF AMERICA
2004
ONE DIME
If the GOP puts
Ronald Reagan on
the dime, what
will they put
George W. Bush on?
CREDIT
CARD
2004
NO LIMIT
NOW IF WE ONLY HAD A
DIME FOR EVERY TIME THEY'VE
COMPLAINED ABOUT OVERSPENDING.
TOLES
UNIVERSAL PRESS SYND.
12 © 2003 THE WASHINGTON POST

12-9-03

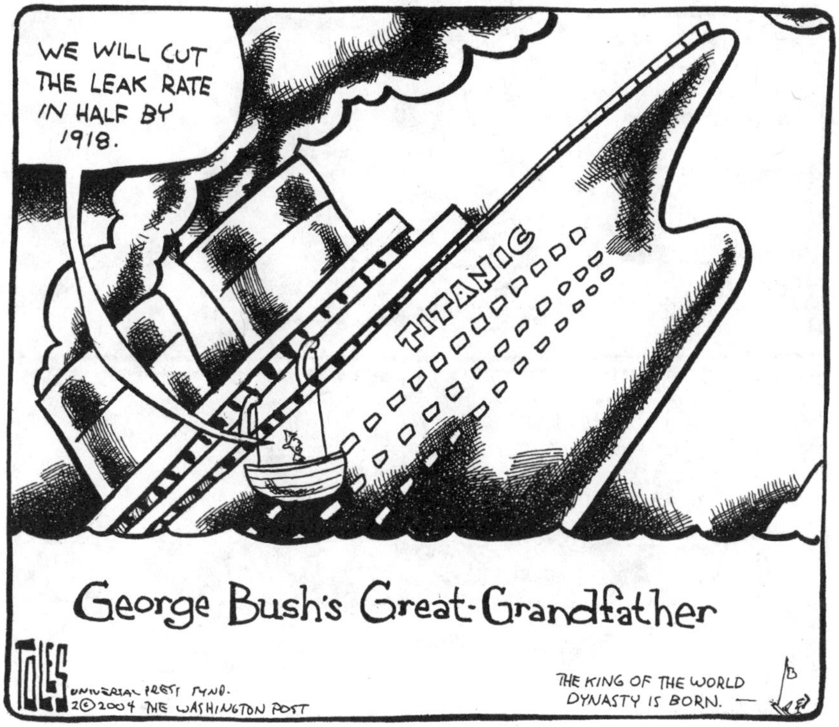
WE WILL CUT THE LEAK RATE IN HALF BY 1918.
TITANIC
George Bush's Great-Grandfather
TOLES
UNIVERSAL PRESS SYND.
©2004 THE WASHINGTON POST
THE KING OF THE WORLD DYNASTY IS BORN.

2-4-04

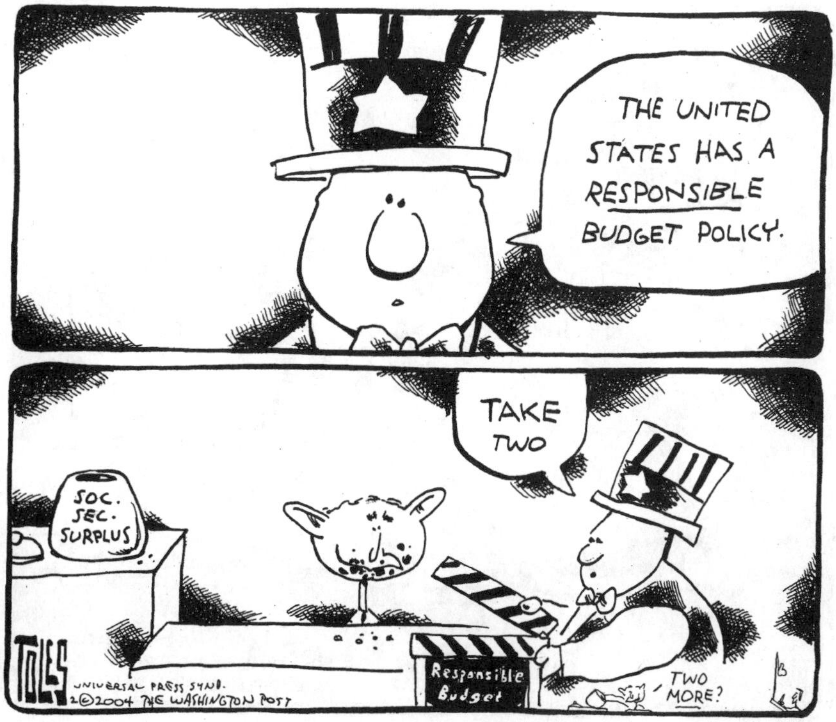
THE UNITED STATES HAS A RESPONSIBLE BUDGET POLICY.
TAKE TWO
SOC. SEC. SURPLUS
Responsible Budget
TWO MORE?
TOLES
UNIVERSAL PRESS SYND.
©2004 THE WASHINGTON POST

2-29-04

I'M FRANKLY FED UP WRITING THESE $2000 CHECKS TO LAWMAKERS TO GET THEM TO DO WHAT I WANT.
ALICE, FIND OUT IF WE CAN'T GET SOME LAWMAKERS IN INDIA TO DO IT FOR $200.
SUDDENLY THERE'S A LAW AGAINST IT.
TOLES
UNIVERSAL PRESS SYND.
3 © 2004 THE WASHINGTON POST

3-1-04

Health of the Nation News
Obesity has nearly overtaken smoking as a metaphor for the deficit.
BETTER EXPLOSION.
TOLES
UNIVERSAL PRESS SYND.
3 © 2004 THE WASHINGTON POST

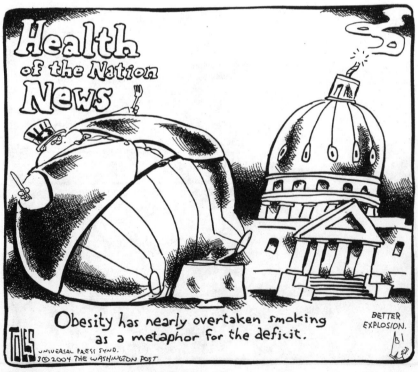

3-15-04

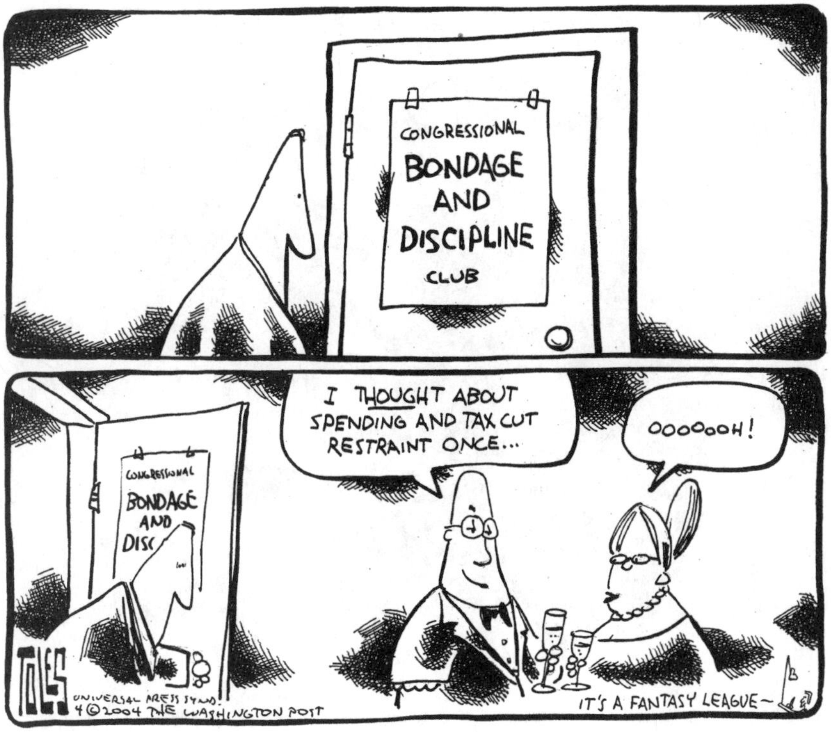
CONGRESSIONAL
BONDAGE
AND
DISCIPLINE
CLUB
CONGRESSIONAL
BONDAGE
AND
DISC
I THOUGHT ABOUT SPENDING AND TAX CUT RESTRAINT ONCE...
OOOOOOH!
TOLES
UNIVERSAL PRESS SYND.
4 © 2004 THE WASHINGTON POST
IT'S A FANTASY LEAGUE~

4-5-04

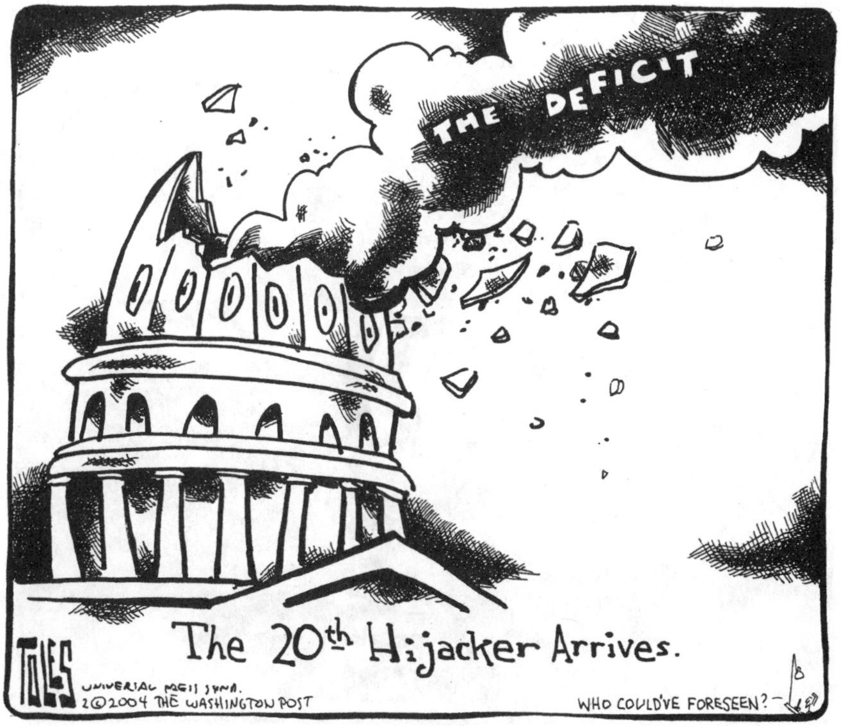
THE DEFICIT
The 20th Hijacker Arrives.
TOLES
UNIVERSAL PRESS SYND.
2 © 2004 THE WASHINGTON POST
WHO COULD'VE FORESEEN?~

2-17-04

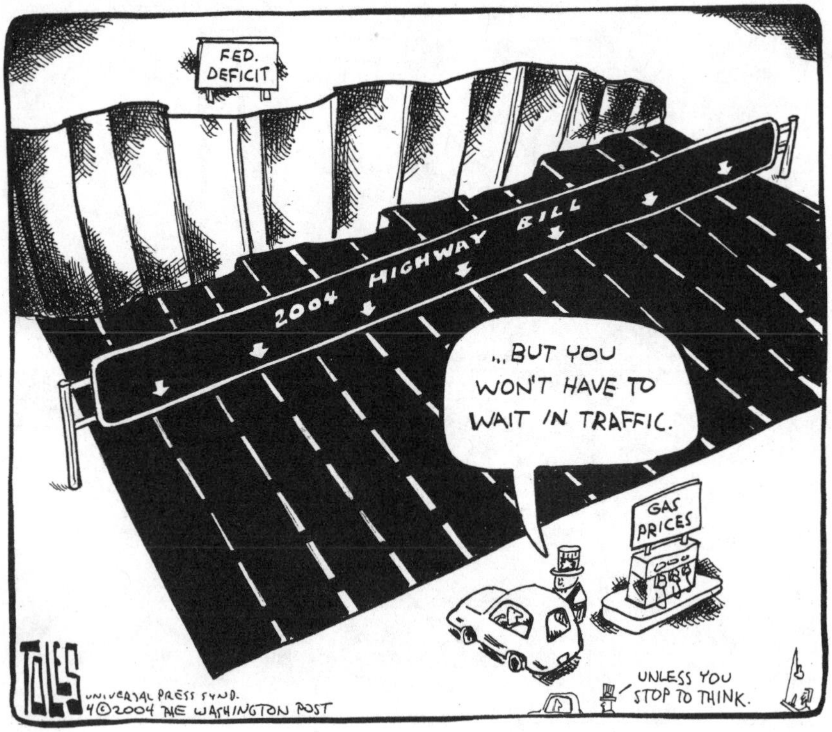
FED. DEFICIT
2004 HIGHWAY BILL
...BUT YOU WON'T HAVE TO WAIT IN TRAFFIC.
GAS PRICES
UNLESS YOU STOP TO THINK.
TOLES
UNIVERSAL PRESS SYND.
4©2004 THE WASHINGTON POST

4-6-04

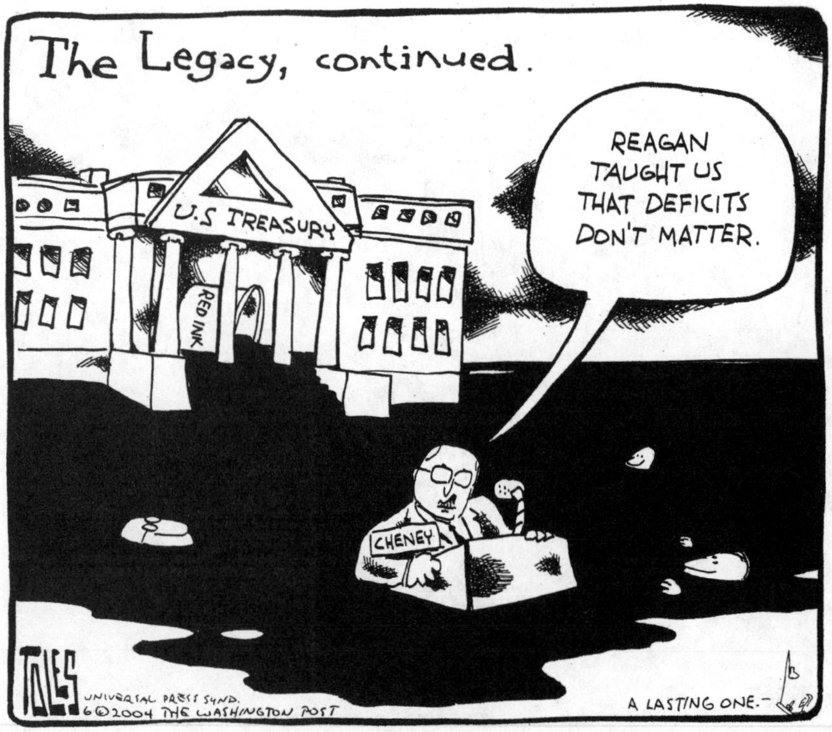
The Legacy, continued.
U.S TREASURY
RED INK
REAGAN TAUGHT US THAT DEFICITS DON'T MATTER.
CHENEY
TOLES
UNIVERSAL PRESS SYND.
6©2004 THE WASHINGTON POST
A LASTING ONE.

6-8-04

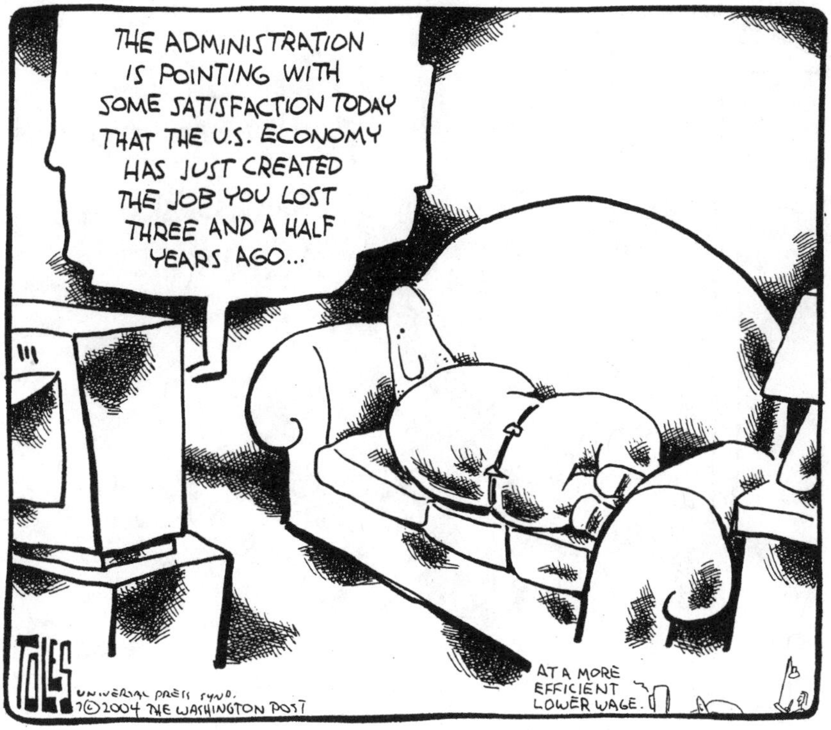
THE ADMINISTRATION IS POINTING WITH SOME SATISFACTION TODAY THAT THE U.S. ECONOMY HAS JUST CREATED THE JOB YOU LOST THREE AND A HALF YEARS AGO...
TOLES
UNIVERSAL PRESS SYND.
7 © 2004 THE WASHINGTON POST
AT A MORE EFFICIENT LOWER WAGE.

7-2-04

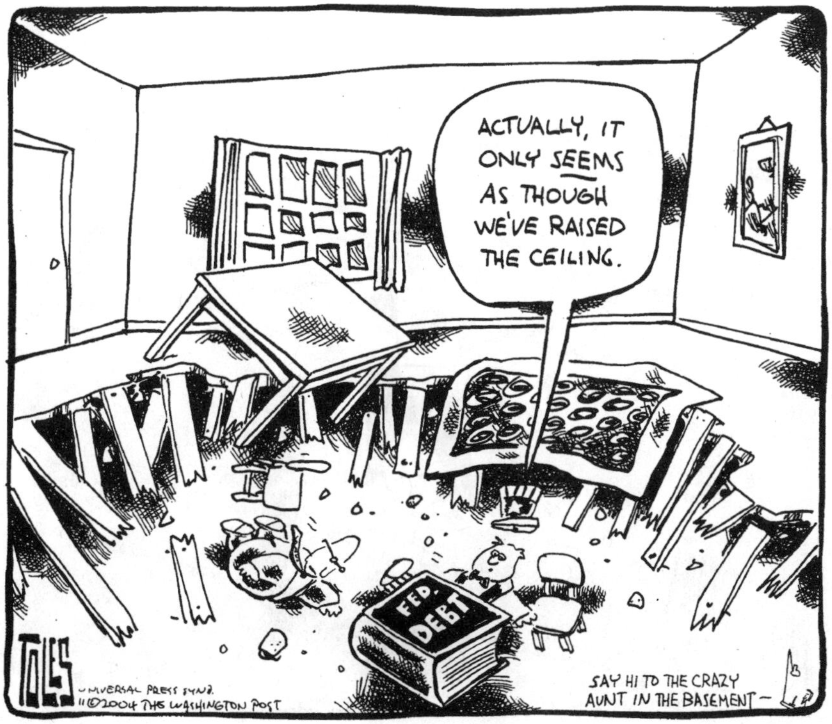
ACTUALLY, IT ONLY SEEMS AS THOUGH WE'VE RAISED THE CEILING.
FED. DEBT
TOLES
UNIVERSAL PRESS SYND.
11 © 2004 THE WASHINGTON POST
SAY HI TO THE CRAZY AUNT IN THE BASEMENT—

11-21-04

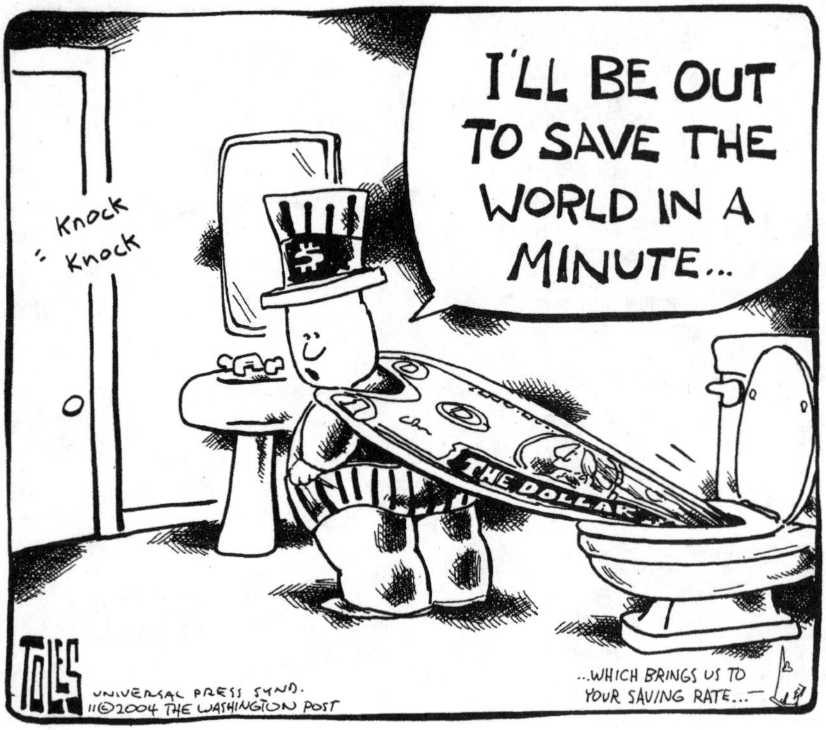
Knock
Knock
I'LL BE OUT TO SAVE THE WORLD IN A MINUTE...
THE DOLLAR
TOLES
UNIVERSAL PRESS SYND.
11©2004 THE WASHINGTON POST
...WHICH BRINGS US TO YOUR SAVING RATE...

11-28-04

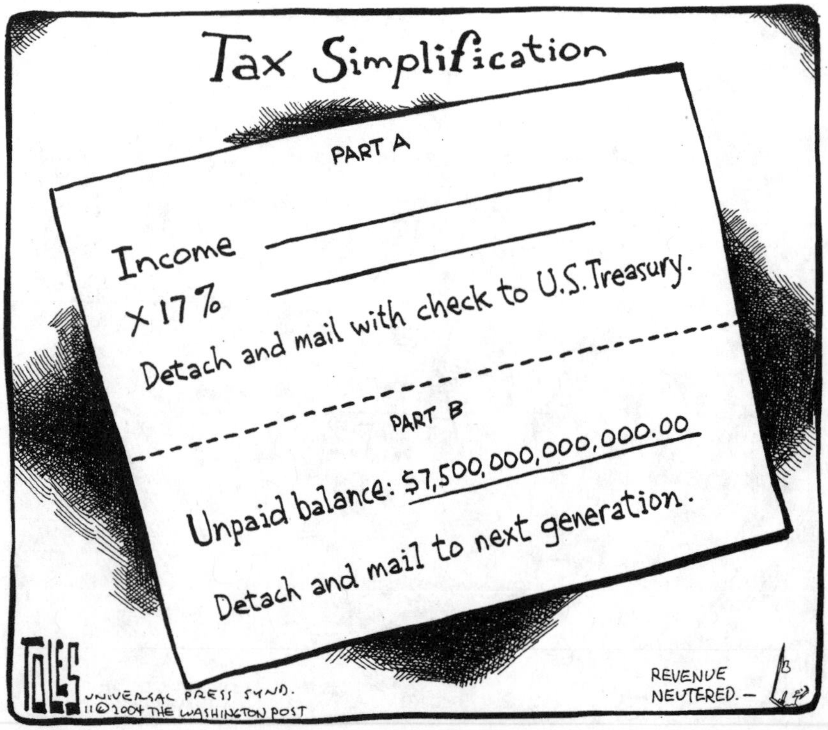
Tax Simplification
PART A
Income
x 17%
Detach and mail with check to U.S. Treasury.
PART B
Unpaid balance: $7,500,000,000,000.00
Detach and mail to next generation.
TOLES
UNIVERSAL PRESS SYND.
11©2004 THE WASHINGTON POST
REVENUE NEUTERED.

11-26-04

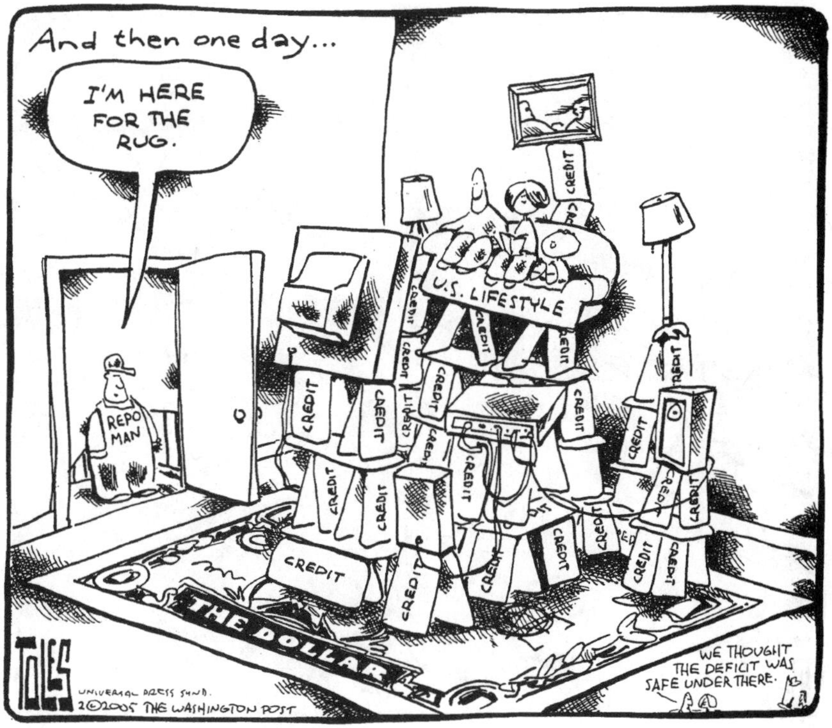
And then one day...
I'M HERE FOR THE RUG.
REPO MAN
U.S. LIFESTYLE
CREDIT
THE DOLLAR
TOLES
UNIVERSAL PRESS SYND.
2 © 2005 THE WASHINGTON POST
WE THOUGHT THE DEFICIT WAS SAFE UNDER THERE.

2-27-05

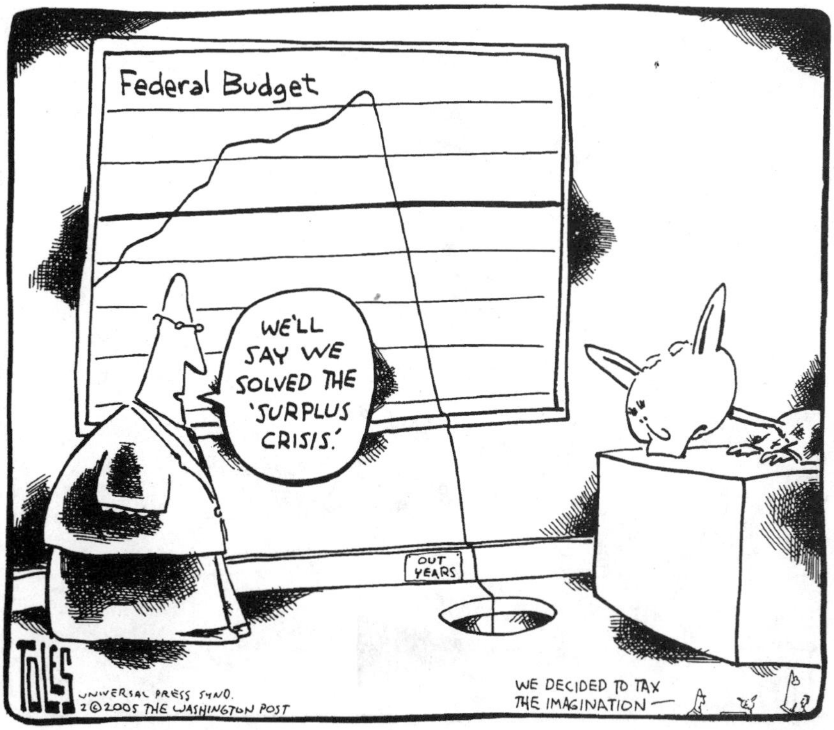
Federal Budget
WE'LL SAY WE SOLVED THE 'SURPLUS CRISIS.'
OUT YEARS
TOLES
UNIVERSAL PRESS SYND.
2 © 2005 THE WASHINGTON POST
WE DECIDED TO TAX THE IMAGINATION—

2-20-05

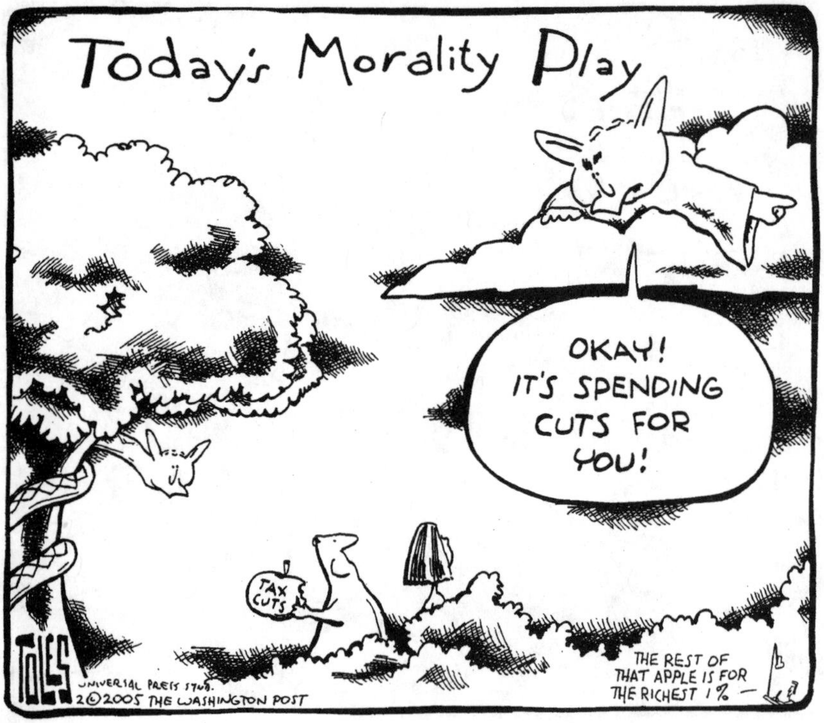
Today's Morality Play
OKAY! IT'S SPENDING CUTS FOR YOU!
TAX CUTS
TOLES
UNIVERSAL PRESS SYND.
2©2005 THE WASHINGTON POST
THE REST OF THAT APPLE IS FOR THE RICHEST 1% —

2-9-05

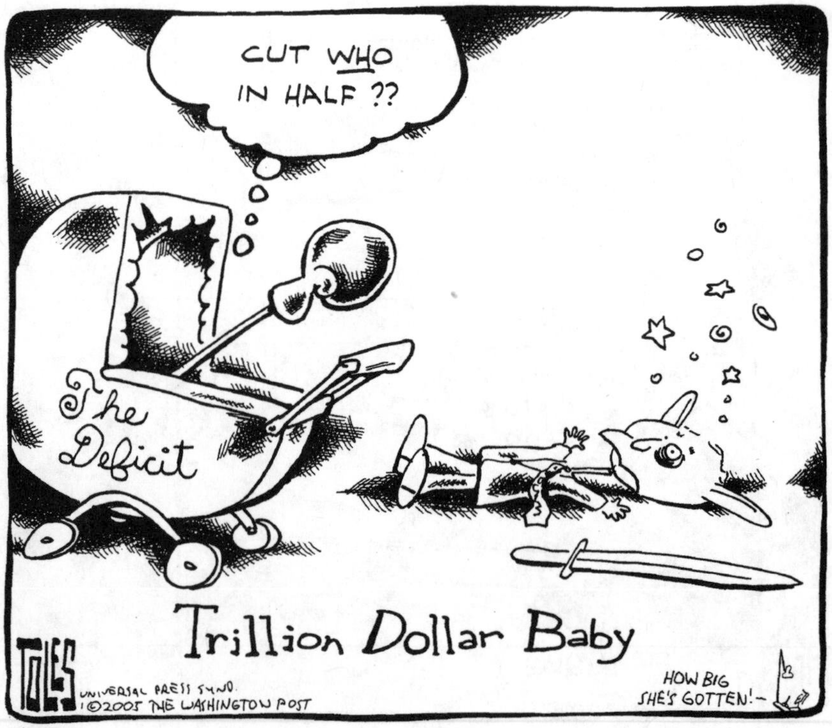
CUT WHO IN HALF ??
The Deficit
Trillion Dollar Baby
TOLES
UNIVERSAL PRESS SYND.
1©2005 THE WASHINGTON POST
HOW BIG SHE'S GOTTEN! —

1-27-05

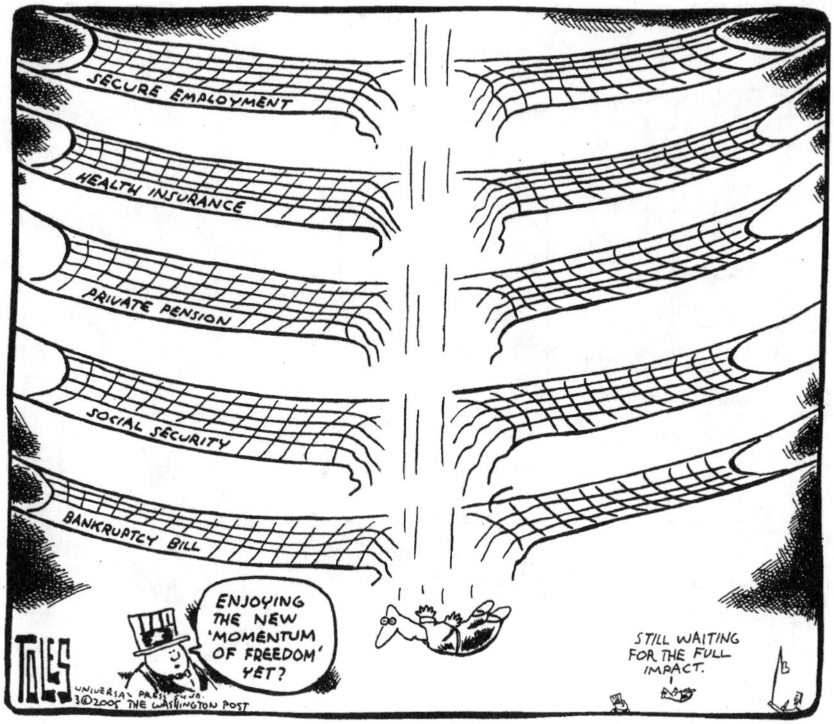
SECURE EMPLOYMENT
HEALTH INSURANCE
PRIVATE PENSION
SOCIAL SECURITY
BANKRUPTCY BILL
ENJOYING THE NEW 'MOMENTUM OF FREEDOM' YET?
TOLES
UNIVERSAL PRESS SYND.
©2005 THE WASHINGTON POST
STILL WAITING FOR THE FULL IMPACT.

3-11-05

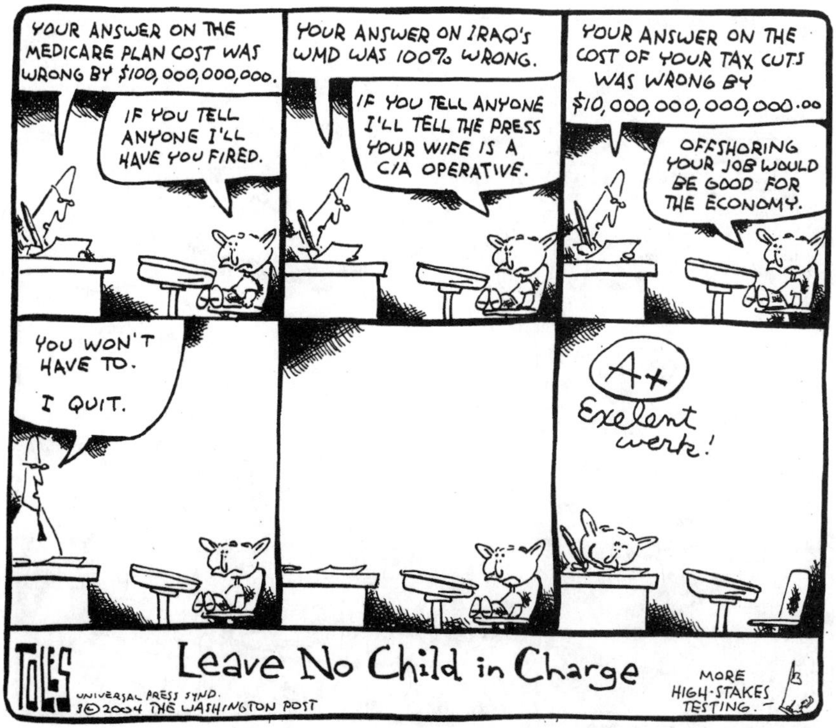
YOUR ANSWER ON THE MEDICARE PLAN COST WAS WRONG BY $100,000,000,000.
IF YOU TELL ANYONE I'LL HAVE YOU FIRED.
YOUR ANSWER ON IRAQ'S WMD WAS 100% WRONG.
IF YOU TELL ANYONE I'LL TELL THE PRESS YOUR WIFE IS A CIA OPERATIVE.
YOUR ANSWER ON THE COST OF YOUR TAX CUTS WAS WRONG BY $10,000,000,000,000.00
OFFSHORING YOUR JOB WOULD BE GOOD FOR THE ECONOMY.
YOU WON'T HAVE TO.
I QUIT.
A+
Exelent werk!
TOLES
Leave No Child in Charge
UNIVERSAL PRESS SYND.
©2004 THE WASHINGTON POST
MORE HIGH-STAKES TESTING.

3-20-04

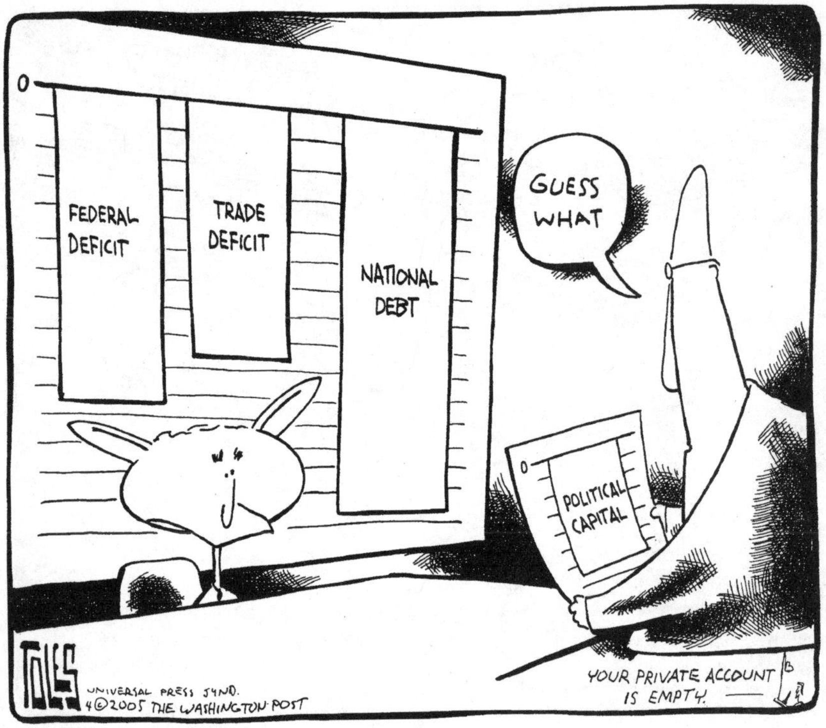

0
FEDERAL DEFICIT
TRADE DEFICIT
NATIONAL DEBT
GUESS WHAT
0
POLITICAL CAPITAL
YOUR PRIVATE ACCOUNT IS EMPTY.
TOLES
UNIVERSAL PRESS SYND.
4©2005 THE WASHINGTON POST

4-10-05

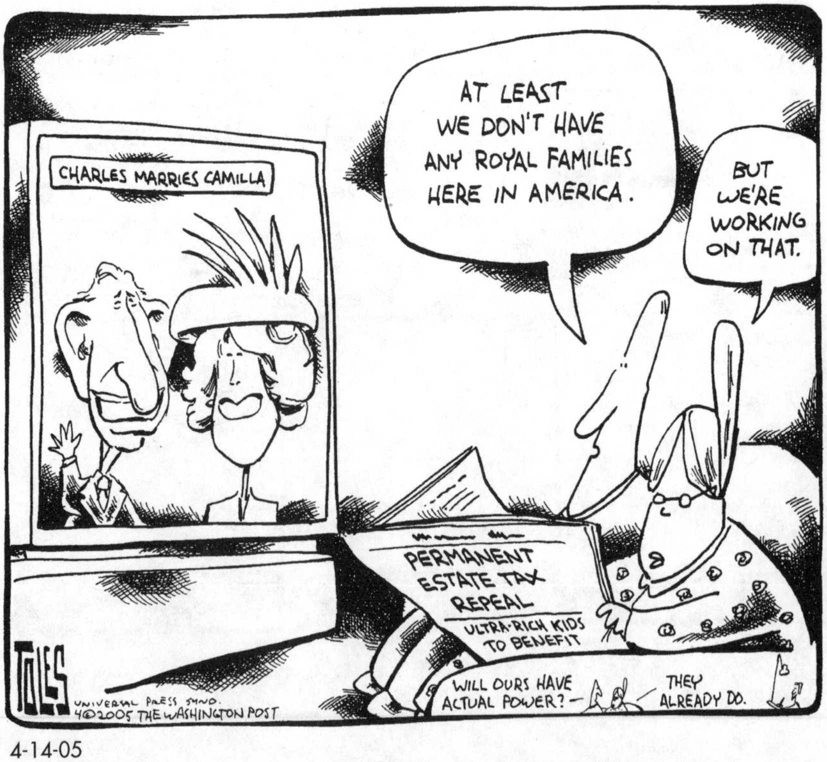

CHARLES MARRIES CAMILLA
AT LEAST WE DON'T HAVE ANY ROYAL FAMILIES HERE IN AMERICA.
BUT WE'RE WORKING ON THAT.
PERMANENT ESTATE TAX REPEAL
ULTRA-RICH KIDS TO BENEFIT
WILL OURS HAVE ACTUAL POWER?
THEY ALREADY DO.
TOLES
UNIVERSAL PRESS SYND.
4©2005 THE WASHINGTON POST

4-14-05

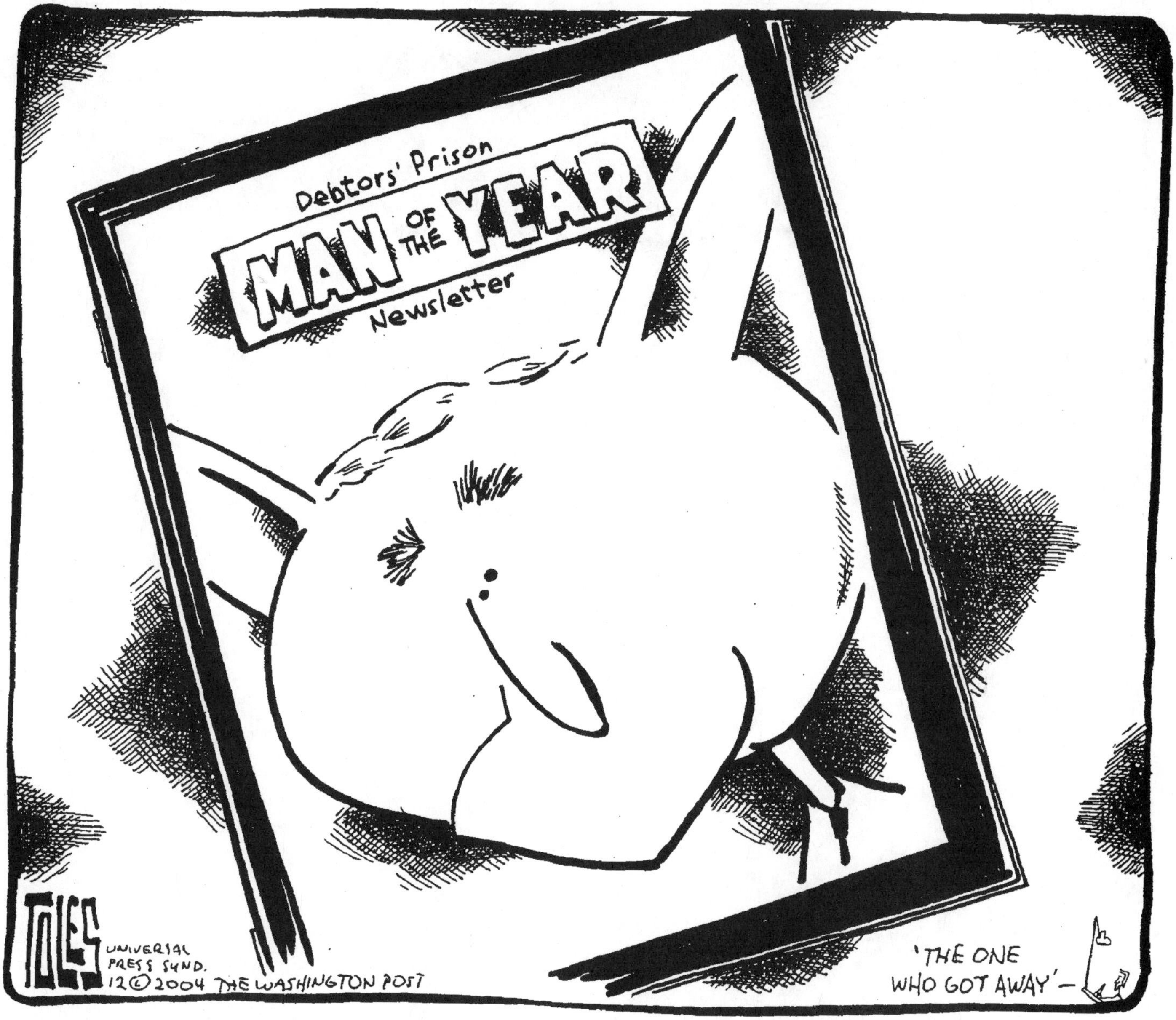
Debtors' Prison
MAN OF THE YEAR
Newsletter
TOLES
UNIVERSAL PRESS SYND.
12 © 2004 THE WASHINGTON POST
'THE ONE WHO GOT AWAY'—

12-21-04

SECURITY

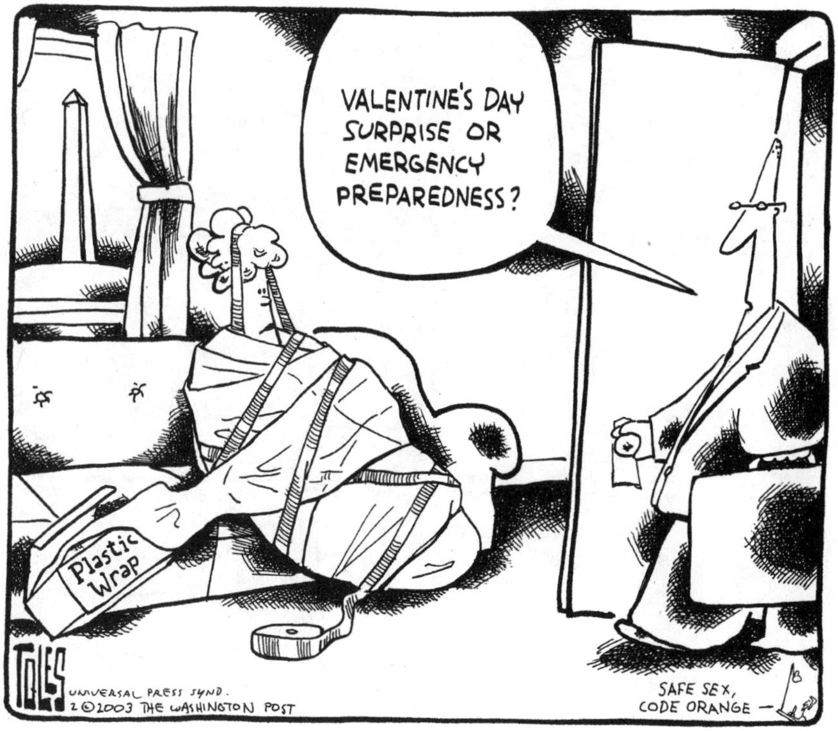
VALENTINE'S DAY SURPRISE OR EMERGENCY PREPAREDNESS?
Plastic Wrap
TOLES
UNIVERSAL PRESS SYND.
2 ©2003 THE WASHINGTON POST
SAFE SEX, CODE ORANGE

2-13-03

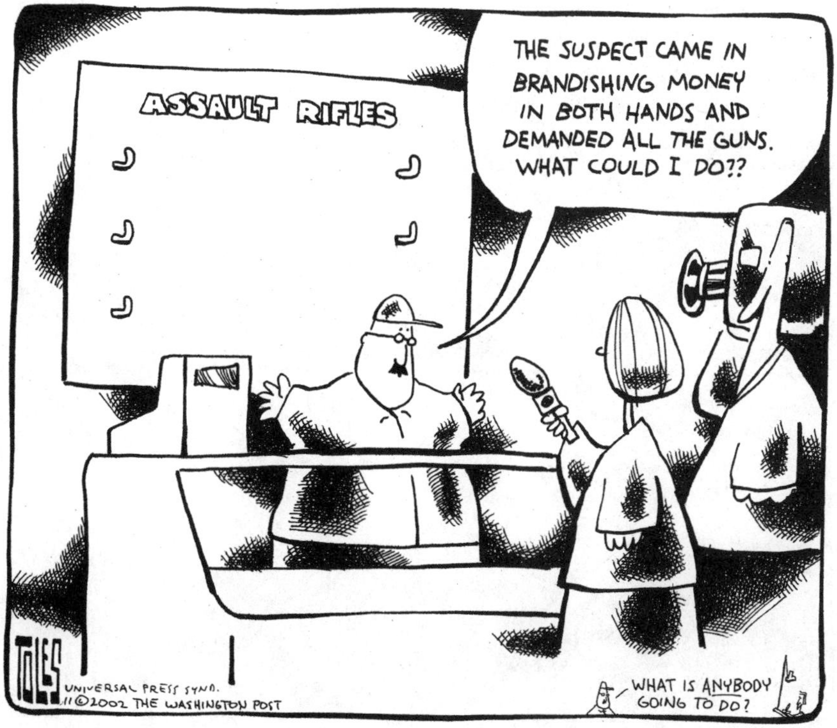
ASSAULT RIFLES
THE SUSPECT CAME IN BRANDISHING MONEY IN BOTH HANDS AND DEMANDED ALL THE GUNS. WHAT COULD I DO??
TOLES
UNIVERSAL PRESS SYND.
11 ©2002 THE WASHINGTON POST
WHAT IS ANYBODY GOING TO DO?

11-4-02

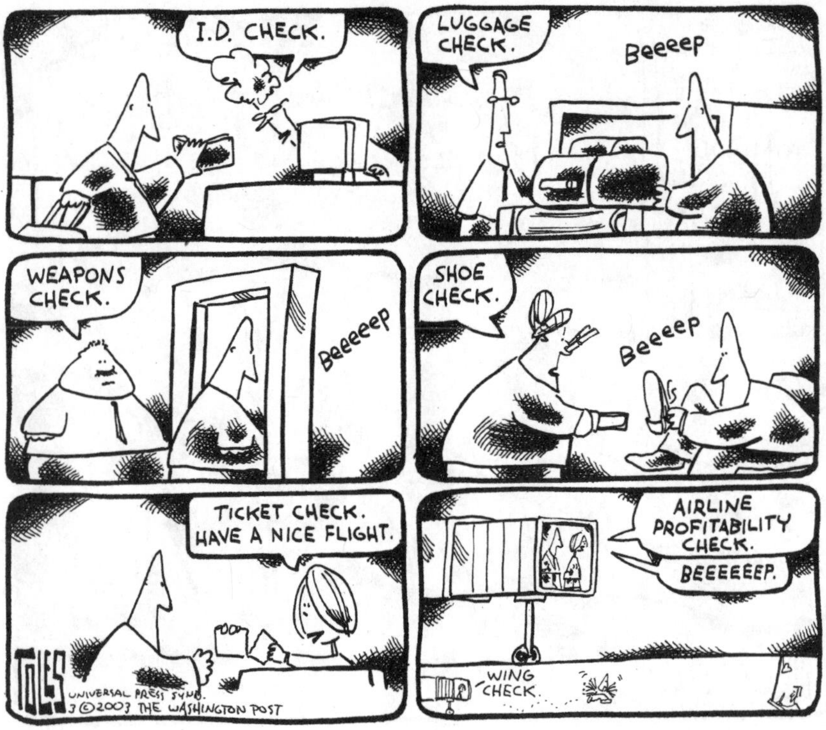
I.D. CHECK.
LUGGAGE CHECK.
Beeeep
WEAPONS CHECK.
Beeeeep
SHOE CHECK.
Beeeep
TICKET CHECK. HAVE A NICE FLIGHT.
TOLES
UNIVERSAL PRESS SYND.
3 © 2003 THE WASHINGTON POST
AIRLINE PROFITABILITY CHECK.
BEEEEEEP.
WING CHECK.

3-16-03

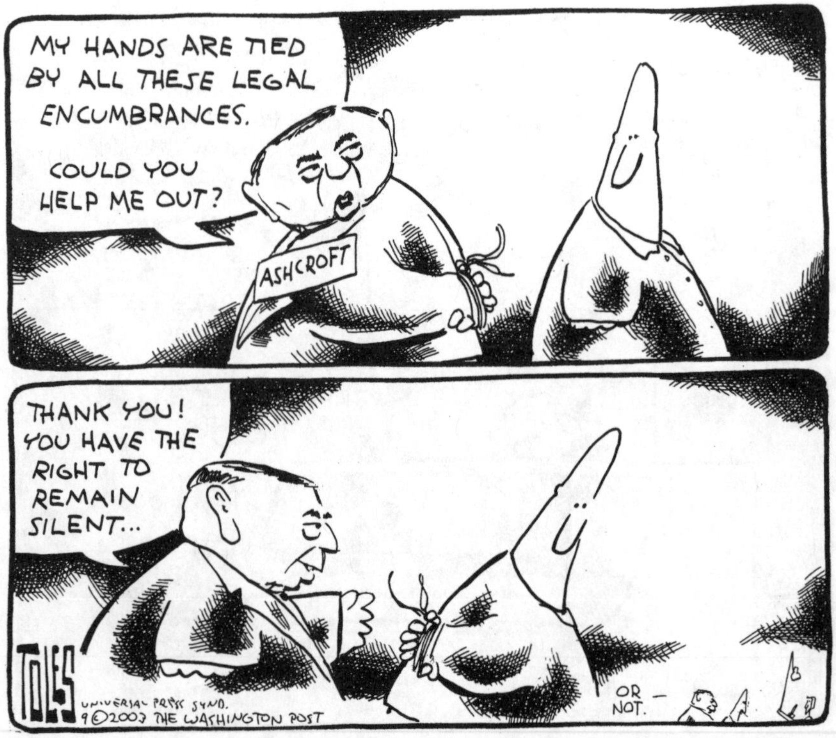
MY HANDS ARE TIED BY ALL THESE LEGAL ENCUMBRANCES.
COULD YOU HELP ME OUT?
ASHCROFT
THANK YOU! YOU HAVE THE RIGHT TO REMAIN SILENT...
TOLES
UNIVERSAL PRESS SYND.
9 © 2003 THE WASHINGTON POST
OR — NOT.

9-21-03

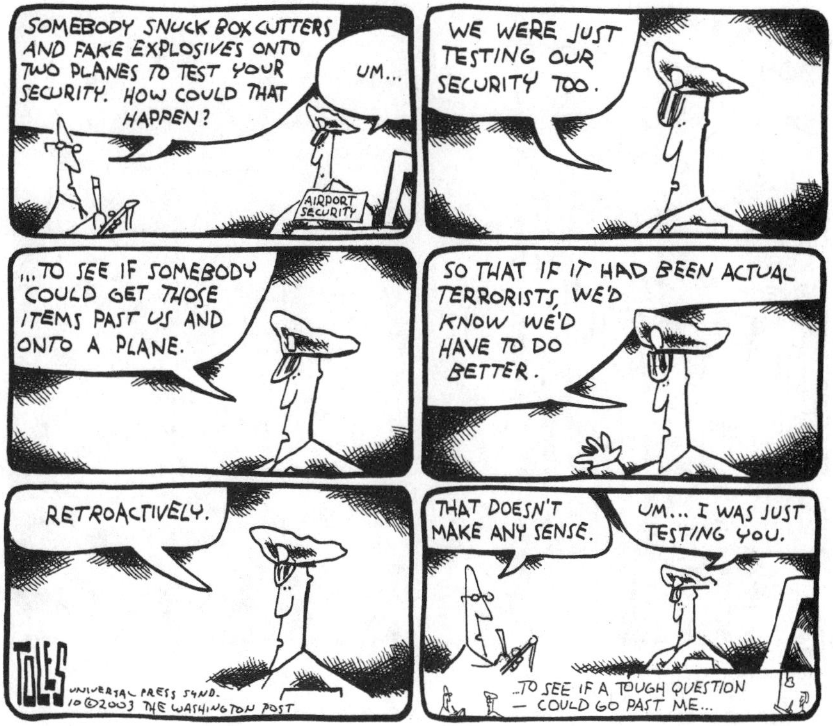
SOMEBODY SNUCK BOX CUTTERS AND FAKE EXPLOSIVES ONTO TWO PLANES TO TEST YOUR SECURITY. HOW COULD THAT HAPPEN?
UM...
AIRPORT SECURITY
WE WERE JUST TESTING OUR SECURITY TOO.
...TO SEE IF SOMEBODY COULD GET THOSE ITEMS PAST US AND ONTO A PLANE.
SO THAT IF IT HAD BEEN ACTUAL TERRORISTS, WE'D KNOW WE'D HAVE TO DO BETTER.
RETROACTIVELY.
THAT DOESN'T MAKE ANY SENSE.
UM... I WAS JUST TESTING YOU.
TOLES
UNIVERSAL PRESS SYND.
10 © 2003 THE WASHINGTON POST
...TO SEE IF A TOUGH QUESTION — COULD GO PAST ME...

10-21-03

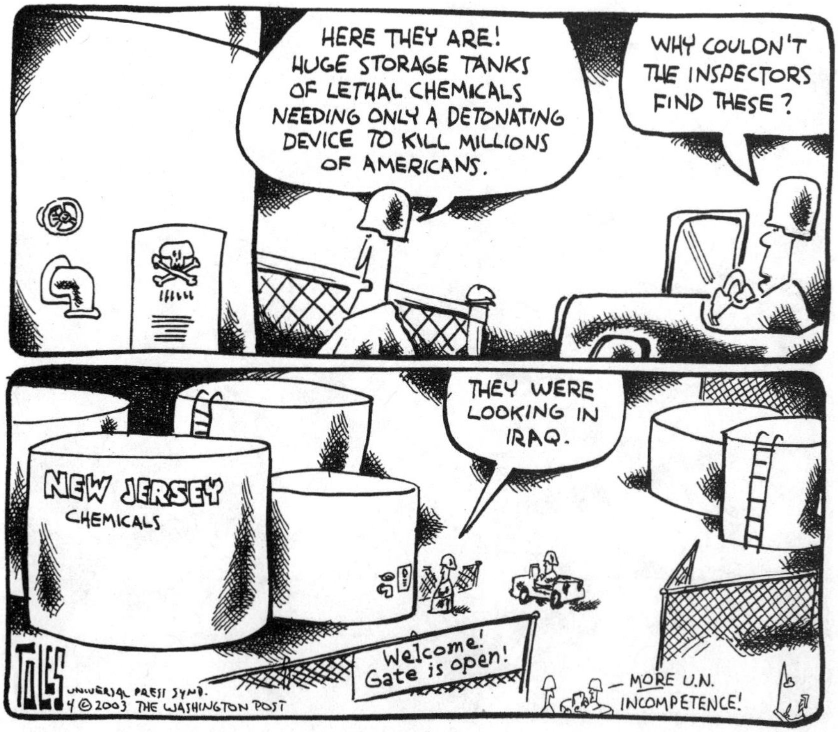
HERE THEY ARE! HUGE STORAGE TANKS OF LETHAL CHEMICALS NEEDING ONLY A DETONATING DEVICE TO KILL MILLIONS OF AMERICANS.
WHY COULDN'T THE INSPECTORS FIND THESE?
THEY WERE LOOKING IN IRAQ.
NEW JERSEY
CHEMICALS
Welcome! Gate is open!
— MORE U.N. INCOMPETENCE!
TOLES
UNIVERSAL PRESS SYND.
4 © 2003 THE WASHINGTON POST

4-29-03

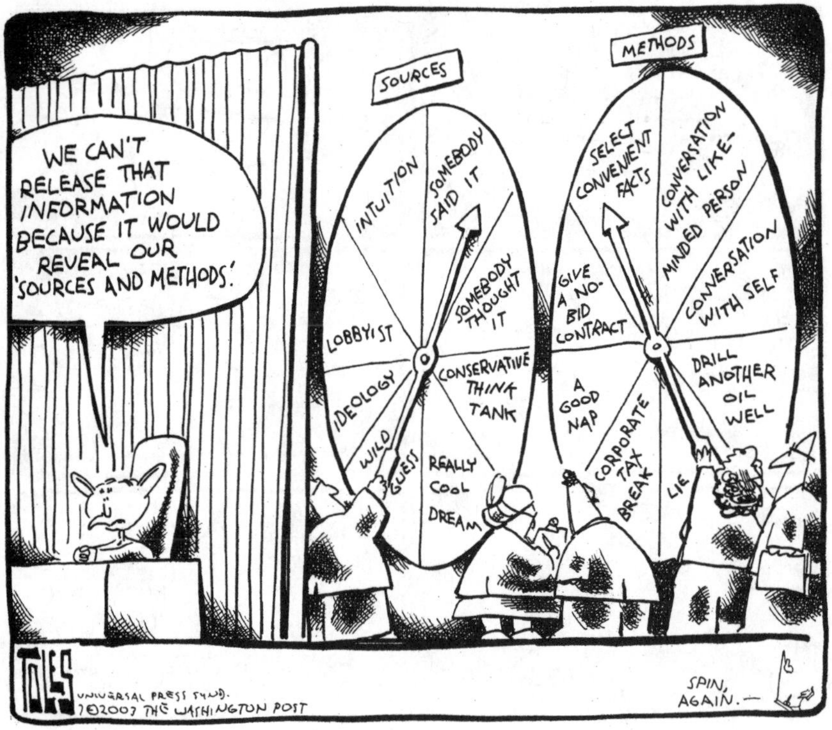
WE CAN'T RELEASE THAT INFORMATION BECAUSE IT WOULD REVEAL OUR 'SOURCES AND METHODS.'
SOURCES
INTUITION
SOMEBODY SAID IT
SOMEBODY THOUGHT IT
LOBBYIST
IDEOLOGY
CONSERVATIVE THINK TANK
WILD GUESS
REALLY COOL DREAM
METHODS
SELECT CONVENIENT FACTS
CONVERSATION WITH LIKE-MINDED PERSON
GIVE A NO-BID CONTRACT
CONVERSATION WITH SELF
A GOOD NAP
DRILL ANOTHER OIL WELL
CORPORATE TAX BREAK
LIE
TOLES
UNIVERSAL PRESS SYND.
7©2003 THE WASHINGTON POST
SPIN, AGAIN.—

7-31-03

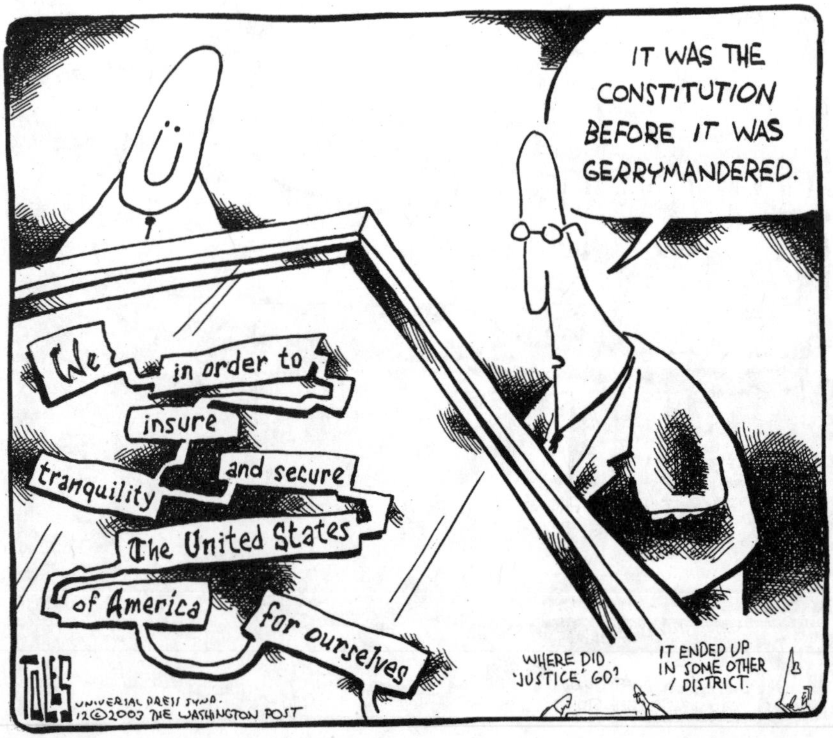
IT WAS THE CONSTITUTION BEFORE IT WAS GERRYMANDERED.
We
in order to
insure
tranquility
and secure
The United States
of America
for ourselves
TOLES
UNIVERSAL PRESS SYND.
12©2003 THE WASHINGTON POST
WHERE DID 'JUSTICE' GO?
IT ENDED UP IN SOME OTHER DISTRICT.

12-15-03

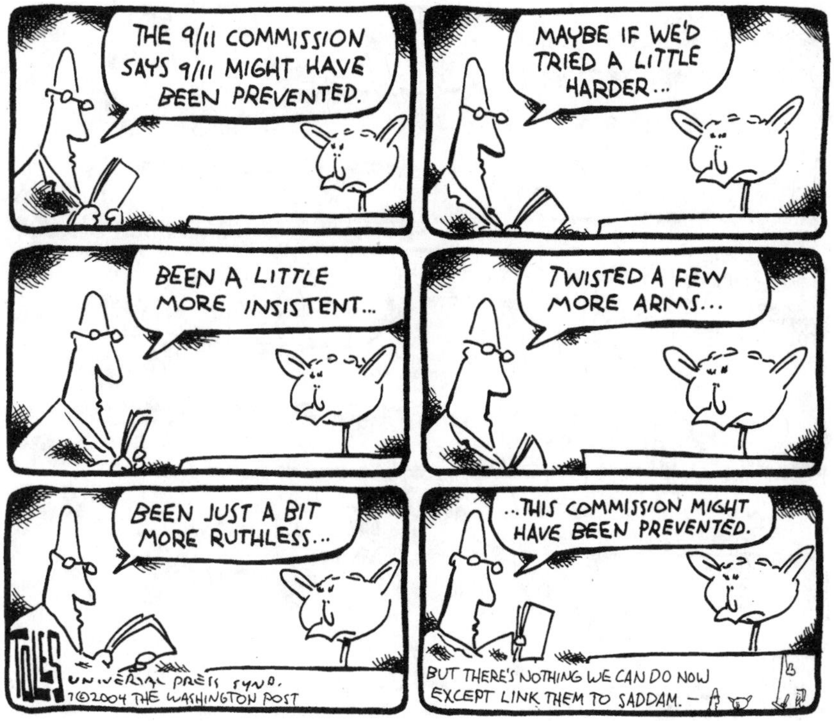
THE 9/11 COMMISSION SAYS 9/11 MIGHT HAVE BEEN PREVENTED.
MAYBE IF WE'D TRIED A LITTLE HARDER...
BEEN A LITTLE MORE INSISTENT...
TWISTED A FEW MORE ARMS...
BEEN JUST A BIT MORE RUTHLESS...
...THIS COMMISSION MIGHT HAVE BEEN PREVENTED.
BUT THERE'S NOTHING WE CAN DO NOW EXCEPT LINK THEM TO SADDAM.
TOLES
UNIVERSAL PRESS SYND.
7©2004 THE WASHINGTON POST

7-22-04

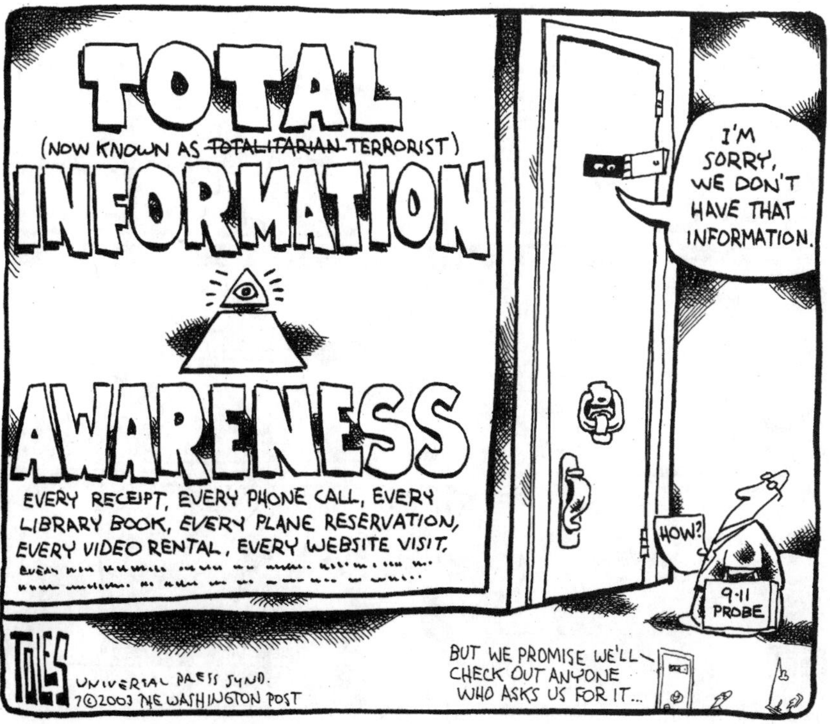
TOTAL
(NOW KNOWN AS TOTALITARIAN TERRORIST)
INFORMATION
AWARENESS
EVERY RECEIPT, EVERY PHONE CALL, EVERY LIBRARY BOOK, EVERY PLANE RESERVATION, EVERY VIDEO RENTAL, EVERY WEBSITE VISIT,
I'M SORRY, WE DON'T HAVE THAT INFORMATION.
HOW?
9-11 PROBE
BUT WE PROMISE WE'LL CHECK OUT ANYONE WHO ASKS US FOR IT...
TOLES
UNIVERSAL PRESS SYND.
7©2003 THE WASHINGTON POST

7-13-03

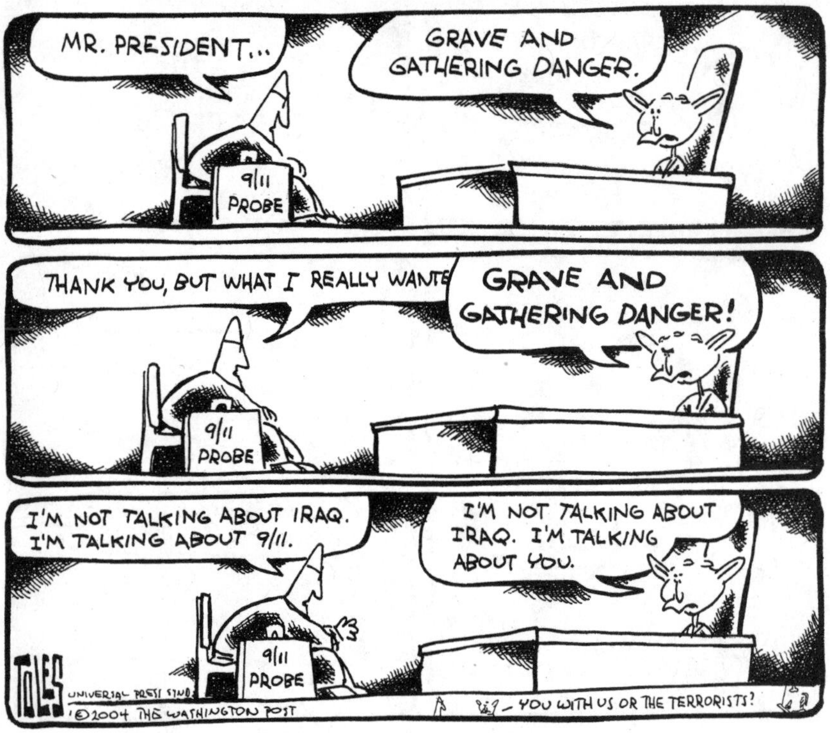
MR. PRESIDENT...
GRAVE AND GATHERING DANGER.
9/11 PROBE
THANK YOU, BUT WHAT I REALLY WANTE
GRAVE AND GATHERING DANGER!
9/11 PROBE
I'M NOT TALKING ABOUT IRAQ. I'M TALKING ABOUT 9/11.
I'M NOT TALKING ABOUT IRAQ. I'M TALKING ABOUT YOU.
9/11 PROBE
TOLES
©2004 THE WASHINGTON POST
YOU WITH US OR THE TERRORISTS?

1-30-04

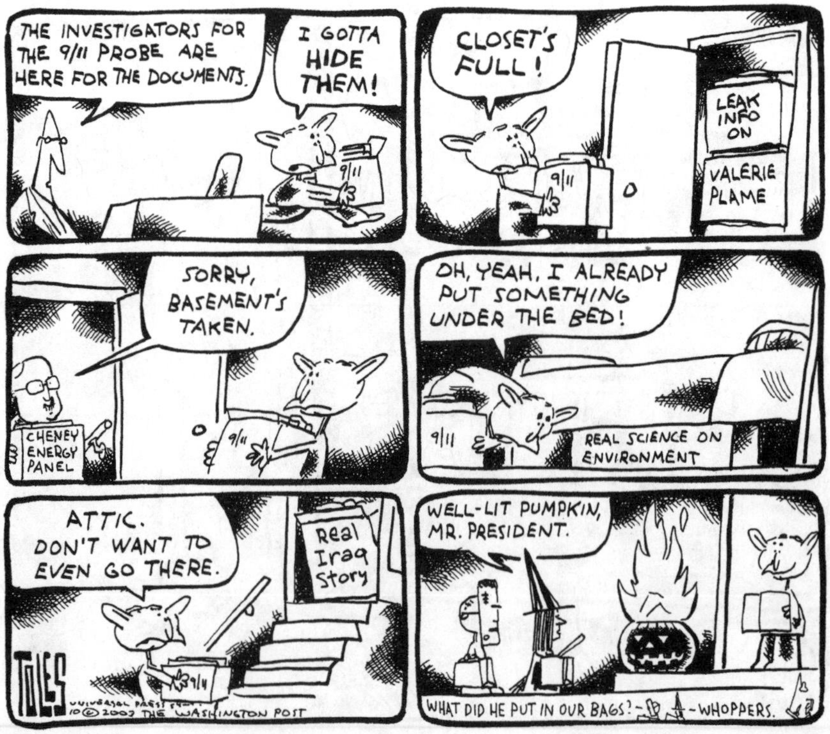
THE INVESTIGATORS FOR THE 9/11 PROBE ARE HERE FOR THE DOCUMENTS.
I GOTTA HIDE THEM!
9/11
CLOSET'S FULL!
LEAK INFO ON
VALERIE PLAME
9/11
SORRY, BASEMENT'S TAKEN.
CHENEY ENERGY PANEL
9/11
OH, YEAH, I ALREADY PUT SOMETHING UNDER THE BED!
9/11
REAL SCIENCE ON ENVIRONMENT
ATTIC. DON'T WANT TO EVEN GO THERE.
Real Iraq Story
9/11
TOLES
THE WASHINGTON POST
WELL-LIT PUMPKIN, MR. PRESIDENT.
WHAT DID HE PUT IN OUR BAGS?
WHOPPERS.

10-27-03

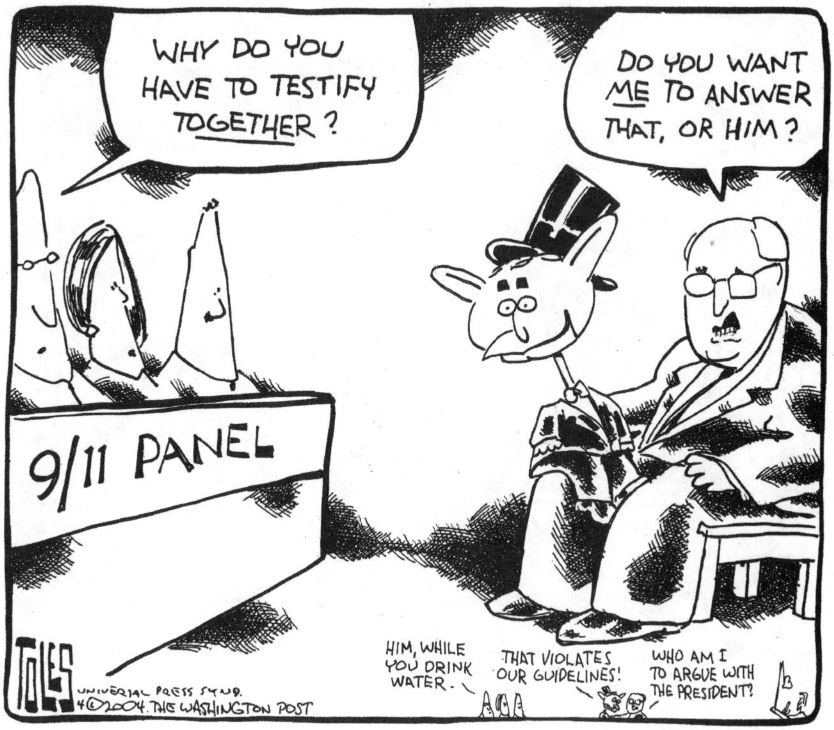
WHY DO YOU HAVE TO TESTIFY TOGETHER ?
DO YOU WANT ME TO ANSWER THAT, OR HIM ?
9/11 PANEL
TOLES
UNIVERSAL PRESS SYND.
4 © 2004 THE WASHINGTON POST
HIM, WHILE YOU DRINK WATER.
THAT VIOLATES OUR GUIDELINES!
WHO AM I TO ARGUE WITH THE PRESIDENT?

4-2-04

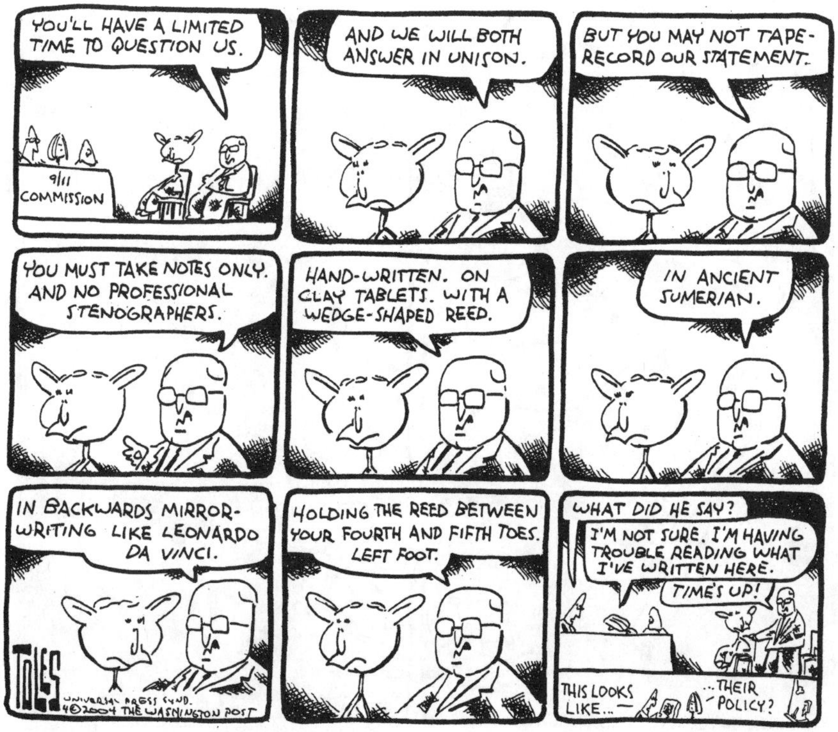
YOU'LL HAVE A LIMITED TIME TO QUESTION US.
9/11 COMMISSION
AND WE WILL BOTH ANSWER IN UNISON.
BUT YOU MAY NOT TAPE-RECORD OUR STATEMENT.
YOU MUST TAKE NOTES ONLY. AND NO PROFESSIONAL STENOGRAPHERS.
HAND-WRITTEN. ON CLAY TABLETS. WITH A WEDGE-SHAPED REED.
IN ANCIENT SUMERIAN.
IN BACKWARDS MIRROR-WRITING LIKE LEONARDO DA VINCI.
HOLDING THE REED BETWEEN YOUR FOURTH AND FIFTH TOES. LEFT FOOT.
WHAT DID HE SAY?
I'M NOT SURE. I'M HAVING TROUBLE READING WHAT I'VE WRITTEN HERE.
TIME'S UP!
THIS LOOKS LIKE...
...THEIR POLICY?
TOLES
UNIVERSAL PRESS SYND.
4 © 2004 THE WASHINGTON POST

4-29-04

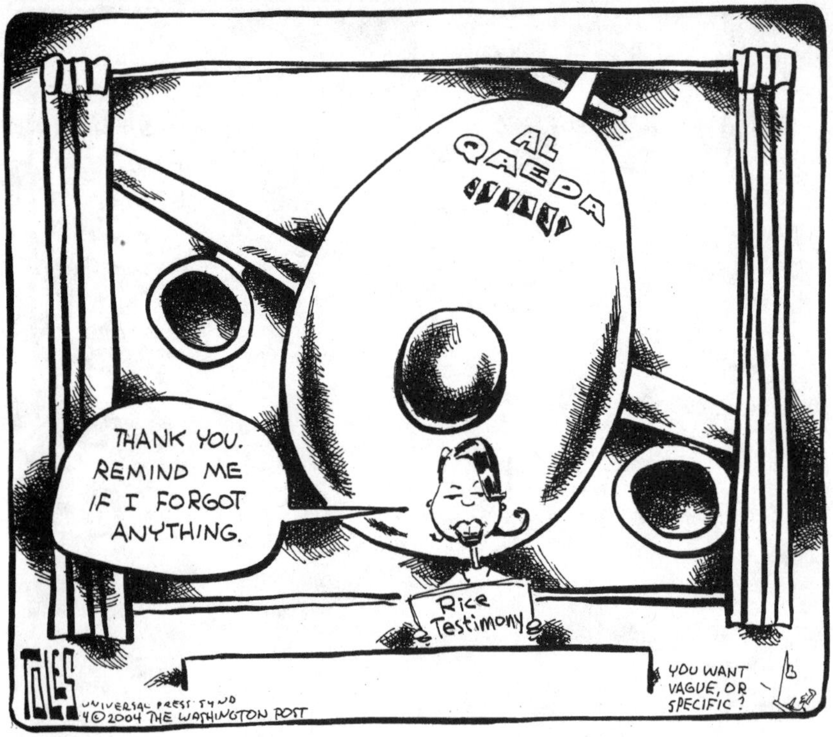
AL QAEDA
THANK YOU. REMIND ME IF I FORGOT ANYTHING.
Rice Testimony
TOLES
UNIVERSAL PRESS SYND
4©2004 THE WASHINGTON POST
YOU WANT VAGUE, OR SPECIFIC?

4-11-04

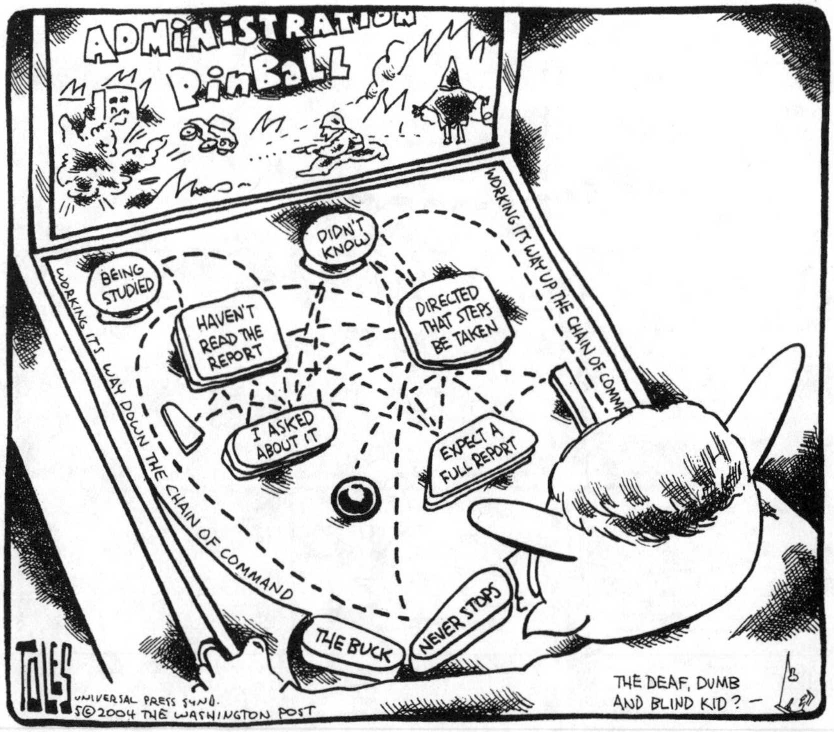
ADMINISTRATION PINBALL
WORKING ITS WAY UP THE CHAIN OF COMMAND
WORKING ITS WAY DOWN THE CHAIN OF COMMAND
BEING STUDIED
DIDN'T KNOW
HAVEN'T READ THE REPORT
DIRECTED THAT STEPS BE TAKEN
I ASKED ABOUT IT
EXPECT A FULL REPORT
THE BUCK
NEVER STOPS
TOLES
UNIVERSAL PRESS SYND.
5©2004 THE WASHINGTON POST
THE DEAF, DUMB AND BLIND KID?

5-6-04

YES, I BELIEVE HE DESCRIBED HIMSELF AS A 'WARP RESIDENT'.
DISTORTED INTELLIGENCE
AT A FUN HOUSE PRESS CONFERENCE?
TOLES
UNIVERSAL PRESS SYND.
7 © 2004 THE WASHINGTON POST

7-13-04

Yes! ♪
THE REORGANIZATION OF THE CIA IS NOW COMPLETE.
THEY ARE READY TO BE PREACHED TO.
TOLES
UNIVERSAL PRESS SYND.
11 © 2004 THE WASHINGTON POST

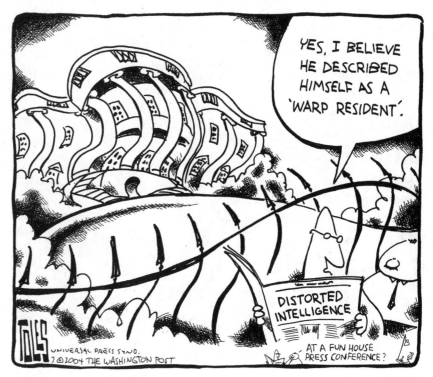

11-18-04

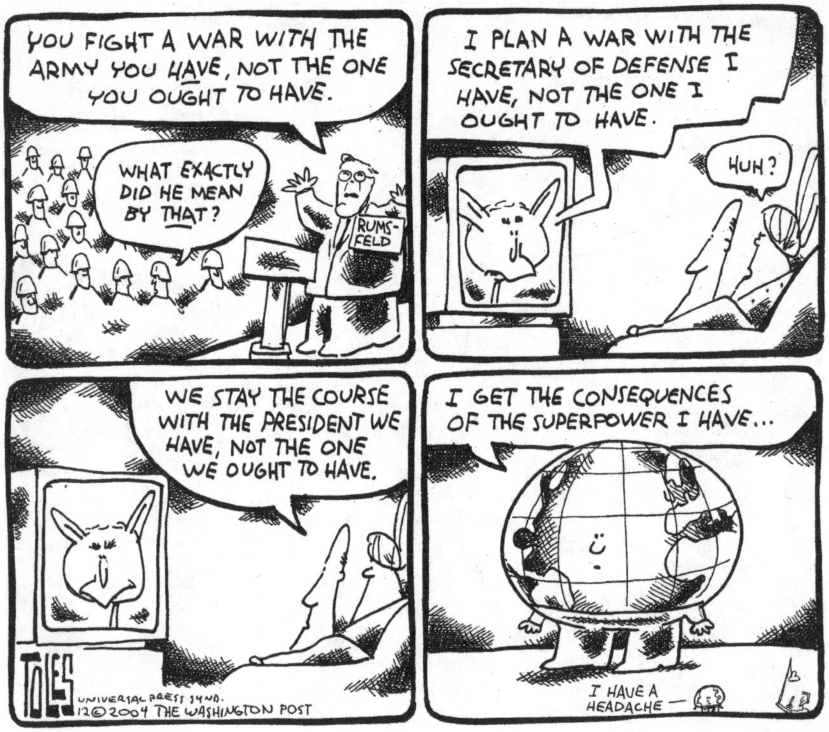
YOU FIGHT A WAR WITH THE ARMY YOU HAVE, NOT THE ONE YOU OUGHT TO HAVE.
WHAT EXACTLY DID HE MEAN BY THAT?
RUMS-FELD
I PLAN A WAR WITH THE SECRETARY OF DEFENSE I HAVE, NOT THE ONE I OUGHT TO HAVE.
HUH?
WE STAY THE COURSE WITH THE PRESIDENT WE HAVE, NOT THE ONE WE OUGHT TO HAVE.
I GET THE CONSEQUENCES OF THE SUPERPOWER I HAVE...
I HAVE A HEADACHE
TOLES
UNIVERSAL PRESS SYND.
12 © 2004 THE WASHINGTON POST

12-10-04

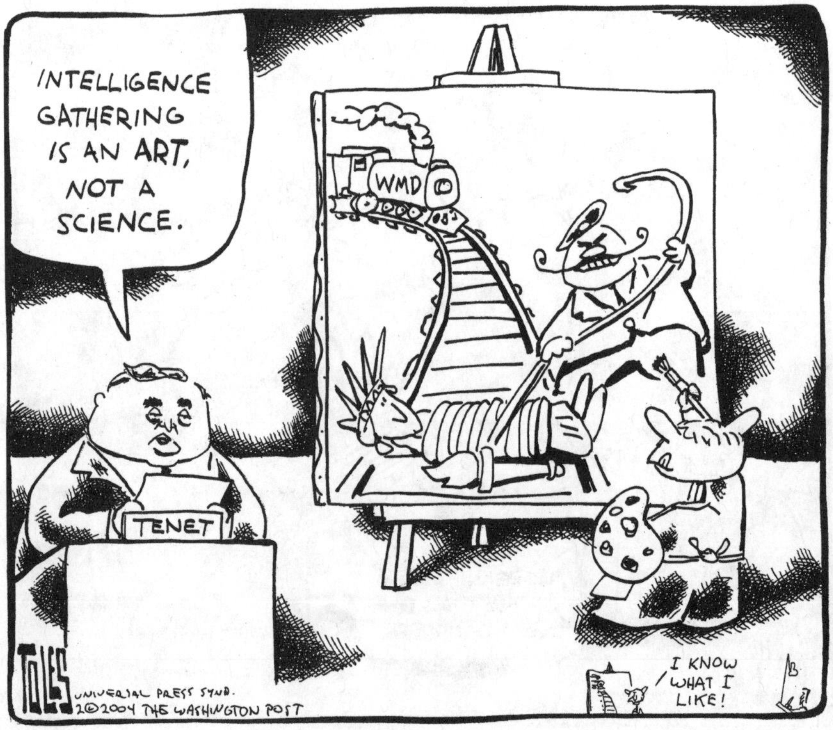
INTELLIGENCE GATHERING IS AN ART, NOT A SCIENCE.
WMD
TENET
I KNOW WHAT I LIKE!
TOLES
UNIVERSAL PRESS SYND.
2 © 2004 THE WASHINGTON POST

2-9-04

SOMEONE SHOULD INVESTIGATE WHY THE CIA GAVE ME A BAD HAMMER.
TOLES
UNIVERSAL PRESS SYND.
2 © 2004 THE WASHINGTON POST
BE CAREFUL WHAT YOU ASK FOR –

2-3-04

WHO COULD HAVE FORESEEN CONGRESS FLYING A BUILDING INTO OUR AIRPLANE ?
INTELLIGENCE REFORM
TOLES
UNIVERSAL PRESS SYND.
11 © 2004 THE WASHINGTON POST
IT MAY HAVE BEEN IN THE PRESIDENTIAL DAILY BRIEFING. –

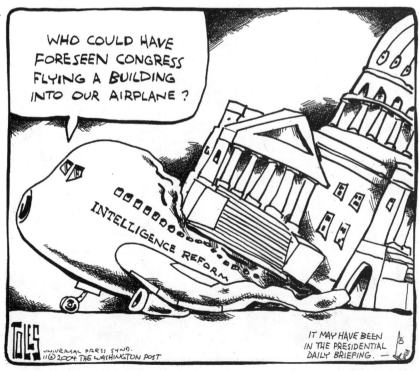

11-24-04

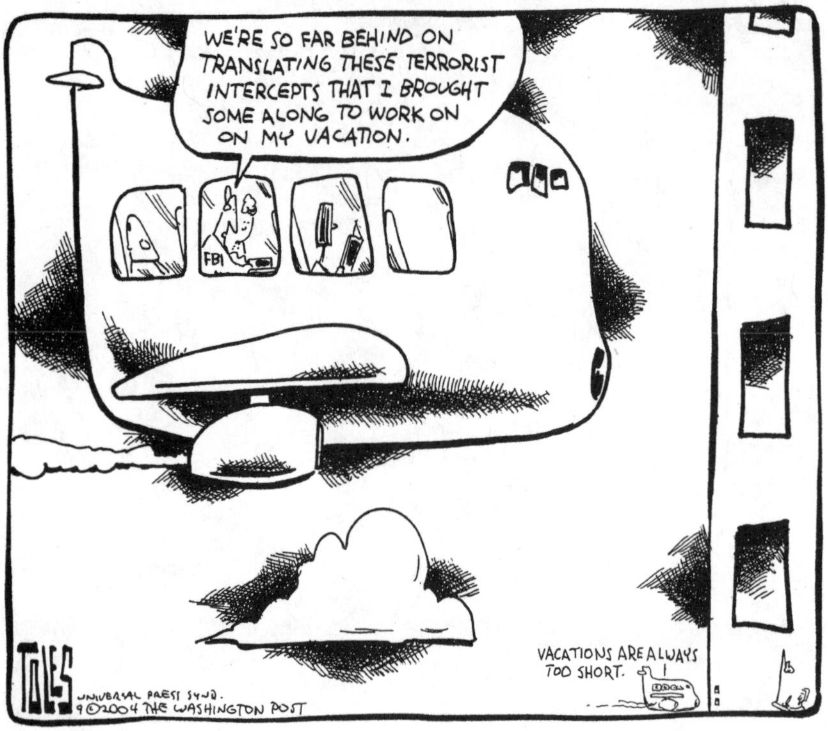
WE'RE SO FAR BEHIND ON TRANSLATING THESE TERRORIST INTERCEPTS THAT I BROUGHT SOME ALONG TO WORK ON ON MY VACATION.
FBI
TOLES
UNIVERSAL PRESS SYND.
9 © 2004 THE WASHINGTON POST
VACATIONS ARE ALWAYS TOO SHORT.

9-30-04

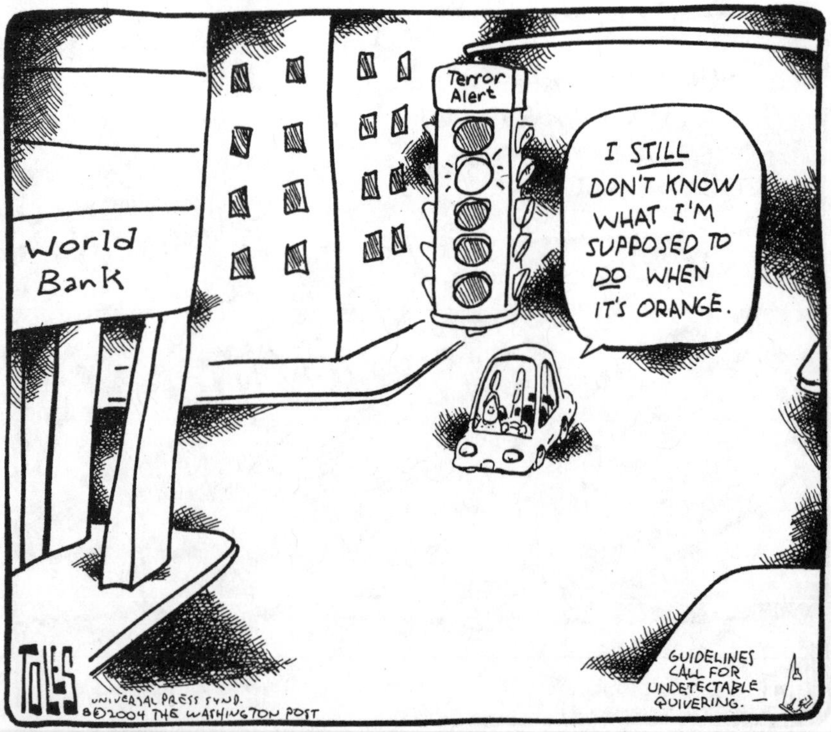
Terror Alert
World Bank
I STILL DON'T KNOW WHAT I'M SUPPOSED TO DO WHEN IT'S ORANGE.
TOLES
UNIVERSAL PRESS SYND.
8 © 2004 THE WASHINGTON POST
GUIDELINES CALL FOR UNDETECTABLE QUIVERING.

8-3-04

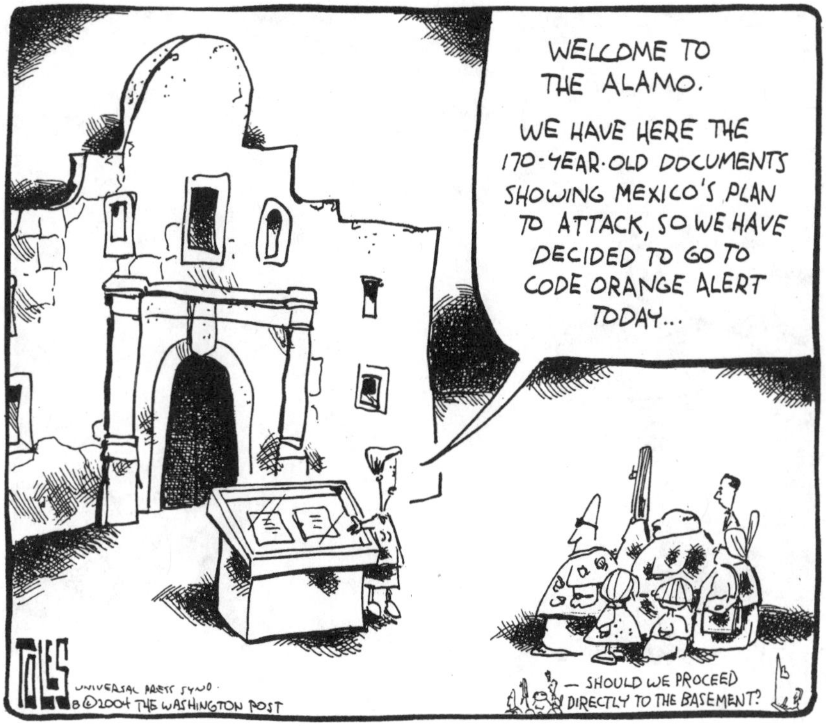
WELCOME TO THE ALAMO.
WE HAVE HERE THE 170-YEAR-OLD DOCUMENTS SHOWING MEXICO'S PLAN TO ATTACK, SO WE HAVE DECIDED TO GO TO CODE ORANGE ALERT TODAY...
TOLES
UNIVERSAL PRESS SYND. 8©2004 THE WASHINGTON POST
— SHOULD WE PROCEED DIRECTLY TO THE BASEMENT?

8-4-04

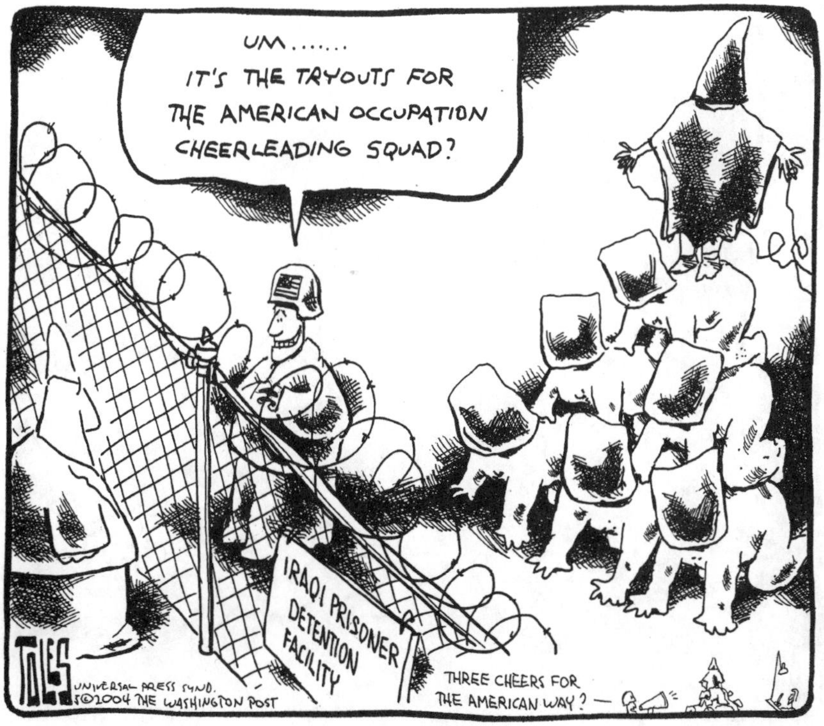
UM.......
IT'S THE TRYOUTS FOR THE AMERICAN OCCUPATION CHEERLEADING SQUAD?
IRAQI PRISONER DETENTION FACILITY
TOLES
UNIVERSAL PRESS SYND. 5©2004 THE WASHINGTON POST
THREE CHEERS FOR THE AMERICAN WAY? —

5-4-04

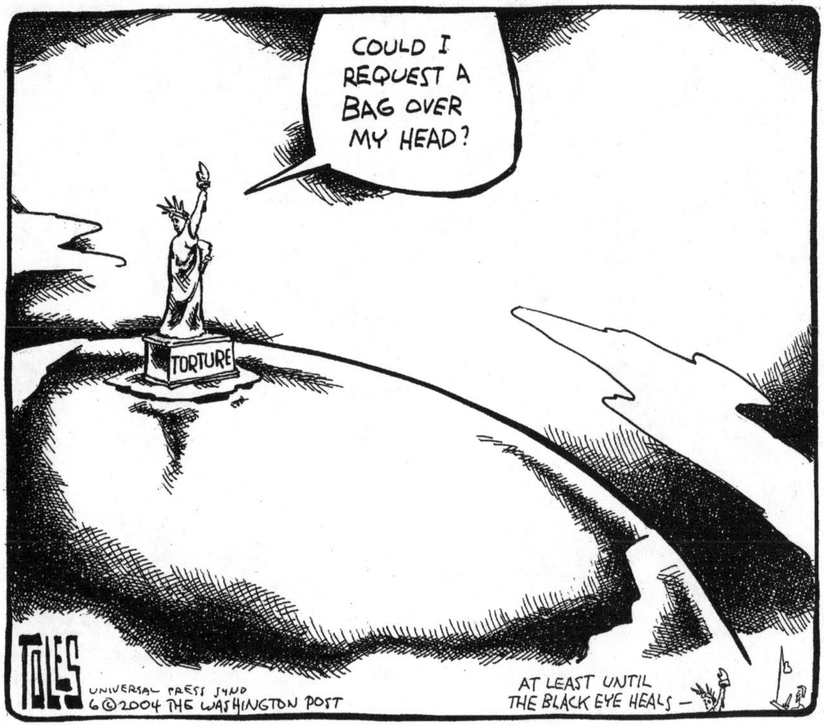
COULD I REQUEST A BAG OVER MY HEAD?
TORTURE
TOLES
UNIVERSAL PRESS SYND
6 © 2004 THE WASHINGTON POST
AT LEAST UNTIL THE BLACK EYE HEALS —

6-27-04

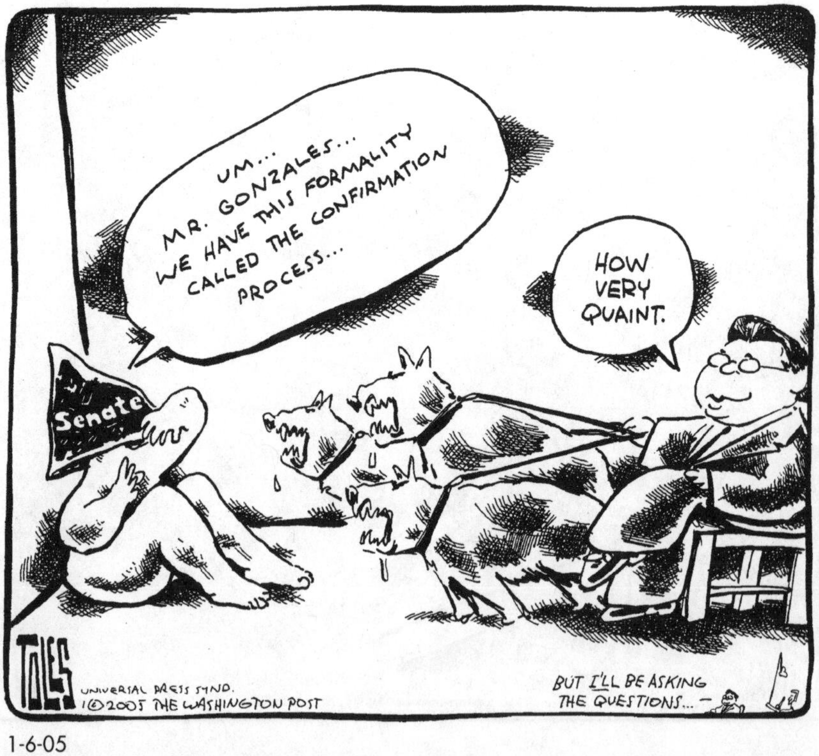
UM... MR. GONZALES... WE HAVE THIS FORMALITY CALLED THE CONFIRMATION PROCESS...
HOW VERY QUAINT.
Senate
TOLES
UNIVERSAL PRESS SYND.
1 © 2005 THE WASHINGTON POST
BUT I'LL BE ASKING THE QUESTIONS... —

1-6-05

SHOCKING! HOW FAR UP THE CHAIN OF COMMAND DOES THIS GO?
IRAQ
TOLES
UNIVERSAL PRESS SYND.
5 © 2004 THE WASHINGTON POST
TO THE WEAKEST LINK.

5-19-04

Administration Lawyers Say Torture is Okay.
NOW ARE YOU WILLING TO SAY OUR IRAQ EXPLANATIONS MAKE SENSE?
LOGIC
TOLES
UNIVERSAL PRESS SYND.
6 © 2004 THE WASHINGTON POST
ENGLISH LANGUAGE, YOU'RE IS NEXT!

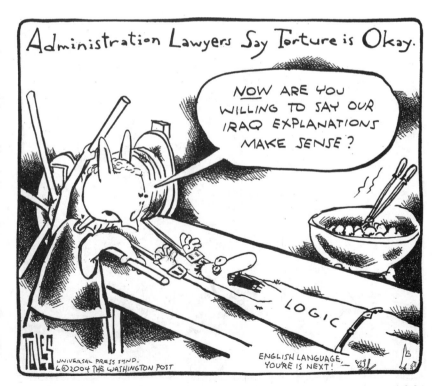

6-9-04

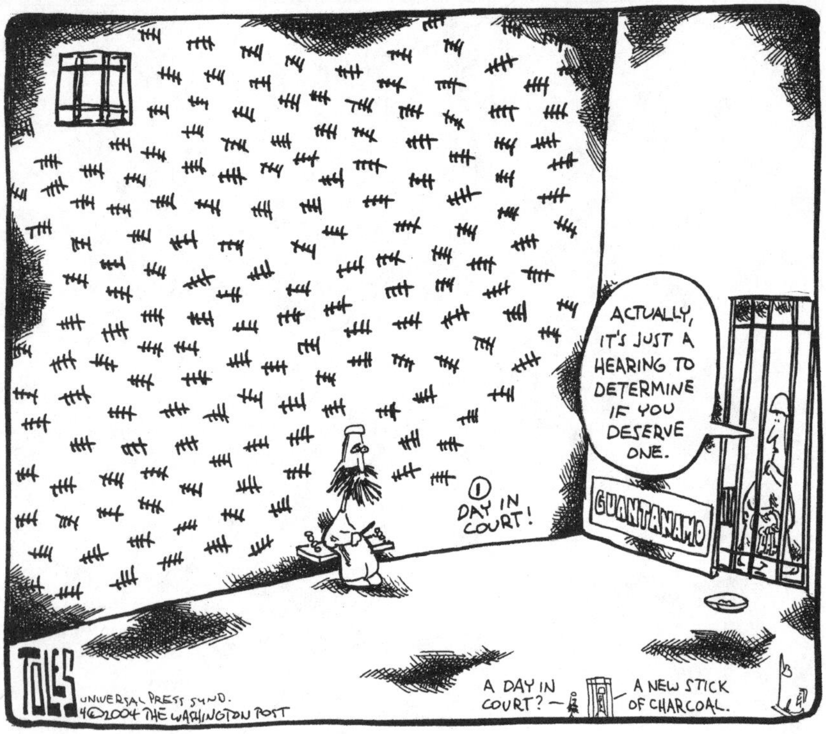
ACTUALLY, IT'S JUST A HEARING TO DETERMINE IF YOU DESERVE ONE.
GUANTANAMO
1 DAY IN COURT!
TOLES
UNIVERSAL PRESS SYND.
4©2004 THE WASHINGTON POST
A DAY IN COURT? —
— A NEW STICK OF CHARCOAL.

4-21-04

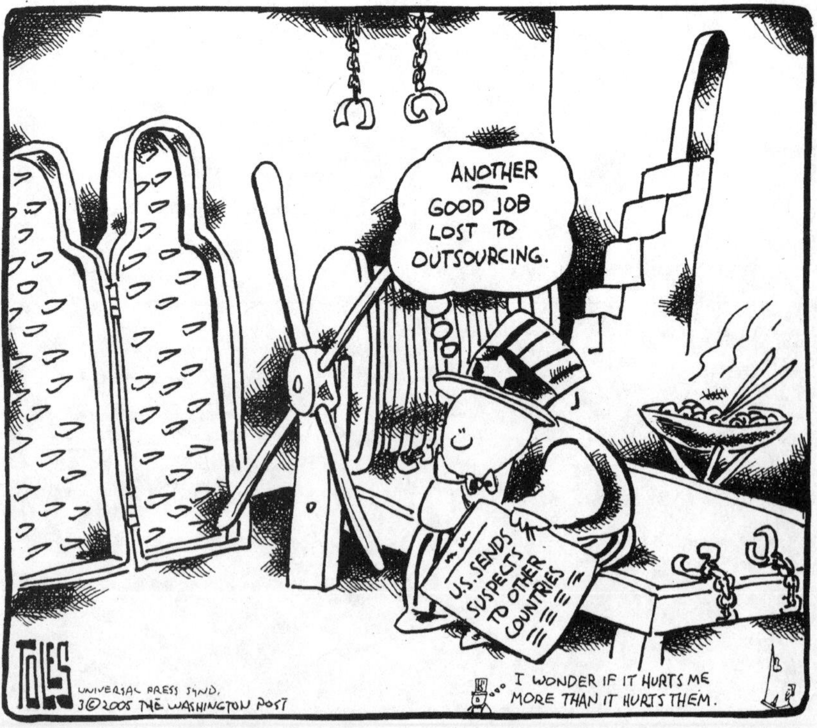
ANOTHER GOOD JOB LOST TO OUTSOURCING.
U.S. SENDS SUSPECTS TO OTHER COUNTRIES
TOLES
UNIVERSAL PRESS SYND.
3©2005 THE WASHINGTON POST
I WONDER IF IT HURTS ME MORE THAN IT HURTS THEM.

3-13-05

WMD AND BEYOND

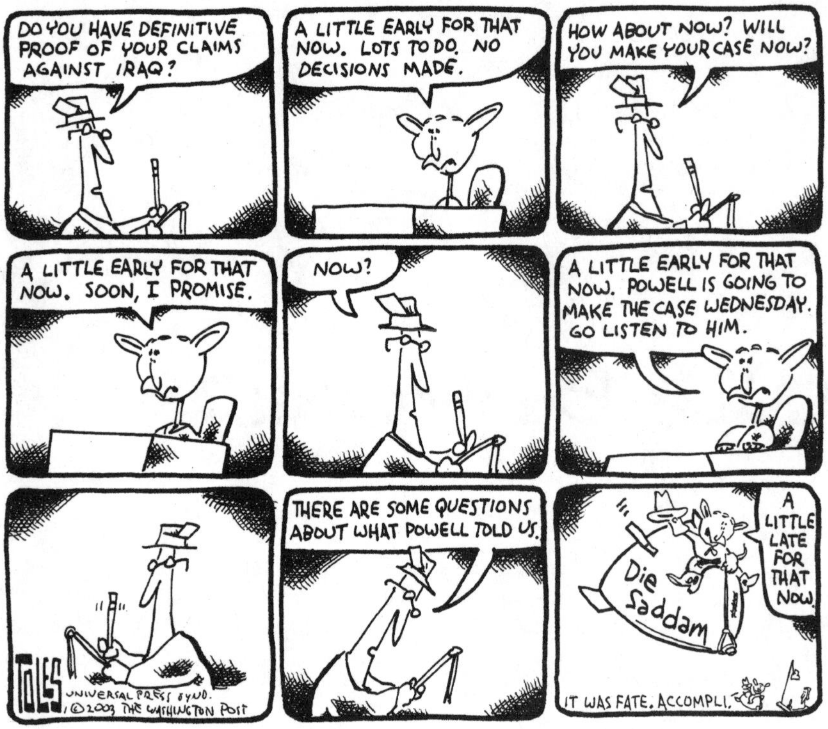
DO YOU HAVE DEFINITIVE PROOF OF YOUR CLAIMS AGAINST IRAQ?
A LITTLE EARLY FOR THAT NOW. LOTS TO DO. NO DECISIONS MADE.
HOW ABOUT NOW? WILL YOU MAKE YOUR CASE NOW?
A LITTLE EARLY FOR THAT NOW. SOON, I PROMISE.
NOW?
A LITTLE EARLY FOR THAT NOW. POWELL IS GOING TO MAKE THE CASE WEDNESDAY. GO LISTEN TO HIM.
TOLES
UNIVERSAL PRESS SYND.
©2003 THE WASHINGTON POST
THERE ARE SOME QUESTIONS ABOUT WHAT POWELL TOLD US.
Die Saddam
A LITTLE LATE FOR THAT NOW.
IT WAS FATE. ACCOMPLI.

1-31-03

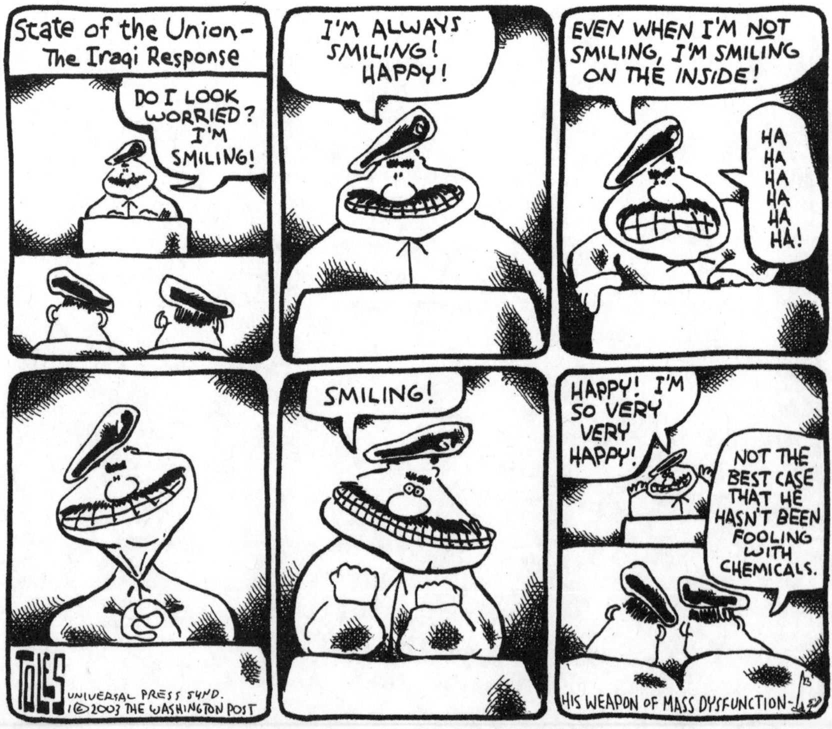
State of the Union-
The Iraqi Response
DO I LOOK WORRIED? I'M SMILING!
I'M ALWAYS SMILING! HAPPY!
EVEN WHEN I'M NOT SMILING, I'M SMILING ON THE INSIDE!
HA HA HA HA HA HA HA!
SMILING!
HAPPY! I'M SO VERY VERY HAPPY!
NOT THE BEST CASE THAT HE HASN'T BEEN FOOLING WITH CHEMICALS.
TOLES
UNIVERSAL PRESS SYND.
©2003 THE WASHINGTON POST
HIS WEAPON OF MASS DYSFUNCTION-

1-30-03

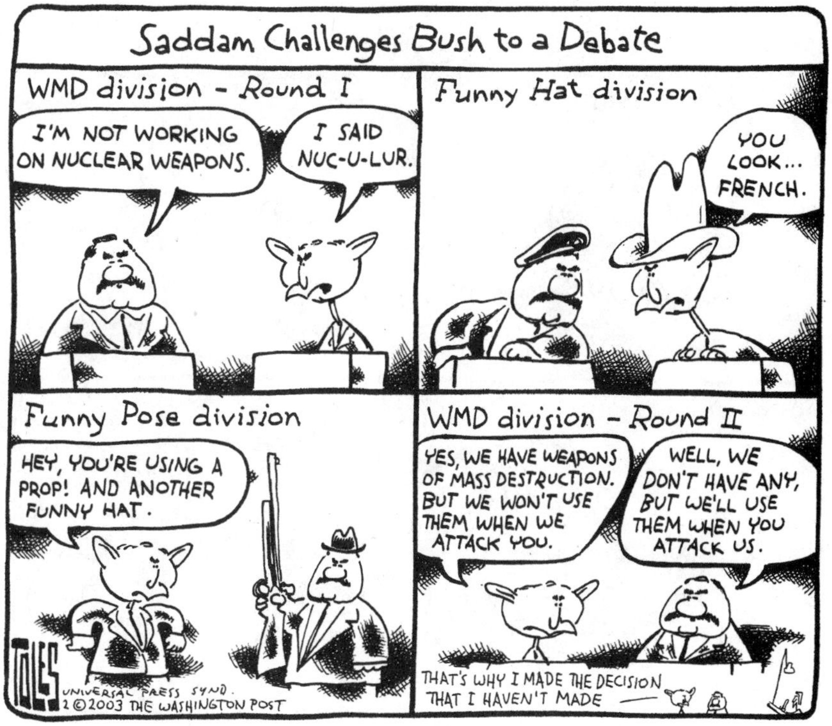
Saddam Challenges Bush to a Debate
WMD division - Round I
I'M NOT WORKING ON NUCLEAR WEAPONS.
I SAID NUC-U-LUR.
Funny Hat division
YOU LOOK... FRENCH.
Funny Pose division
HEY, YOU'RE USING A PROP! AND ANOTHER FUNNY HAT.
WMD division - Round II
YES, WE HAVE WEAPONS OF MASS DESTRUCTION. BUT WE WON'T USE THEM WHEN WE ATTACK YOU.
WELL, WE DON'T HAVE ANY, BUT WE'LL USE THEM WHEN YOU ATTACK US.
THAT'S WHY I MADE THE DECISION THAT I HAVEN'T MADE
TOLES
UNIVERSAL PRESS SYND.
2 © 2003 THE WASHINGTON POST

2-26-03

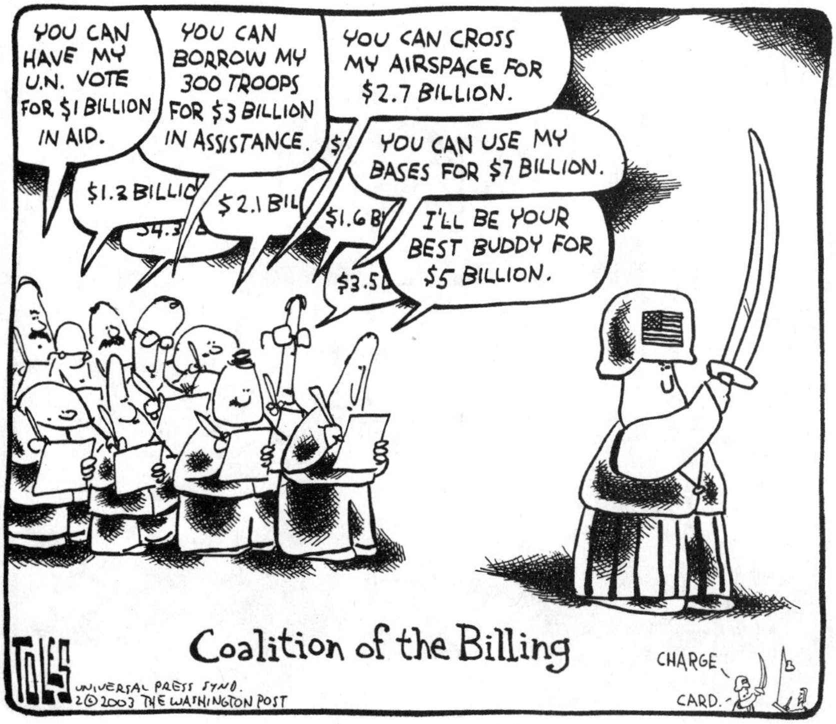
YOU CAN HAVE MY U.N. VOTE FOR $1 BILLION IN AID.
YOU CAN BORROW MY 300 TROOPS FOR $3 BILLION IN ASSISTANCE.
YOU CAN CROSS MY AIRSPACE FOR $2.7 BILLION.
YOU CAN USE MY BASES FOR $7 BILLION.
I'LL BE YOUR BEST BUDDY FOR $5 BILLION.
Coalition of the Billing
CHARGE
CARD.
TOLES
UNIVERSAL PRESS SYND.
2 © 2003 THE WASHINGTON POST

2-25-03

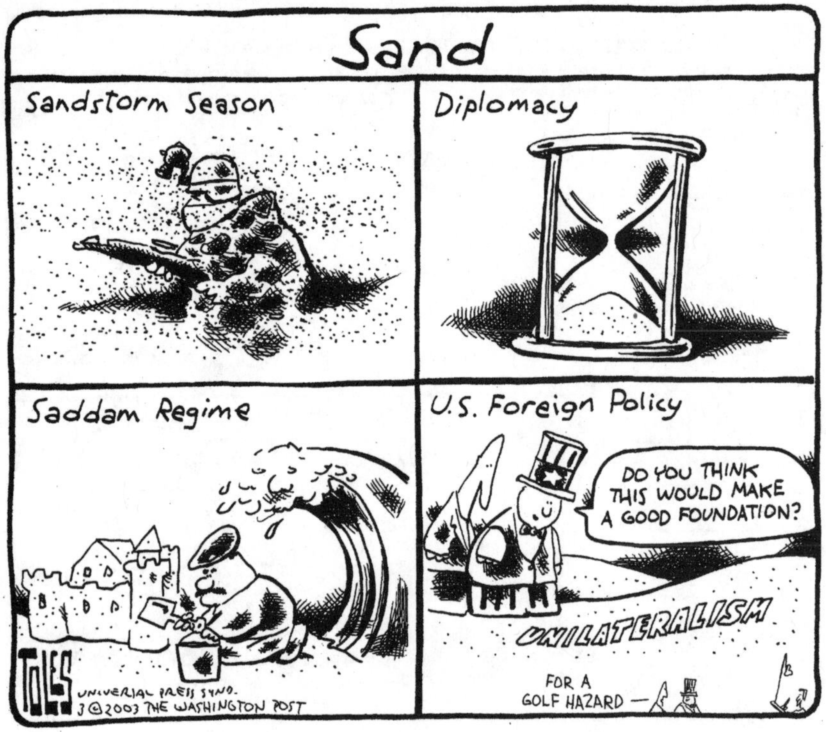
Sand
Sandstorm Season
Diplomacy
Saddam Regime
U.S. Foreign Policy
DO YOU THINK THIS WOULD MAKE A GOOD FOUNDATION?
UNILATERALISM
FOR A GOLF HAZARD
TOLES
UNIVERSAL PRESS SYND.
3 © 2003 THE WASHINGTON POST

3-23-03

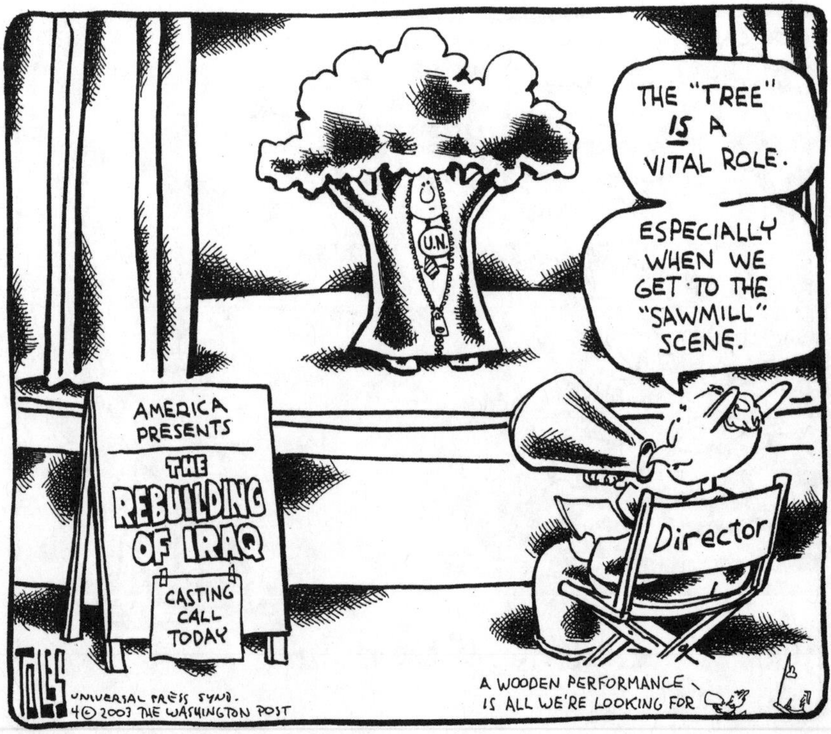
THE "TREE" IS A VITAL ROLE.
ESPECIALLY WHEN WE GET TO THE "SAWMILL" SCENE.
U.N.
AMERICA PRESENTS
THE REBUILDING OF IRAQ
CASTING CALL TODAY
Director
TOLES
UNIVERSAL PRESS SYND.
4 © 2003 THE WASHINGTON POST
A WOODEN PERFORMANCE IS ALL WE'RE LOOKING FOR

4-10-03

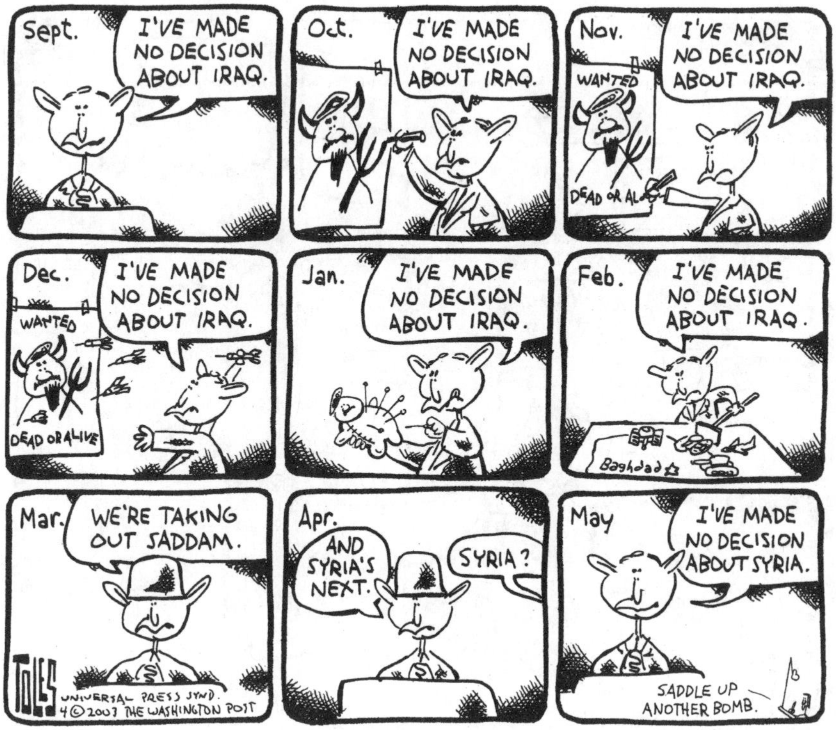
Sept.
I'VE MADE NO DECISION ABOUT IRAQ.
Oct.
I'VE MADE NO DECISION ABOUT IRAQ.
Nov.
I'VE MADE NO DECISION ABOUT IRAQ.
WANTED
DEAD OR AL
Dec.
I'VE MADE NO DECISION ABOUT IRAQ.
WANTED
DEAD OR ALIVE
Jan.
I'VE MADE NO DECISION ABOUT IRAQ.
Feb.
I'VE MADE NO DECISION ABOUT IRAQ.
Baghdad
Mar.
WE'RE TAKING OUT SADDAM.
Apr.
AND SYRIA'S NEXT.
SYRIA?
May
I'VE MADE NO DECISION ABOUT SYRIA.
TOLES
UNIVERSAL PRESS SYND.
4 © 2003 THE WASHINGTON POST
SADDLE UP ANOTHER BOMB.

4-14-03

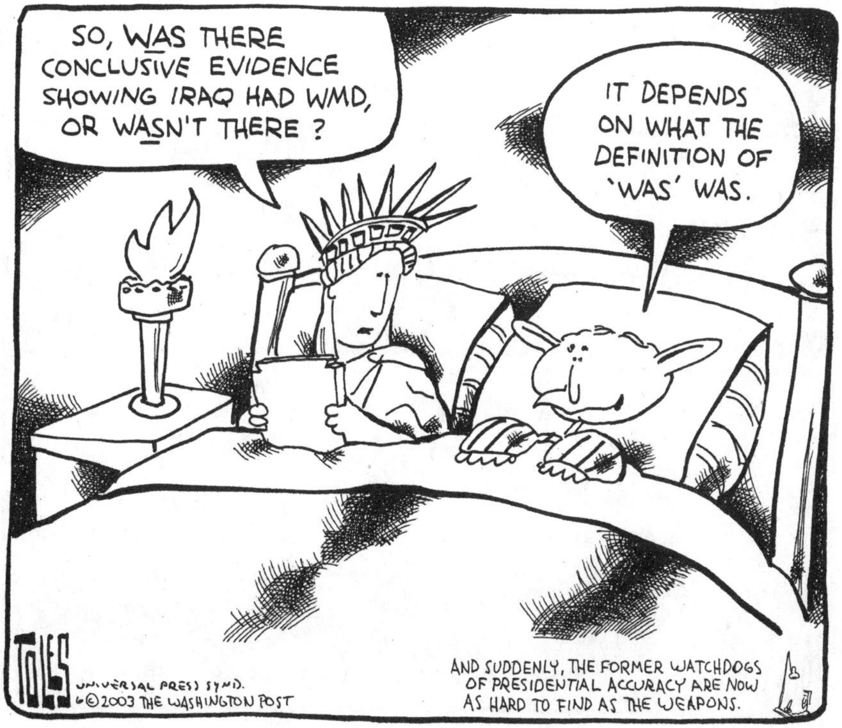
SO, WAS THERE CONCLUSIVE EVIDENCE SHOWING IRAQ HAD WMD, OR WASN'T THERE?
IT DEPENDS ON WHAT THE DEFINITION OF 'WAS' WAS.
TOLES
UNIVERSAL PRESS SYND.
6 © 2003 THE WASHINGTON POST
AND SUDDENLY, THE FORMER WATCHDOGS OF PRESIDENTIAL ACCURACY ARE NOW AS HARD TO FIND AS THE WEAPONS.

6-12-03

Real Facts
Fake Facts
Out-of-date Facts
Made up Facts
Hyped Facts
Fun Facts
Misleading Facts
Selective Facts
Changing Facts
Speculative Facts
RUMS-FELD
PARTS IS PARTS.
CASE FOR WAR
TOLES
UNIVERSAL PRESS SYND.
7 © 2003 THE WASHINGTON POST
I PLAY MINE.

7-11-03

Today's Vocabulary Word:
Debunker: n
one who exposes false or exaggerated opinions or claims.
Synonym: Truth-teller
Dictionary
Antonym: Where Cheney spent most of last year.
I WANT YOU TO MAKE THE INTELLIGENCE COME OUT THE WAY I WANT IT TO COME OUT.
CIA
WE'LL COME OUT WHEN IT DOES.
TOLES
UNIVERSAL PRESS SYND.
7 © 2003 THE WASHINGTON POST

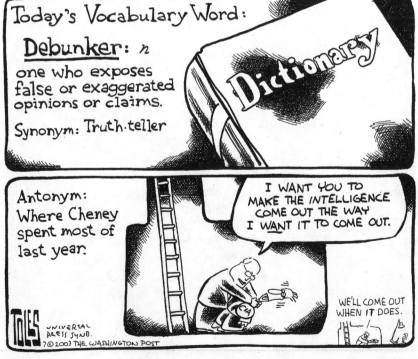

7-18-03

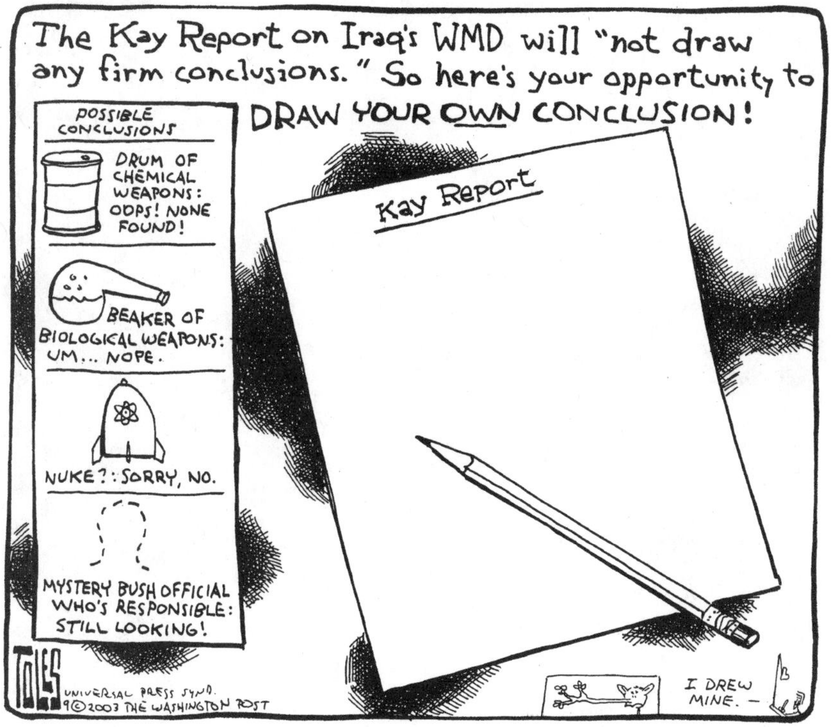
The Kay Report on Iraq's WMD will "not draw any firm conclusions." So here's your opportunity to DRAW YOUR OWN CONCLUSION!
POSSIBLE CONCLUSIONS
DRUM OF CHEMICAL WEAPONS: OOPS! NONE FOUND!
BEAKER OF BIOLOGICAL WEAPONS: UM... NOPE.
NUKE?: SORRY, NO.
MYSTERY BUSH OFFICIAL WHO'S RESPONSIBLE: STILL LOOKING!
Kay Report
I DREW MINE. —
TOLES
UNIVERSAL PRESS SYND.
9©2003 THE WASHINGTON POST

9-28-03

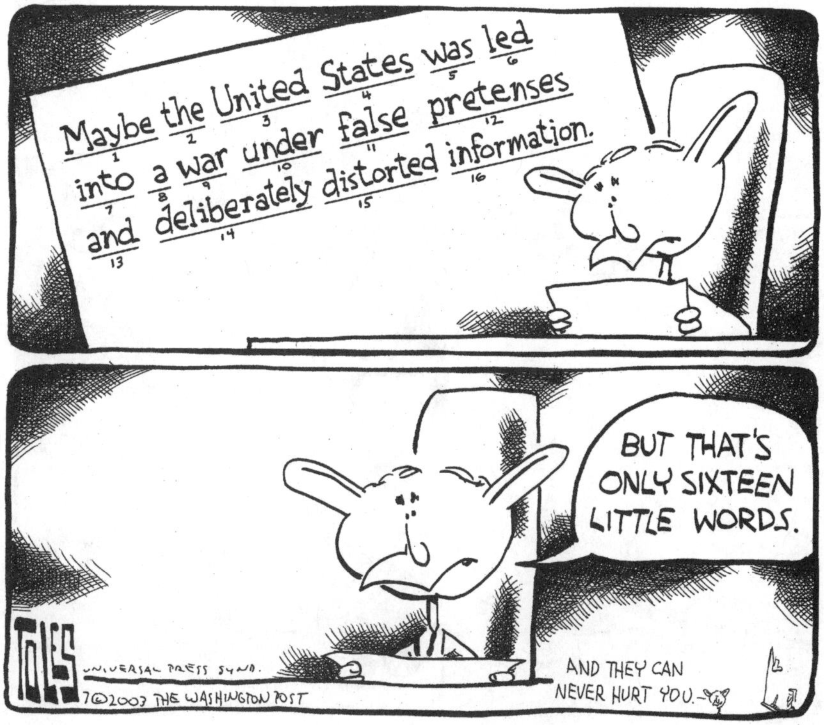
Maybe the United States was led into a war under false pretenses and deliberately distorted information.
1 2 3 4 5 6 7 8 9 10 11 12 13 14 15 16
BUT THAT'S ONLY SIXTEEN LITTLE WORDS.
AND THEY CAN NEVER HURT YOU. —
TOLES
UNIVERSAL PRESS SYND.
7©2003 THE WASHINGTON POST

7-20-03

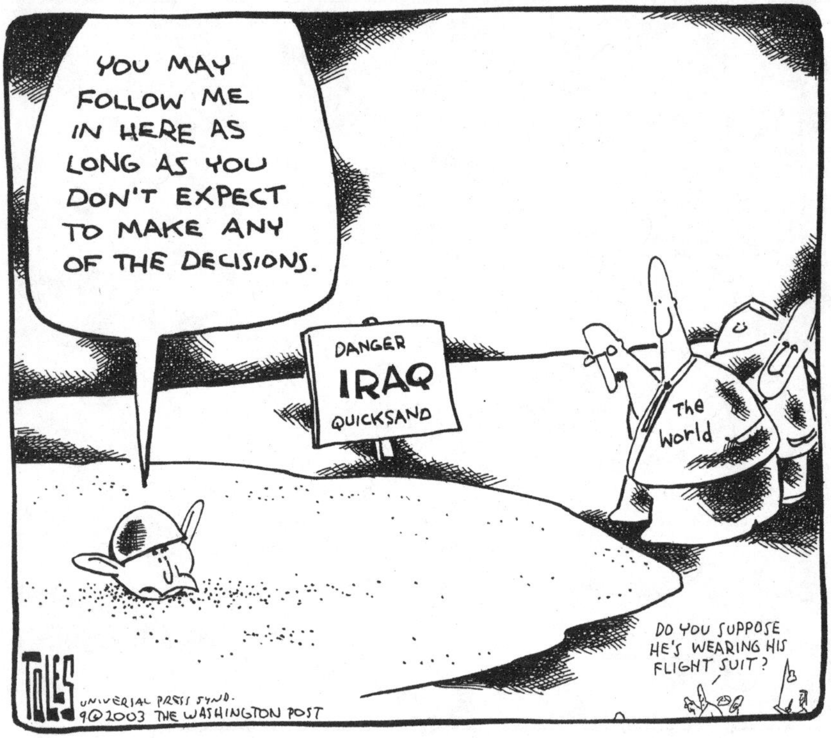

YOU MAY FOLLOW ME IN HERE AS LONG AS YOU DON'T EXPECT TO MAKE ANY OF THE DECISIONS.
DANGER
IRAQ
QUICKSAND
The World
DO YOU SUPPOSE HE'S WEARING HIS FLIGHT SUIT?
TOLES
UNIVERSAL PRESS SYND.
9 © 2003 THE WASHINGTON POST

9-5-03

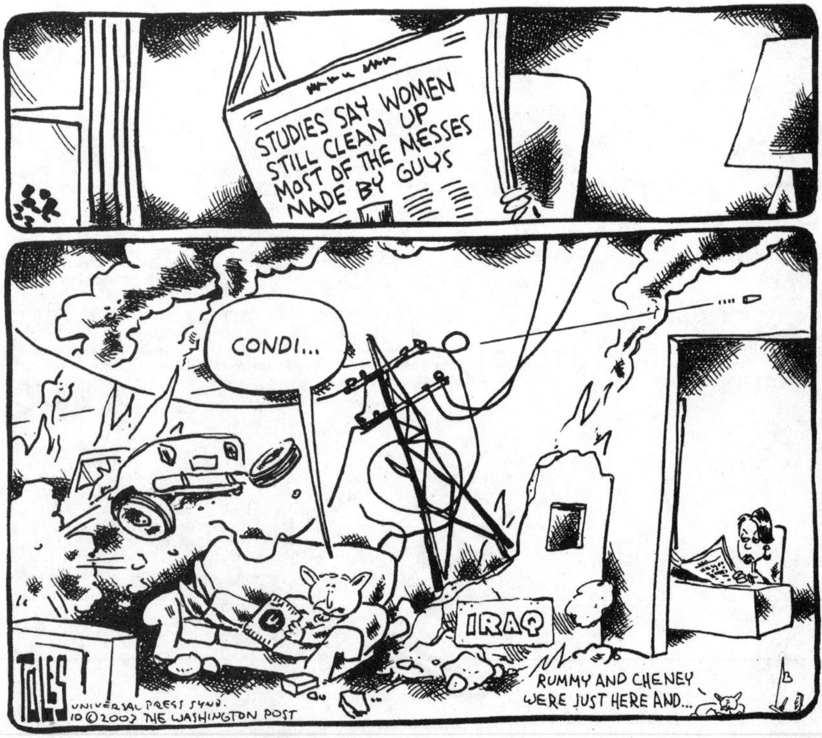

STUDIES SAY WOMEN STILL CLEAN UP MOST OF THE MESSES MADE BY GUYS
CONDI...
IRAQ
RUMMY AND CHENEY WERE JUST HERE AND...
TOLES
UNIVERSAL PRESS SYND.
10 © 2003 THE WASHINGTON POST

10-8-03

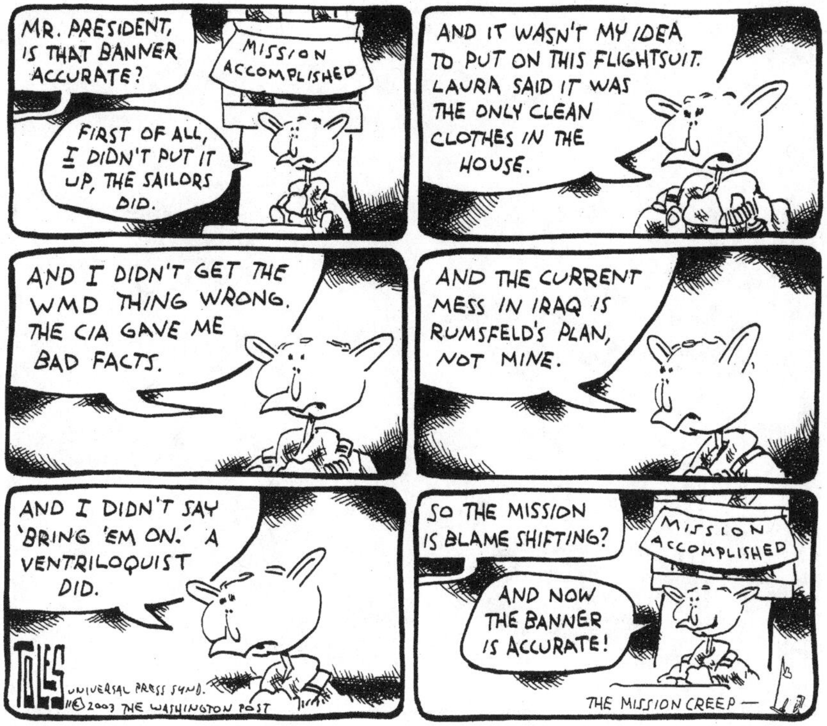
MR. PRESIDENT, IS THAT BANNER ACCURATE?
MISSION ACCOMPLISHED
FIRST OF ALL, I DIDN'T PUT IT UP, THE SAILORS DID.
AND IT WASN'T MY IDEA TO PUT ON THIS FLIGHTSUIT. LAURA SAID IT WAS THE ONLY CLEAN CLOTHES IN THE HOUSE.
AND I DIDN'T GET THE WMD THING WRONG. THE CIA GAVE ME BAD FACTS.
AND THE CURRENT MESS IN IRAQ IS RUMSFELD'S PLAN, NOT MINE.
AND I DIDN'T SAY 'BRING 'EM ON.' A VENTRILOQUIST DID.
SO THE MISSION IS BLAME SHIFTING?
MISSION ACCOMPLISHED
AND NOW THE BANNER IS ACCURATE!
TOLES
UNIVERSAL PRESS SYND.
11 © 2003 THE WASHINGTON POST
THE MISSION CREEP —

11-2-03

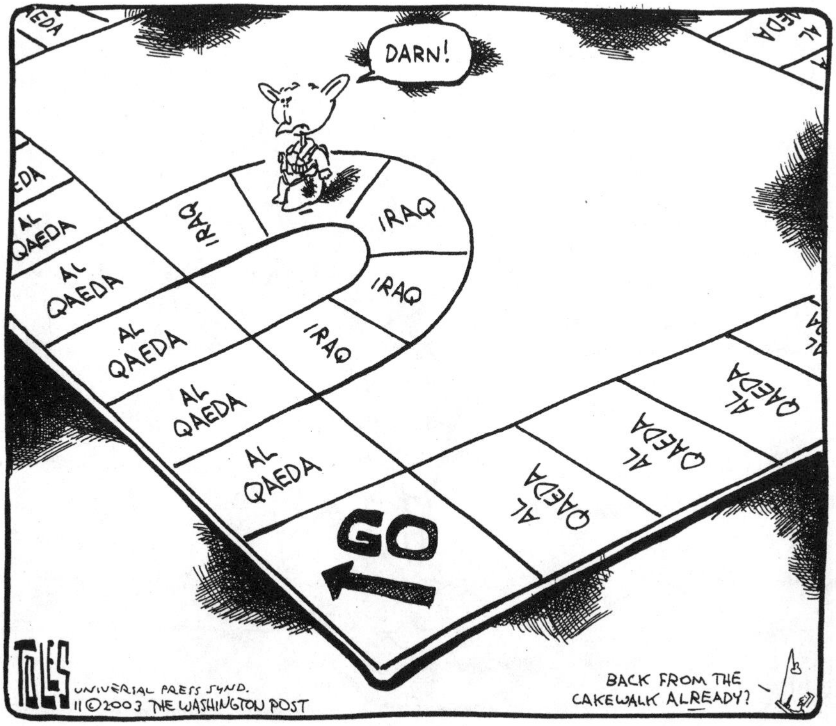
DARN!
IRAQ
IRAQ
IRAQ
IRAQ
AL QAEDA
AL QAEDA
AL QAEDA
AL QAEDA
AL QAEDA
AL QAEDA
AL QAEDA
AL QAEDA
GO
TOLES
UNIVERSAL PRESS SYND.
11 © 2003 THE WASHINGTON POST
BACK FROM THE CAKEWALK ALREADY?

11-23-03

WAR PRESIDENT
WMD BASIS
TOLES
UNIVERSAL PRESS SYND.
1 ©2005 THE WASHINGTON POST
ALL THOSE IN FAVOR OF IGNORING THE OBVIOUS...

1-16-05

SADDAM'S ACTUAL THREAT -Report
TOLES
UNIVERSAL PRESS SYND.
10 ©2004 THE WASHINGTON POST
IT WILL LOOK BIGGER IN THE CAMPAIGN AD. -

10-10-04

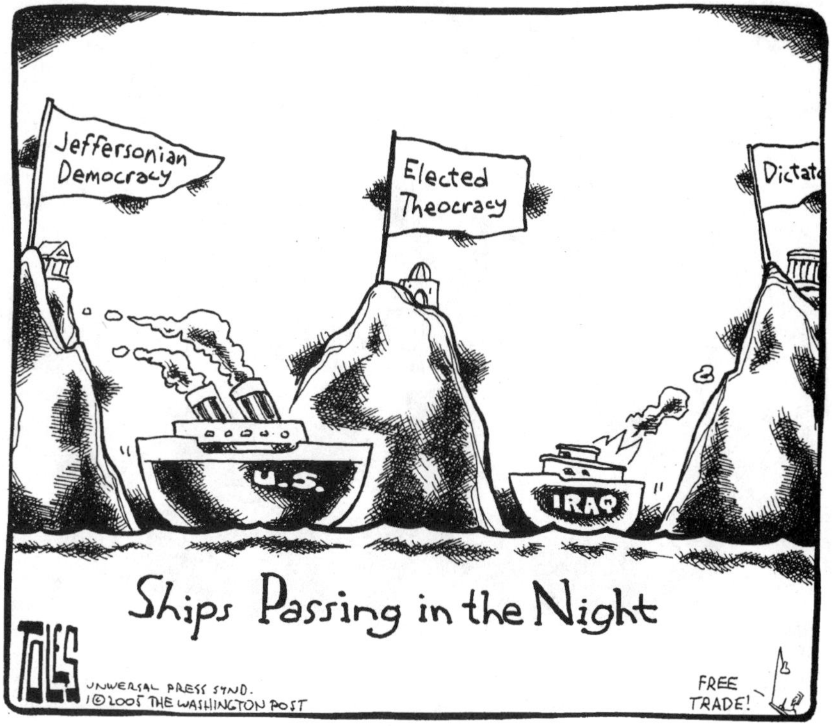
Jeffersonian Democracy
Elected Theocracy
Dictato
U.S.
IRAQ
Ships Passing in the Night
TOLES
UNIVERSAL PRESS SYND.
1©2005 THE WASHINGTON POST
FREE TRADE!

1-20-05

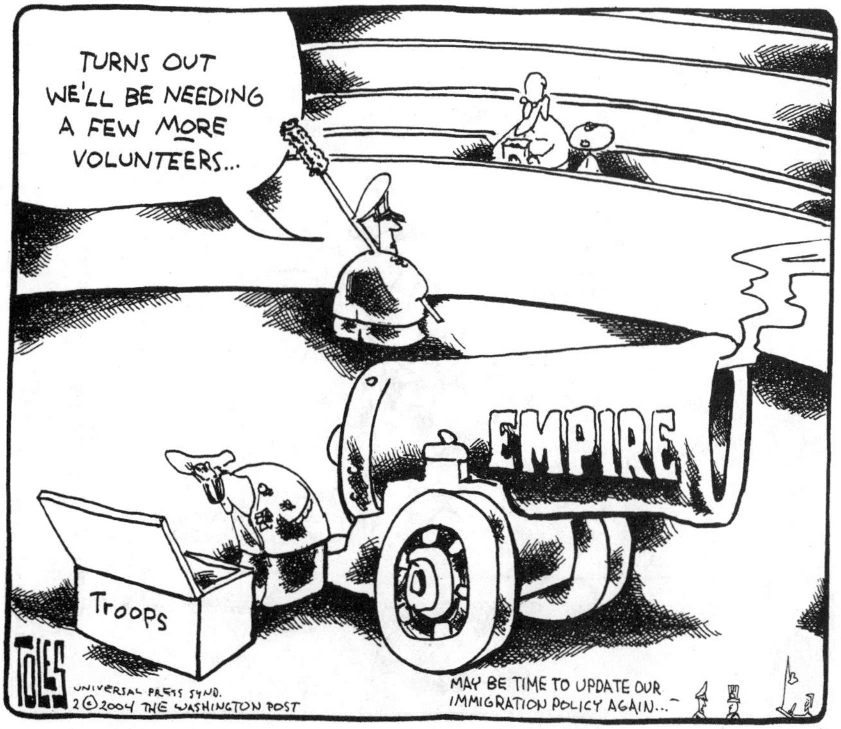
TURNS OUT WE'LL BE NEEDING A FEW MORE VOLUNTEERS...
EMPIRE
Troops
TOLES
UNIVERSAL PRESS SYND.
2©2004 THE WASHINGTON POST
MAY BE TIME TO UPDATE OUR IMMIGRATION POLICY AGAIN...

2-2-04

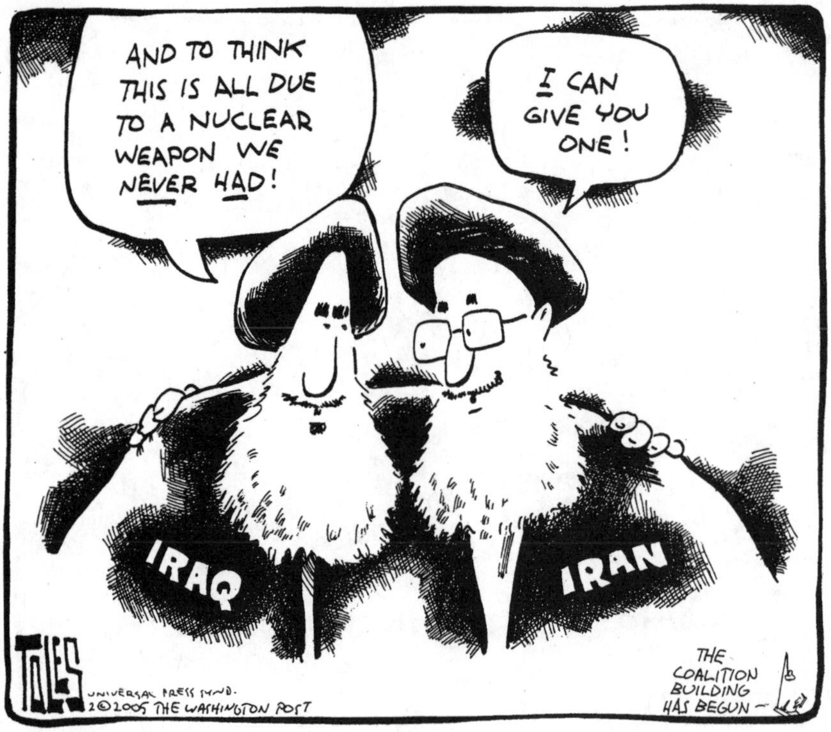
AND TO THINK THIS IS ALL DUE TO A NUCLEAR WEAPON WE NEVER HAD!
I CAN GIVE YOU ONE!
IRAQ
IRAN
TOLES
UNIVERSAL PRESS SYND.
2©2005 THE WASHINGTON POST
THE COALITION BUILDING HAS BEGUN —

2-15-05

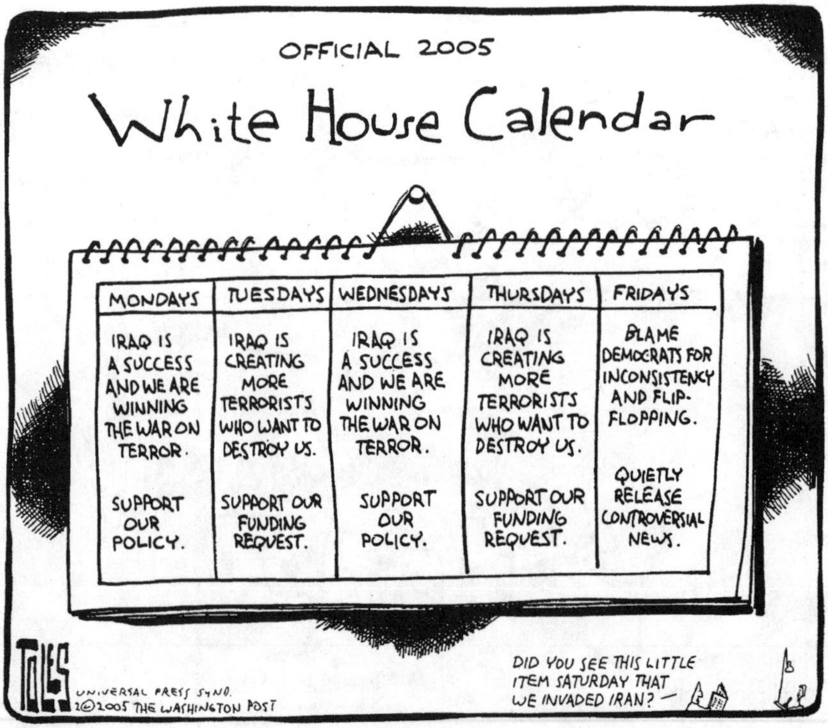
OFFICIAL 2005
White House Calendar
MONDAYS
IRAQ IS A SUCCESS AND WE ARE WINNING THE WAR ON TERROR.
SUPPORT OUR POLICY.
TUESDAYS
IRAQ IS CREATING MORE TERRORISTS WHO WANT TO DESTROY US.
SUPPORT OUR FUNDING REQUEST.
WEDNESDAYS
IRAQ IS A SUCCESS AND WE ARE WINNING THE WAR ON TERROR.
SUPPORT OUR POLICY.
THURSDAYS
IRAQ IS CREATING MORE TERRORISTS WHO WANT TO DESTROY US.
SUPPORT OUR FUNDING REQUEST.
FRIDAYS
BLAME DEMOCRATS FOR INCONSISTENCY AND FLIP-FLOPPING.
QUIETLY RELEASE CONTROVERSIAL NEWS.
TOLES
UNIVERSAL PRESS SYND.
2©2005 THE WASHINGTON POST
DID YOU SEE THIS LITTLE ITEM SATURDAY THAT WE INVADED IRAN? —

2-21-05

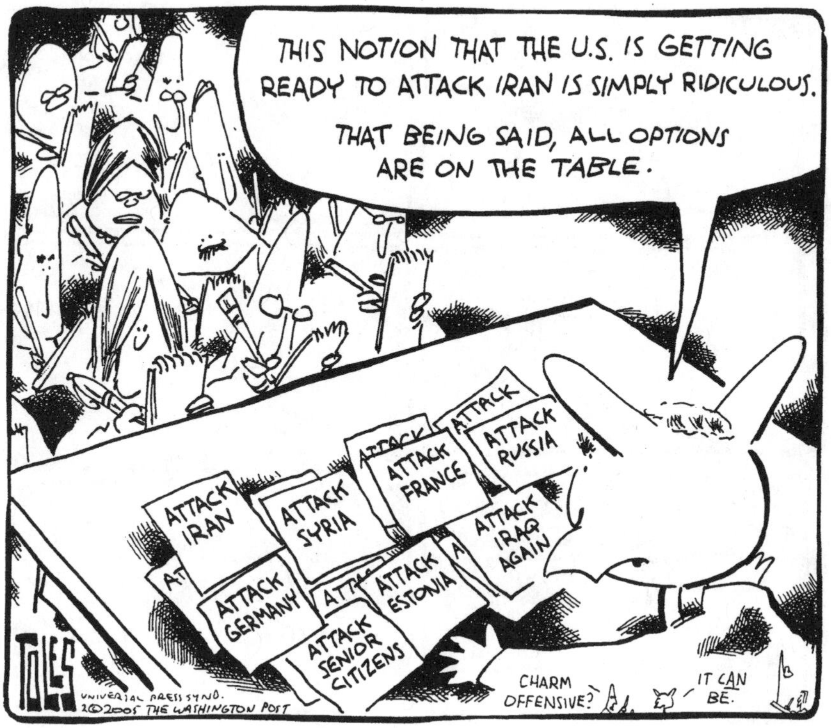
THIS NOTION THAT THE U.S. IS GETTING READY TO ATTACK IRAN IS SIMPLY RIDICULOUS.
THAT BEING SAID, ALL OPTIONS ARE ON THE TABLE.
ATTACK IRAN
ATTACK SYRIA
ATTACK FRANCE
ATTACK RUSSIA
ATTACK IRAQ AGAIN
ATTACK GERMANY
ATTACK ESTONIA
ATTACK SENIOR CITIZENS
TOLES
UNIVERSAL PRESS SYND.
2©2005 THE WASHINGTON POST
CHARM OFFENSIVE?
IT CAN BE.

2-25-05

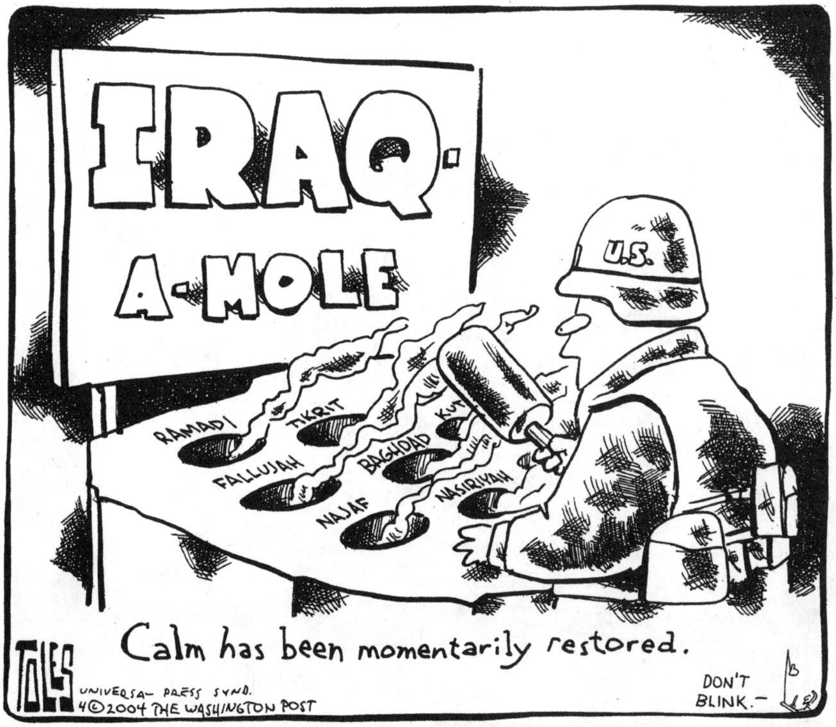
IRAQ-A-MOLE
U.S.
RAMADI
TIKRIT
FALLUJAH
BAGHDAD
NAJAF
NASIRIYAH
Calm has been momentarily restored.
TOLES
UNIVERSAL PRESS SYND.
4©2004 THE WASHINGTON POST
DON'T BLINK.

4-8-04

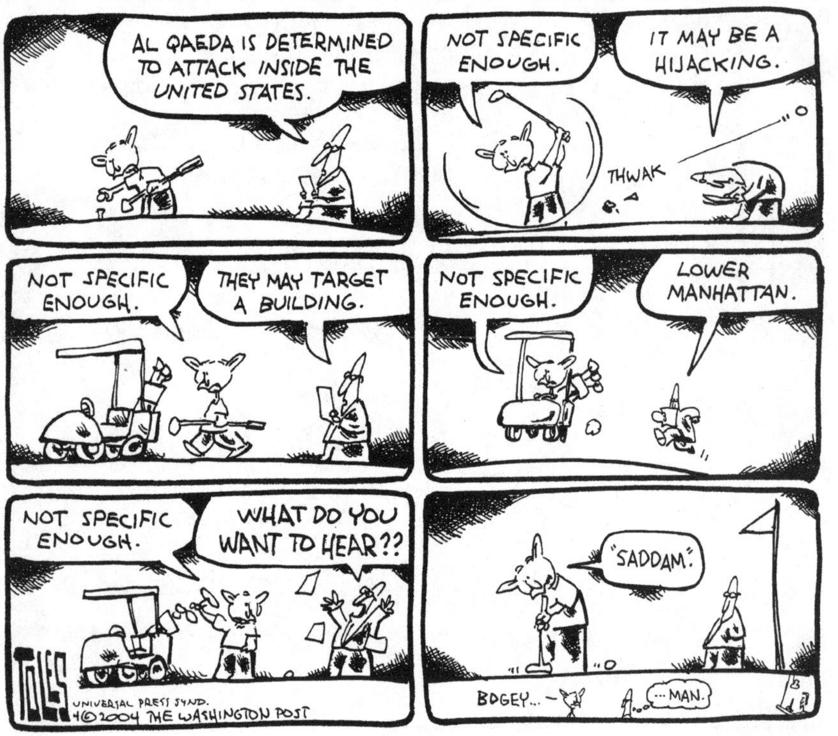
AL QAEDA IS DETERMINED TO ATTACK INSIDE THE UNITED STATES.
NOT SPECIFIC ENOUGH.
IT MAY BE A HIJACKING.
THWAK
NOT SPECIFIC ENOUGH.
THEY MAY TARGET A BUILDING.
NOT SPECIFIC ENOUGH.
LOWER MANHATTAN.
NOT SPECIFIC ENOUGH.
WHAT DO YOU WANT TO HEAR??
"SADDAM."
BOGEY...
...MAN.
TOLES
UNIVERSAL PRESS SYND.
4©2004 THE WASHINGTON POST

4-13-04

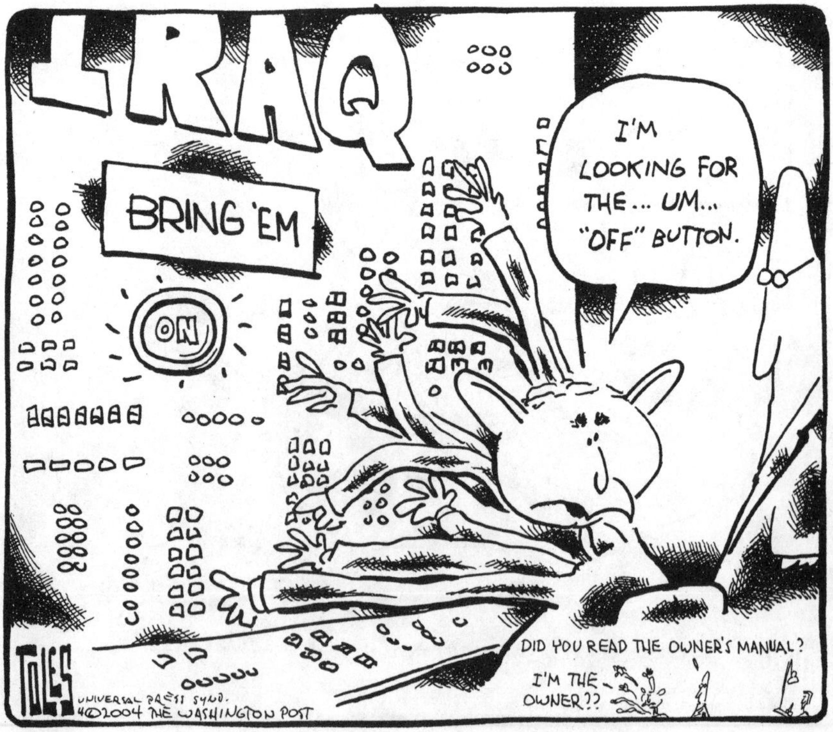
IRAQ
BRING 'EM
ON
I'M LOOKING FOR THE... UM... "OFF" BUTTON.
DID YOU READ THE OWNER'S MANUAL?
I'M THE OWNER??
TOLES
UNIVERSAL PRESS SYND.
4©2004 THE WASHINGTON POST

4-20-04

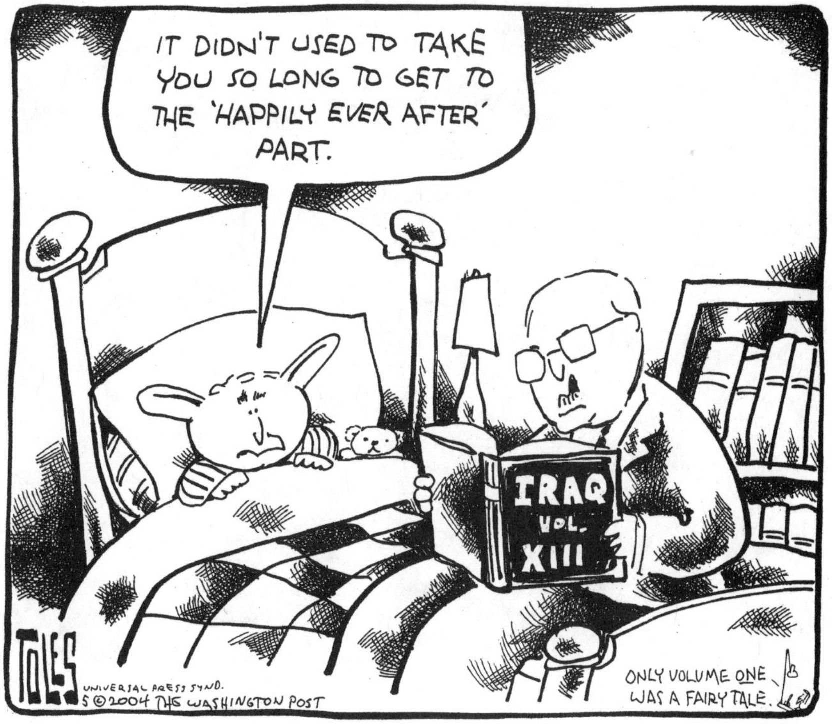
IT DIDN'T USED TO TAKE YOU SO LONG TO GET TO THE 'HAPPILY EVER AFTER' PART.
IRAQ VOL. XIII
TOLES
UNIVERSAL PRESS SYND.
5 ©2004 THE WASHINGTON POST
ONLY VOLUME ONE WAS A FAIRY TALE.

5-16-04

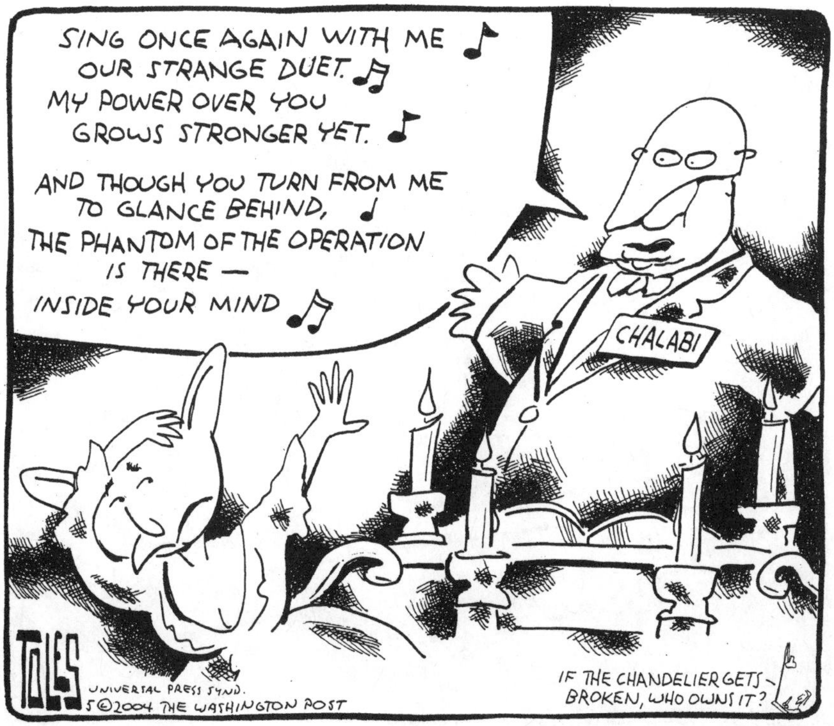
SING ONCE AGAIN WITH ME
OUR STRANGE DUET.
MY POWER OVER YOU
GROWS STRONGER YET.
AND THOUGH YOU TURN FROM ME
TO GLANCE BEHIND,
THE PHANTOM OF THE OPERATION
IS THERE —
INSIDE YOUR MIND
CHALABI
TOLES
UNIVERSAL PRESS SYND.
5 ©2004 THE WASHINGTON POST
IF THE CHANDELIER GETS BROKEN, WHO OWNS IT?

5-30-04

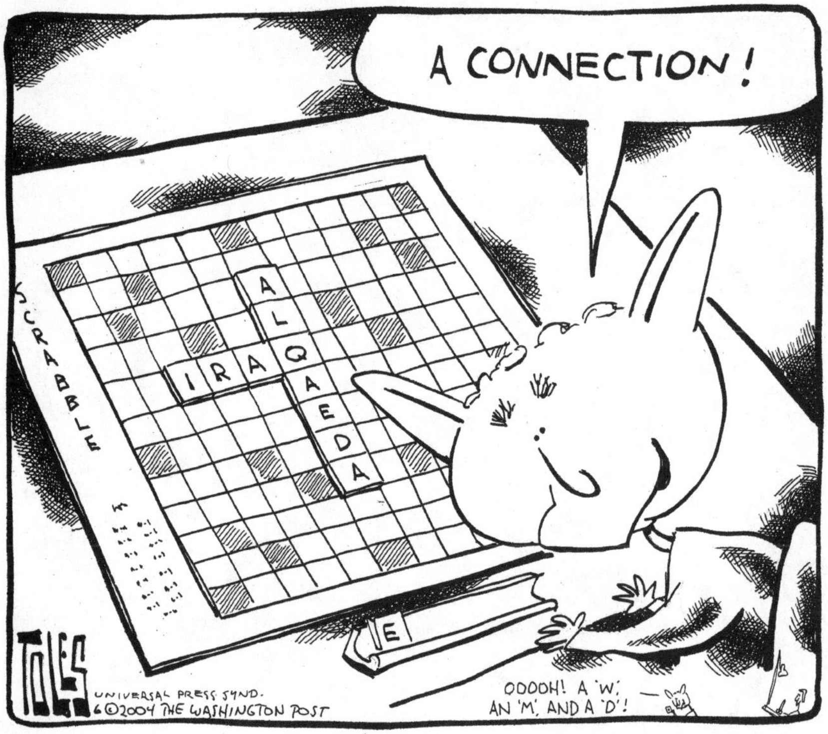
A CONNECTION!
SCRABBLE
IRA
ALQAEDA
E
TOLES
UNIVERSAL PRESS SYND.
6 ©2004 THE WASHINGTON POST
OOOOH! A 'W', AN 'M', AND A 'D'!

6-23-04

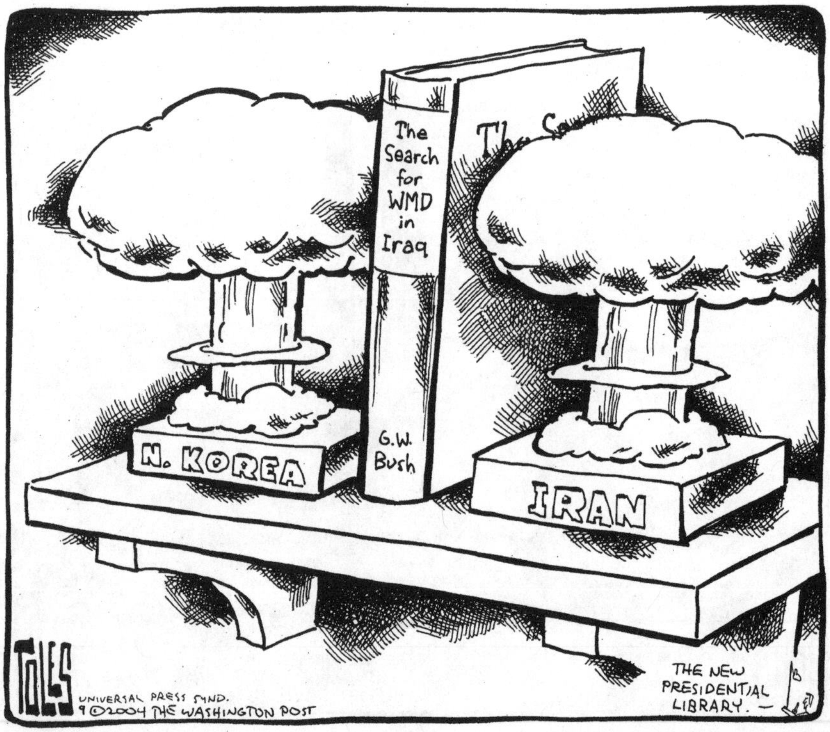
The Search for WMD in Iraq
G.W. Bush
N. KOREA
IRAN
TOLES
UNIVERSAL PRESS SYND.
9 ©2004 THE WASHINGTON POST
THE NEW PRESIDENTIAL LIBRARY.

9-27-04

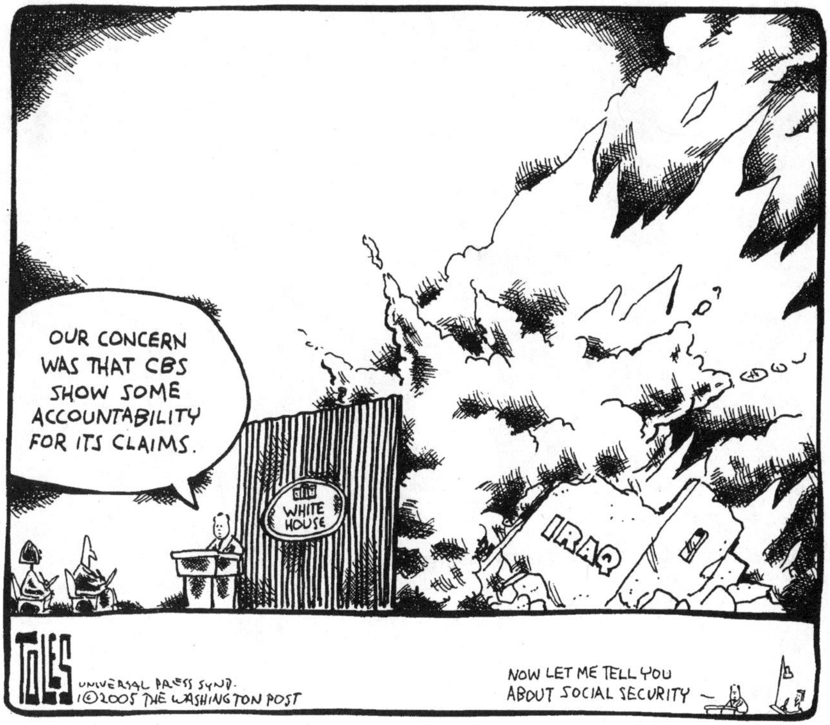
OUR CONCERN WAS THAT CBS SHOW SOME ACCOUNTABILITY FOR ITS CLAIMS.
WHITE HOUSE
IRAQ
TOLES
UNIVERSAL PRESS SYND.
1©2005 THE WASHINGTON POST
NOW LET ME TELL YOU ABOUT SOCIAL SECURITY

1-13-05

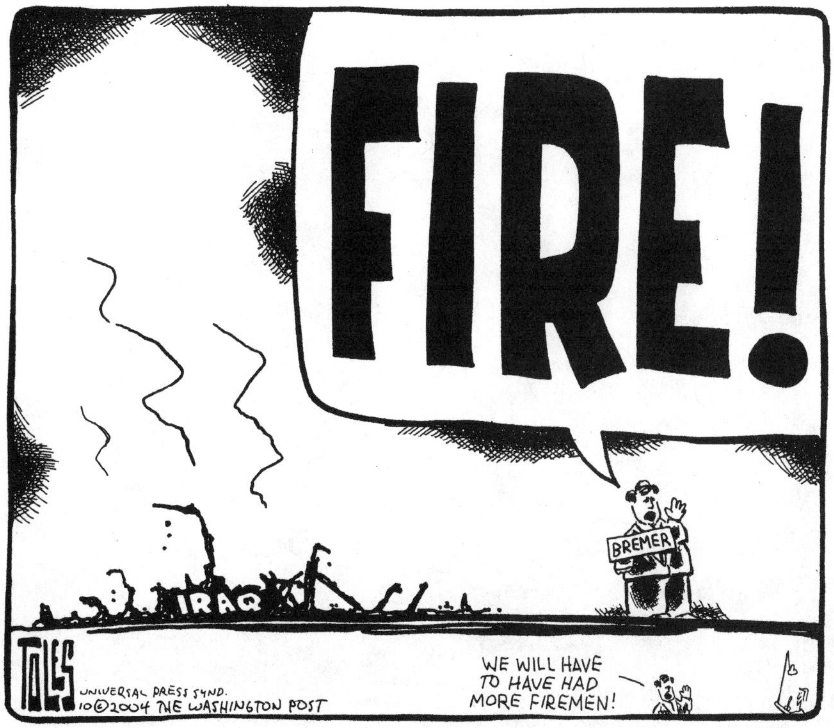
FIRE!
IRAQ
BREMER
TOLES
UNIVERSAL PRESS SYND.
10©2004 THE WASHINGTON POST
WE WILL HAVE TO HAVE HAD MORE FIREMEN!

10-6-04

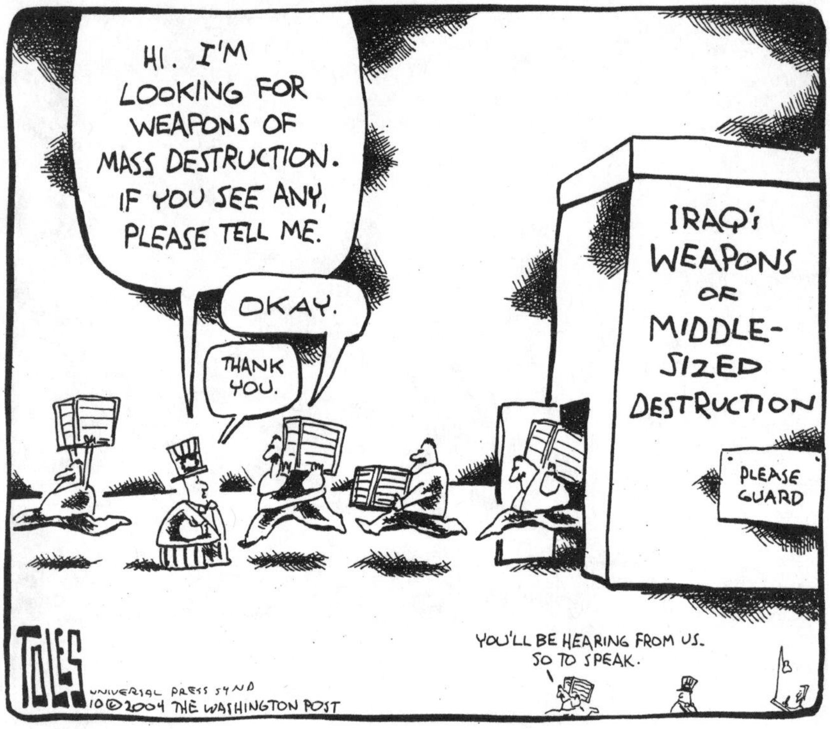
HI. I'M LOOKING FOR WEAPONS OF MASS DESTRUCTION. IF YOU SEE ANY, PLEASE TELL ME.
OKAY.
THANK YOU.
IRAQ's WEAPONS OF MIDDLE-SIZED DESTRUCTION
PLEASE GUARD
YOU'LL BE HEARING FROM US. SO TO SPEAK.
TOLES
UNIVERSAL PRESS SYND
10 © 2004 THE WASHINGTON POST

10-31-04

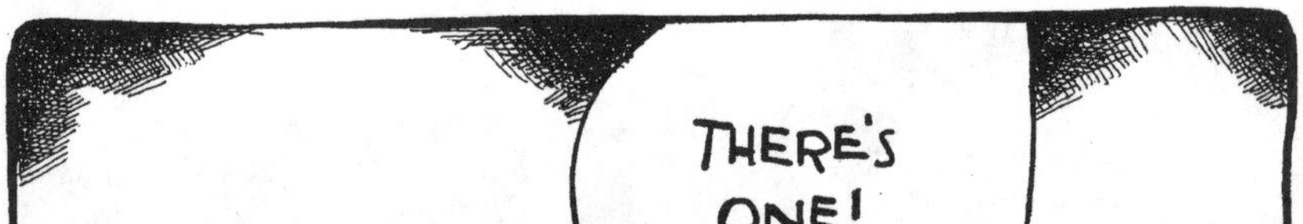
THERE'S ONE!
ebay
democracy, incipient, barely used. for sale by Russia
IRAQ
DO YOU MIND FINGER MARKS AROUND ITS THROAT?
NO.
TOLES
UNIVERSAL PRESS SYND.
9 © 2004 THE WASHINGTON POST

9-19-04

Dec, 2004. ON A REMOTE PACIFIC ISLAND, THE LAST JAPANESE SOLDIER FIGHTING WORLD WAR II RUNS OUT OF AMMO.
HE SURRENDERS TO THE LAST AMERICAN G.I., WHO HAD KEPT HIM PINNED DOWN FOR ALL THESE YEARS.
THE JAPANESE SOLDIER, RETURNING TO TOKYO, WAS SURPRISED BY HOW MUCH IT HAD CHANGED.
THE AMERICAN SOLDIER, RETURNING TO HIS BASE, WAS SURPRISED TO HAVE HIS TOUR OF DUTY EXTENDED IN IRAQ FOR THIRTEEN YEARS.
TOLES
UNIVERSAL PRESS SYND.
12©2004 THE WASHINGTON POST
AT LEAST NOW I'LL GET ALL THE EQUIPMENT I NEED.

12-12-04

NOPE... NO DRAFT, THEY SAID AGAIN TODAY. NO PLANS FOR A DRAFT AT ALL AT THIS TIME, THEY INSISTED. WE HAVE ALL THE TROOPS WE NEED, THEY DECLARED. CONGRESS JUST INTRODUCED DRAFT LEGISLATION THIS WEEK, BUT ONLY SO THEY COULD VOTE AGAINST IT AND PROVE THEY'RE NOT THINKING ABOUT DRAFTING ANYONE ANY TIME RIGHT AWAY...
CANADA
TOLES
UNIVERSAL PRESS SYND.
10©2004 THE WASHINGTON POST
HAVE YOU CONSIDERED THE NATIONAL GUARD?

10-7-04

WHEN YOU GET A MINUTE, VLADIMIR, I'D LIKE TO TAKE A SECOND LOOK INTO THAT SOUL OF YOURS...
IRAQ
PUTIN
IRAN
N. KOREA
TOLES
UNIVERSAL PRESS SYND.
8 ©2002 THE WASHINGTON POST
THE ENTIRE AXIS! AND HERE IN THE LINCOLN BEDROOM, OF ALL PLACES!

8-20-02

THE STATE OF THE UNION CLAIM WAS IN SOME SENSE TRUE.
CONDI
MAYBE IT WASN'T 'YELLOWCAKE' URANIUM, MAYBE IT WASN'T FROM 'NIGER', MAYBE SOME OF THE DOCUMENTS WERE 'FORGERIES'...
BUT SOMEBODY WAS SEEKING TO GET NUCLEAR FUEL FROM SOMEWHERE TO MAKE BOMBS...
N. KOREA
TOLES
UNIVERSAL PRESS SYND.
7 © 2003 THE WASHINGTON POST
'BAD GUY.' THE PRESIDENT SPECIFICALLY MENTIONED A BAD GUY.

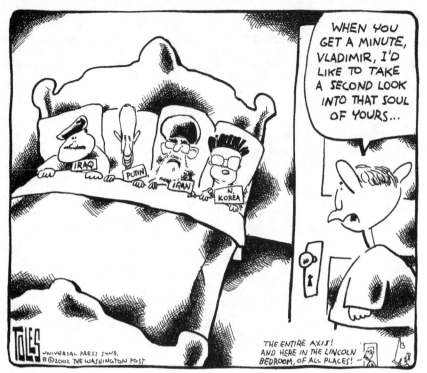

7-16-03

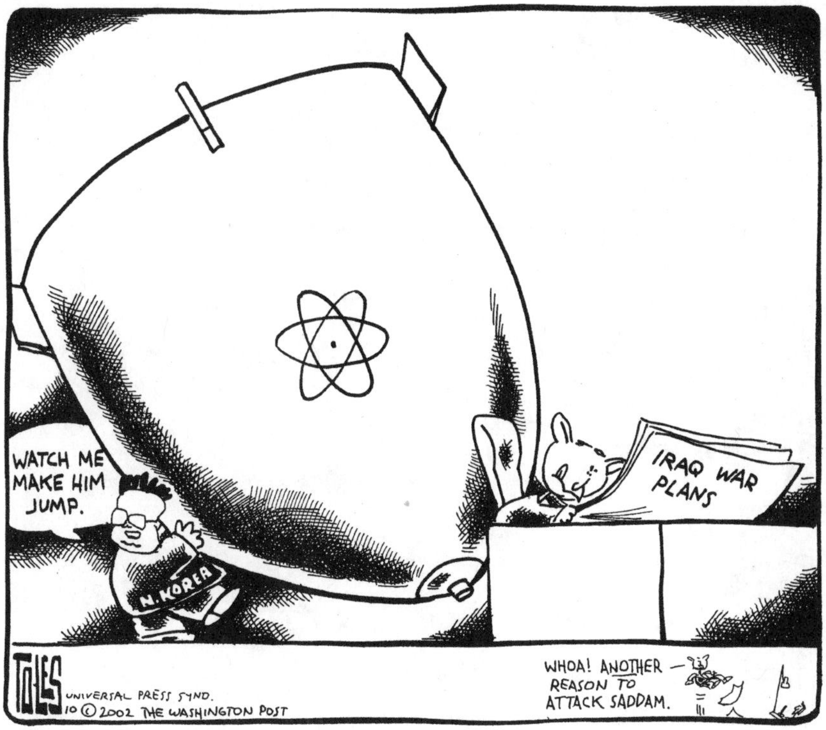
WATCH ME MAKE HIM JUMP.
N. KOREA
IRAQ WAR PLANS
WHOA! ANOTHER REASON TO ATTACK SADDAM.
TOLES
UNIVERSAL PRESS SYND.
10 © 2002 THE WASHINGTON POST

10-18-02

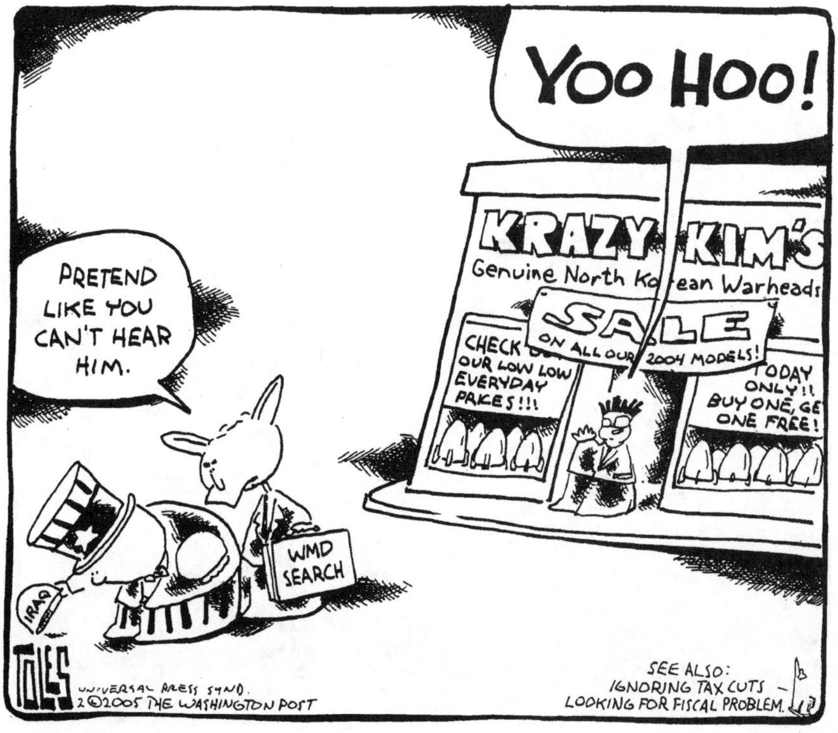
YOO HOO!
KRAZY KIM'S
Genuine North Korean Warheads
SALE
ON ALL OUR 2004 MODELS!
CHECK OUT OUR LOW LOW EVERYDAY PRICES!!!
TODAY ONLY!! BUY ONE, GET ONE FREE!
PRETEND LIKE YOU CAN'T HEAR HIM.
WMD SEARCH
IRAQ
SEE ALSO: IGNORING TAX CUTS — LOOKING FOR FISCAL PROBLEM.
TOLES
UNIVERSAL PRESS SYND.
2 ©2005 THE WASHINGTON POST

2-13-05

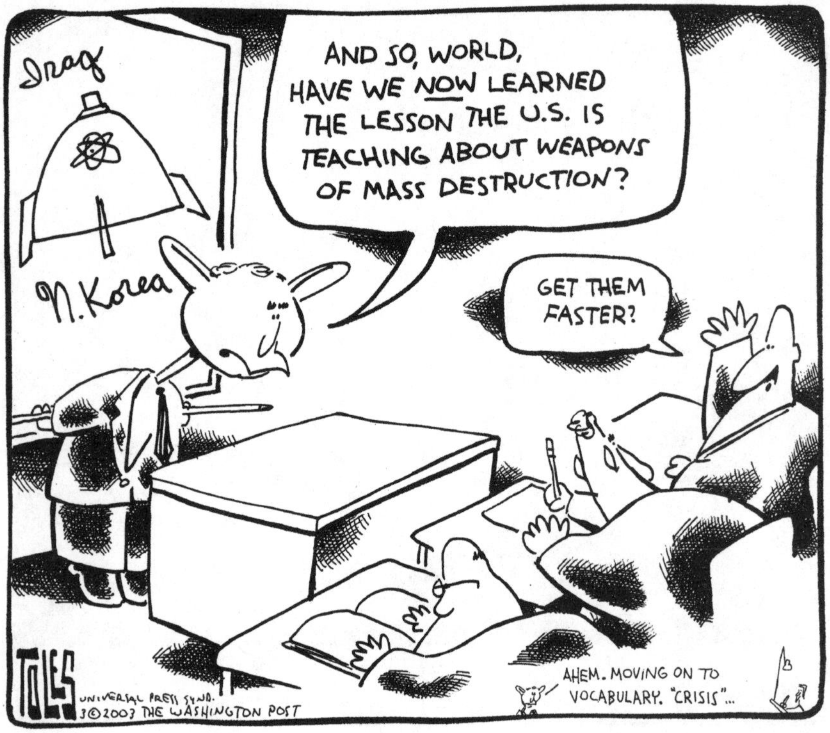
Iraq
N. Korea
AND SO, WORLD, HAVE WE NOW LEARNED THE LESSON THE U.S. IS TEACHING ABOUT WEAPONS OF MASS DESTRUCTION?
GET THEM FASTER?
AHEM. MOVING ON TO VOCABULARY. "CRISIS"...
TOLES
UNIVERSAL PRESS SYND.
3©2003 THE WASHINGTON POST

3-9-03

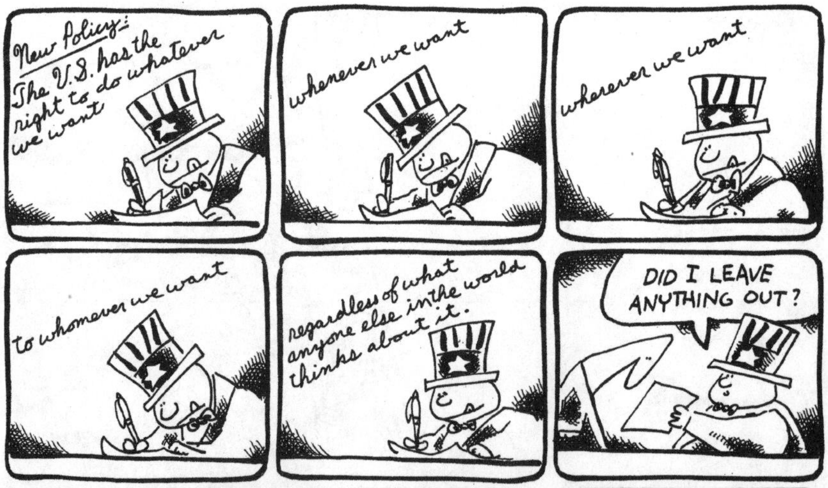
New Policy:
The U.S. has the right to do whatever we want
whenever we want
wherever we want
to whomever we want
regardless of what anyone else in the world thinks about it.
DID I LEAVE ANYTHING OUT?
WITH RIGHTS, DON'T THERE ALSO COME RESPONSIBILITIES?
It is the responsibility of the rest of the world to help us pay for it.
We have the right to make them pay for it
TOLES
UNIVERSAL PRESS SYND.
9©2002 THE WASHINGTON POST

9-24-02

THIS COWBOY ROUTINE ISN'T WORKING SO WELL WITH THE REST OF THE WORLD.
TIME TO TRY A DIFFERENT LOOK.
HEY BABY. WANT TO FORM AN ALLIANCE?
BUT I STILL GET TO CALL ALL THE SHOTS
TOLES
UNIVERSAL PRESS SYND.
12 © 2004 THE WASHINGTON POST

12-5-04

I'VE DECIDED TO MAKE A GESTURE OF COOPERATION.
U.S. Foreign Policy
EUROPE
YOU CAN STOP SMILING AND MOVING AROUND ERRATICALLY NOW...
TOLES
UNIVERSAL PRESS SYND.
2 © 2005 THE WASHINGTON POST

2-23-05

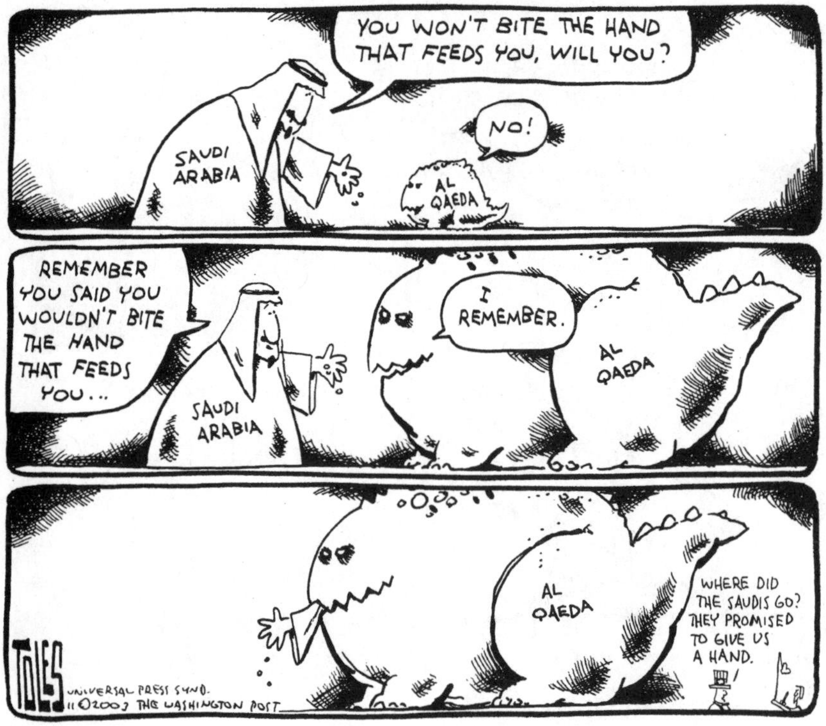
YOU WON'T BITE THE HAND THAT FEEDS YOU, WILL YOU?
NO!
SAUDI ARABIA
AL QAEDA
REMEMBER YOU SAID YOU WOULDN'T BITE THE HAND THAT FEEDS YOU...
I REMEMBER.
SAUDI ARABIA
AL QAEDA
AL QAEDA
WHERE DID THE SAUDIS GO? THEY PROMISED TO GIVE US A HAND!
TOLES
UNIVERSAL PRESS SYND.
11©2003 THE WASHINGTON POST

11-11-03

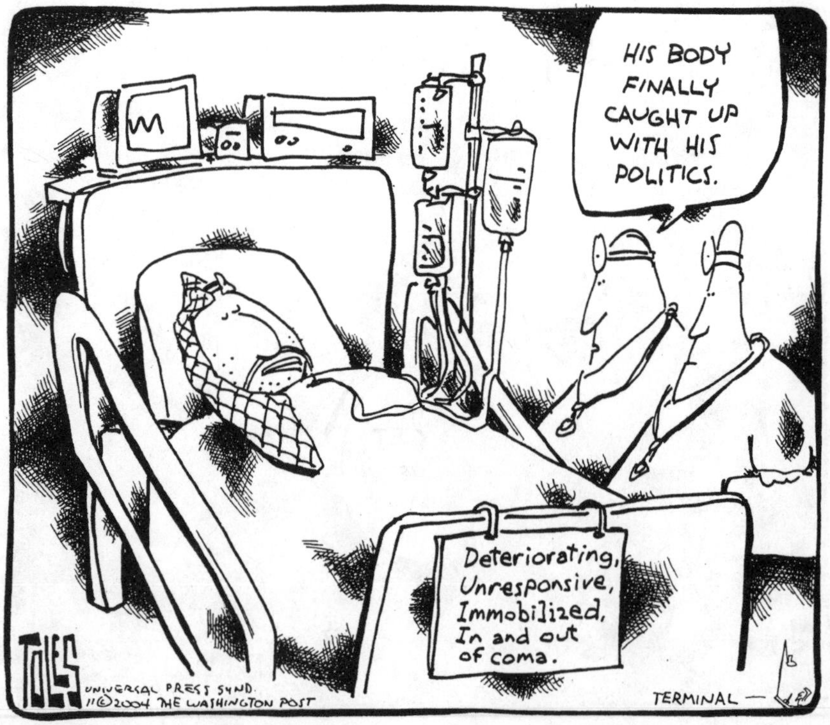
HIS BODY FINALLY CAUGHT UP WITH HIS POLITICS.
Deteriorating, Unresponsive, Immobilized, In and out of coma.
TERMINAL
TOLES
UNIVERSAL PRESS SYND.
11©2004 THE WASHINGTON POST

11-10-04

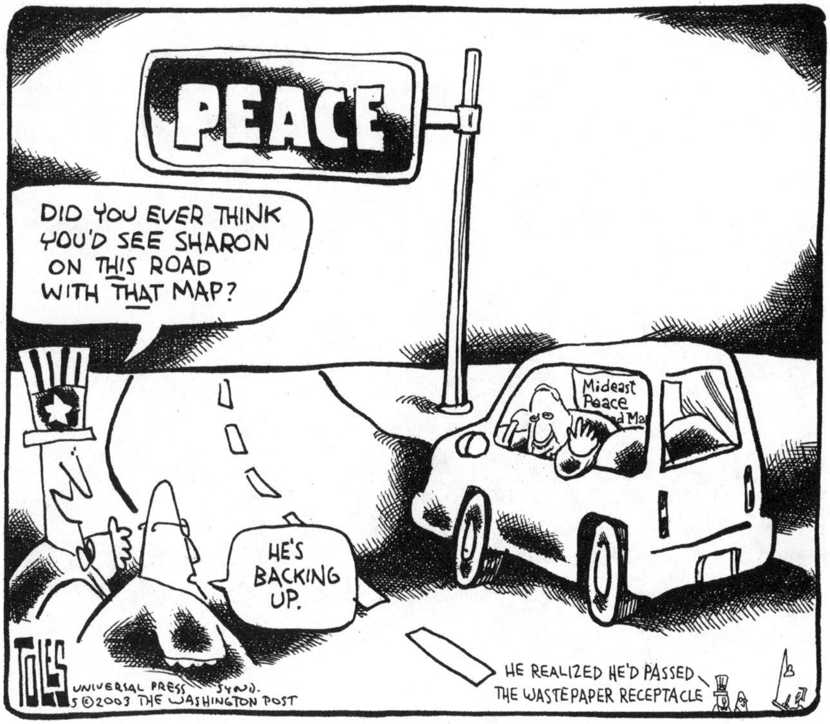
PEACE
DID YOU EVER THINK YOU'D SEE SHARON ON THIS ROAD WITH THAT MAP?
Mideast Peace
HE'S BACKING UP.
TOLES
UNIVERSAL PRESS SYND.
5 © 2003 THE WASHINGTON POST
HE REALIZED HE'D PASSED THE WASTEPAPER RECEPTACLE

5-12-03

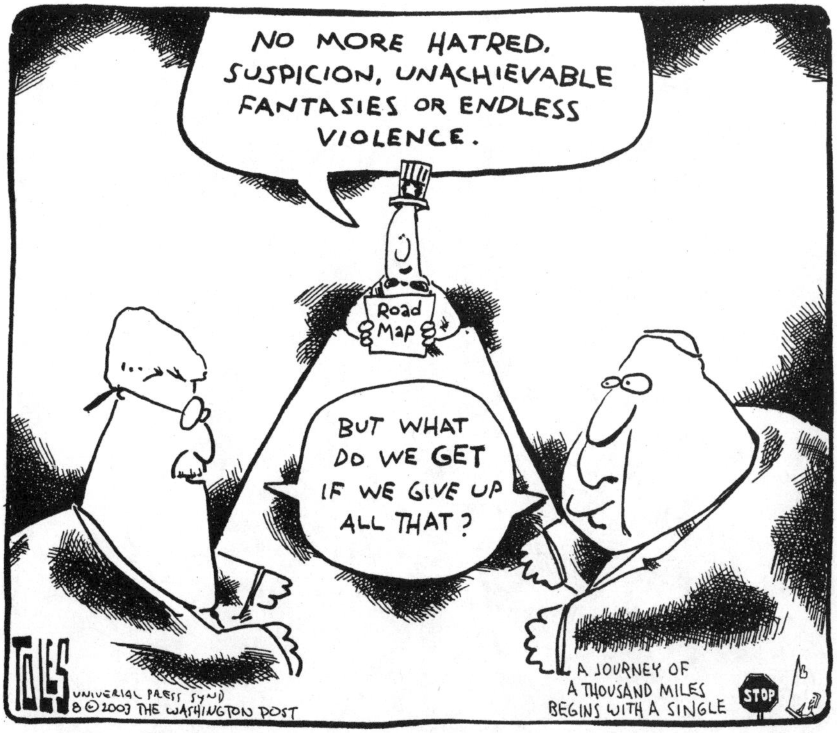
NO MORE HATRED, SUSPICION, UNACHIEVABLE FANTASIES OR ENDLESS VIOLENCE.
Road Map
BUT WHAT DO WE GET IF WE GIVE UP ALL THAT?
TOLES
UNIVERSAL PRESS SYND
8 © 2003 THE WASHINGTON POST
A JOURNEY OF A THOUSAND MILES BEGINS WITH A SINGLE
STOP

8-26-03

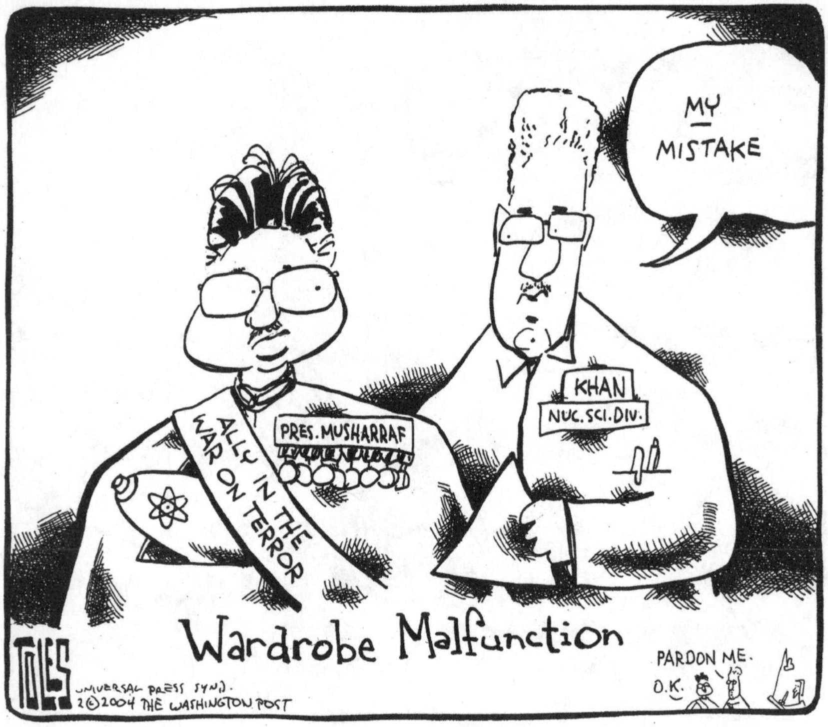
MY MISTAKE
KHAN
NUC. SCI. DIV.
PRES. MUSHARRAF
ALLY IN THE WAR ON TERROR
Wardrobe Malfunction
TOLES
UNIVERSAL PRESS SYND.
2 © 2004 THE WASHINGTON POST
PARDON ME.
O.K.

2-6-04

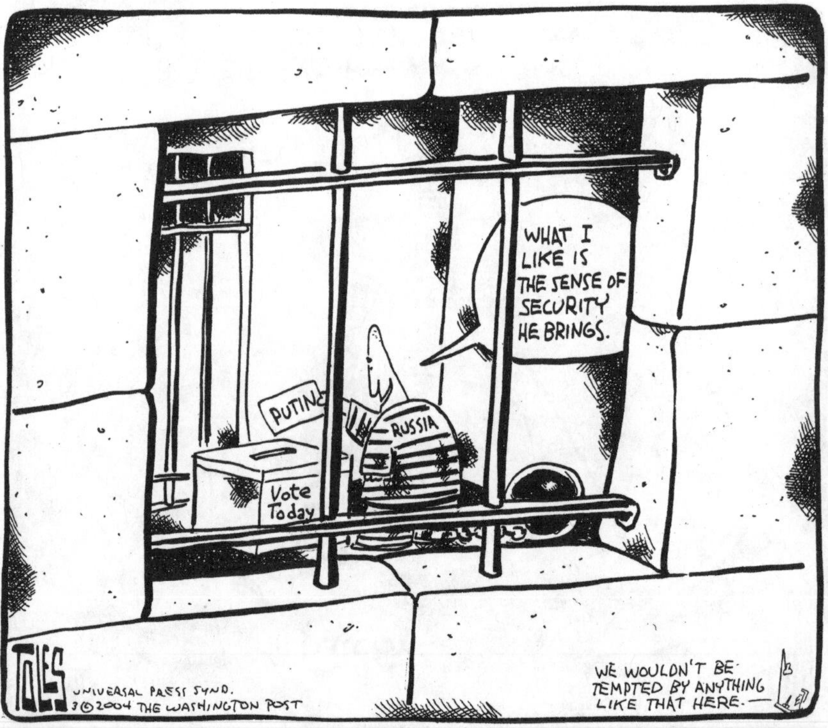
WHAT I LIKE IS THE SENSE OF SECURITY HE BRINGS.
PUTIN
RUSSIA
Vote Today
TOLES
UNIVERSAL PRESS SYND.
3 © 2004 THE WASHINGTON POST
WE WOULDN'T BE TEMPTED BY ANYTHING LIKE THAT HERE.

3-12-04

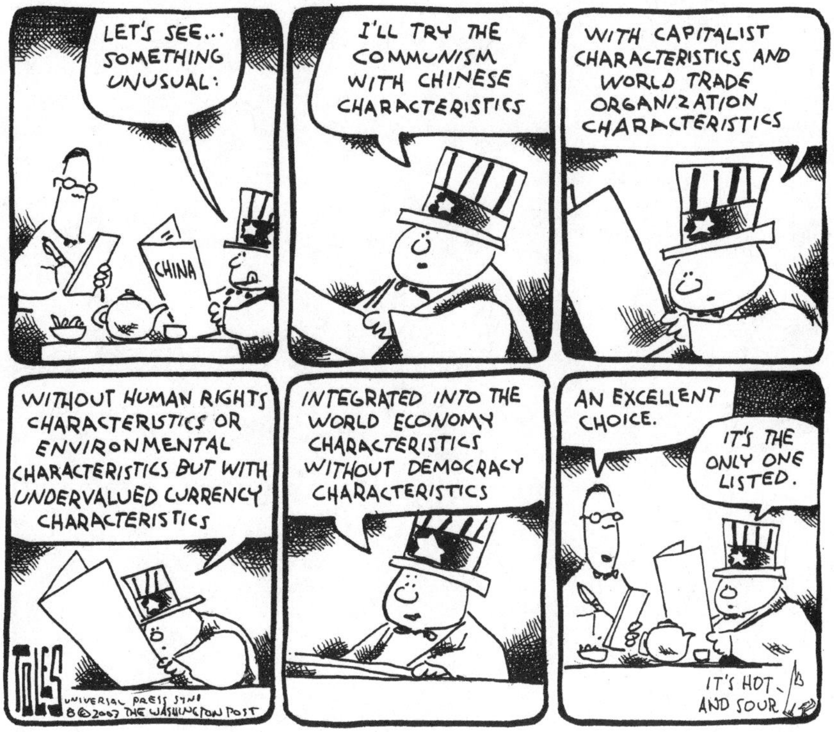
LET'S SEE... SOMETHING UNUSUAL:
CHINA
I'LL TRY THE COMMUNISM WITH CHINESE CHARACTERISTICS
WITH CAPITALIST CHARACTERISTICS AND WORLD TRADE ORGANIZATION CHARACTERISTICS
WITHOUT HUMAN RIGHTS CHARACTERISTICS OR ENVIRONMENTAL CHARACTERISTICS BUT WITH UNDERVALUED CURRENCY CHARACTERISTICS
INTEGRATED INTO THE WORLD ECONOMY CHARACTERISTICS WITHOUT DEMOCRACY CHARACTERISTICS
AN EXCELLENT CHOICE.
IT'S THE ONLY ONE LISTED.
TOLES
UNIVERSAL PRESS SYND
THE WASHINGTON POST
IT'S HOT AND SOUR

8-24-03

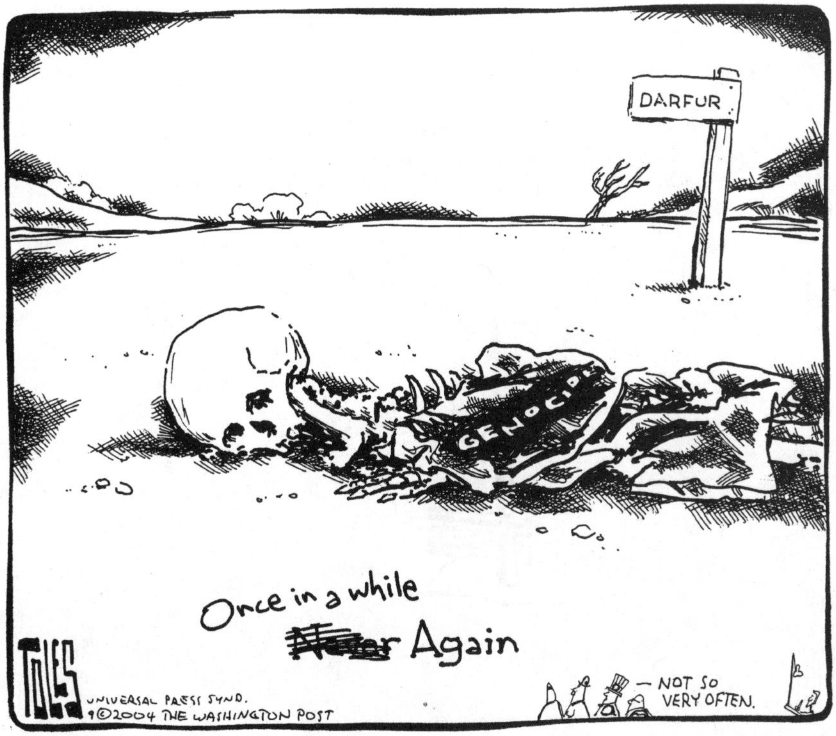
DARFUR
GENOCIDE
Once in a while
~~Never~~ Again
TOLES
UNIVERSAL PRESS SYND.
9 © 2004 THE WASHINGTON POST
— NOT SO VERY OFTEN.

9-16-04